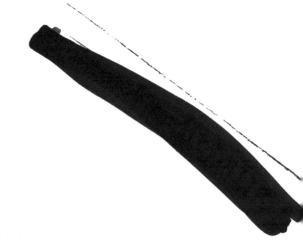

D1570450

Overruled?

Overruled?

Legislative
Overrides, Pluralism,
and Contemporary
Court-Congress
Relations

Jeb Barnes

STANFORD UNIVERSITY PRESS

Stanford, California 2004

Stanford University Press
Stanford, California
© 2004 by the Board of Trustees of the Leland Stanford Junior University.
All rights reserved.
Printed in the United States of America on acid-free, archival-quality paper

Library of Congress Cataloging-in-Publication Data

Barnes, Jeb.
  Overruled? : legislative overrides, pluralism, and contemporary
court-Congress relations / Jeb Barnes.
      p. cm.
  Includes bibliographical references and index.
  ISBN 0-8047-4883-7 (cloth : alk. paper)
  1. Statutes—United States. 2. Judicial review—United States. 3.
Law—United States—Interpretation and construction. 4. Political
questions and judicial power—United States. I. Title.
KF425 .B37 2004
347.73'12—dc22
                                                      2003023971

Typeset by Interactive Composition Corporation in 9.7/11.5 Sabon
Original Printing 2004
Last figure below indicates year of this printing:
13 12 11 10 09 08 07 06 05 04

Contents

Tables and Figures

Tables

Acknowledgments

This book began as a dissertation at the University of California, Berkeley, which I attended after four long years of practicing law as a commercial litigator. Upon arrival, I felt like Charlie entering the Willy Wonka Chocolate Factory; I could not believe my luck as I passed its gates and entered a world of new ideas and challenges. At Berkeley, I was blessed to learn from my fellow graduate students, in particular Trevor Nakagawa, Jonathan Koppell, Eric Shultzke, Ken Greene, Dorie Appollonia, Ray Laraja, and Eric McGee (who shared the rigors of "stats camp" with me). Among the faculty, I would like to thank especially Ernie Haas, David Collier, Sandy Muir, David Leonard, Todd LaPorte, Greg Noble, and my extraordinary dissertation committee: Nelson Polsby, Judith Gruber, Martin Shapiro, and Eric Schickler.

Special thanks are owed to Bob Kagan, who chaired my dissertation committee. I met Bob before applying to graduate school. At the time, I doubted whether returning to school for five or six years was a good idea. In that first meeting, I discussed some of my interests with Bob, and in his inimitable way, he found the best of what I was trying to say, gently indicated where I had gone off track, and encouraged me to keep thinking. I was hooked. As a graduate student, I had the honor of being Bob's student, research assistant, and advisee. In return, he taught me most of what I know about the courts, both here and abroad, and has encouraged me every step of the way. I cannot begin to thank him properly.

After leaving Berkeley, I joined the faculty at the University of Southern California (USC), where I have been graced with talented colleagues, who have commented on all or parts of the manuscript in various stages, including Howard Gillman, Elizabeth Garrett, Jeffrey Sellars,

Janelle Wong, and Ann Crigler; as well as promising graduate students, who have helped to collect facts and offered insights on the manuscript, including Art Auerbach, Joseph Bae, and Jason Whitehead. I am also deeply grateful to the Cal Tech-USC Center for the Study of Law and Politics and the Jesse M. Unruh Center for the Study of Politics, which provided generous grants that allowed me to hire Wayne LeCheminant, a top graduate student at USC, as a research assistant. Over the past year and a half, Wayne has tirelessly delved into the legislative record and pushed my arguments. In the process, he has become a valued colleague and friend. I look forward to returning the favor and reading his books.

I am also very grateful to the faculty at Northwestern University's political science department as well as members of the American Bar Foundation, who invited me to present an earlier version of the manuscript and offered insightful and constructive comments that greatly stimulated my thinking. Similarly, I owe a considerable debt to the editors at Stanford University Press, Amanda Moran and Kate Wahl, and outside reviewers Edward Rubin and Shep Melnick, whose razor sharp comments led to major improvements in the manuscript.

My unreasonably good fortune continued when a fellowship with the Robert Wood Johnson (RWJ) Scholars in Health Policy Research Program allowed me to return to Berkeley, where I put the finishing touches on the manuscript. I thank the site administrator and faculty for all their support and dedication to the scholars, and the RWJ Foundation for creating this innovative and generous program.

Outside the academic community, I would like to thank my parents, Peter Barnes and Pam Heminway, and my sister, Tracy Barnes. The decision to leave the relative security of legal practice and pursue an academic career was not easy. Throughout, they have encouraged me to follow my heart, or as Nelson Polsby would say, to "eat dessert first" in life. Since leaving the law, I have done just that, and it has been delicious.

Above all, I want to thank my wife, Annie Barnes. More than anyone else, she has supported and encouraged me. For all her patience, love, and intelligent contributions to my work, she deserves an equal share in every award, honor, and degree I have received since embarking on an academic career. I dedicate this book to her.

Background

1 The Questions, Debate, and Overview

[T]he reach of a law may never be appreciated by the enacting body until it has been passed and put into practice. Congress is not omniscient; no matter how careful the draftsmen, all contingencies cannot possibly be foreseen; words are treacherous for the transmission of ideas. That is why constant legislative reappraisal of statutes as construed by the courts . . . is a healthy practice.

> —*Justice William O. Douglas[1]*

It's never over [in Washington].

> —*Lament of Former Secretary of State George Schultz[2]*

The Questions

In 1992, twin sisters Karen Sutton and Kimberly Hinton applied to become global pilots for United Airlines. As experienced pilots for a regional airline, they met the company's basic age, education, and Federal Aviation Administration certification requirements, and were asked for interviews. Upon arrival at United, they were told that a mistake had been made. United requires their pilots to have *uncorrected* vision of 20/100 or better, and neither sister met this requirement. Indeed, both were severely myopic; they had vision of 20/200 or worse in their right eyes and 20/400 or worse in their left eyes.[3] At the same time, both sisters had 20/20 vision or better with glasses or contact lenses, which means that their *corrected* vision was as good or better than most. Nevertheless, United rejected their applications.[4]

The sisters sued, claiming that United's vision requirements violated the Americans with Disabilities Act (ADA), which bans discrimination on the basis of physical disabilities. The lawsuit turned on the following question: does the ADA apply to workers whose disabilities can be treated, such as individuals with poor eyesight? The statute was silent on this question and subject to conflicting interpretations.

The sisters advocated a broad reading of the law. They argued that the ADA defined *disability* as a "physical or mental impairment that substantially limits one or more of the major life activities of the individual."[5]

Surely, they contended, severe myopia falls within this definition. After all, without corrective lenses, the sisters could not drive a car, shop in a store, or view a computer screen from a reasonable distance. In fact, only 2 percent of the population suffers from such poor eyesight.[6] In support of their argument, the sisters pointed to Senate and House Committee reports[7] as well as interpretive guidelines from the Equal Employment Opportunity Commission, Justice Department, and Department of Transportation, which explicitly stated that disability under the ADA should be determined without regard to "mitigating measures."[8]

United pressed for a narrower construction. Specifically, it agreed that "disabilities" under the ADA were ailments that substantially impair major life activities. But United asked: how could the sisters' eyesight impair *any* life activities, when both could see perfectly with glasses? In support of its argument, United pointed to legislative findings in the statute. These findings state that the ADA applies to 43 million Americans, which is far less than the estimated 160 million U.S. workers with "correctable" disabilities.[9] United added that the statute's text should trump any inconsistent statements in the legislative history or federal agency rules.

The U.S. District Court agreed with United. It dismissed the sisters' lawsuit, arguing that poor eyesight, which could be corrected, was not a disability under the statute.[10] The Tenth Circuit for the U.S. Court of Appeals affirmed.[11] However, other circuits had ruled differently. Indeed, the majority of federal appellate courts sided with the sisters' position, holding that a person's physical or mental condition should be examined in its untreated state when determining disability under the ADA.[12]

The U.S. Supreme Court granted certiorari to resolve this split, but struggled itself with the issue. During oral argument, Justice David Souter admitted he was "at sea."[13] Justice Stephen Breyer added, "I don't see how to get this statute to work."[14] Nevertheless, the Court had to rule and, in so doing, make a significant policy choice. On one hand, a restrictive interpretation of the ADA would deny millions of workers legal protection from potential discrimination; on the other hand, an expansive construction would require employers to accommodate a wide range of workers claiming disabilities.

In a divided decision, the Supreme Court affirmed the Tenth Circuit's decision and construed the ADA narrowly.[15] In rejecting the sisters' claims, the majority explained as follows: "A 'disability' exists only where an impairment 'substantially limits' a major life activity, not where it 'might,' 'could,' or 'would' be substantially limiting if mitigating measures were not taken."[16] The dissent rejoined that the majority's reasoning was flawed, producing the "counterintuitive conclusion that the ADA's safeguards vanish when individuals make themselves more employable by ascertaining ways to overcome their physical or mental limitations."[17]

Sutton, moreover, did not end controversy over the proper interpretation of the ADA; rather, it angered advocates for the disabled. For example, Professor Chai Feldblum of Georgetown Law School, who helped draft the ADA, charged that the Supreme Court's ruling left the statute with "a gaping hole right at its heart."[18] Senator Tom Harkin, a Democrat from Iowa and a chief sponsor of the ADA, warned that *Sutton* would "send a shock wave through the disability community," adding that he was considering "some kind of remedial legislation" to reverse the decision.[19]

This example highlights crucial lessons about contemporary American policy-making and "statutory construction": the process by which the meaning of laws is defined and refined. First, *Sutton* underscores that statutory language is often vague. Indeed, the ADA's definition of *disability* permitted two plausible and diametrically opposed interpretations. As a result, policy-making from the bench need not involve conservative or liberal judicial activism, in which judges bend the letter of the law to fit their preferences. Instead, judges must sometimes read between the lines when interpreting statutory texts, filling gaps left by Congress. Second, *Sutton* emphasizes that even ostensibly arcane statutory questions may have broad policy consequences. Thus, the question of whether the ADA's definition of *disability* applied to treatable conditions was not a legal quibble; it affected the rights of literally millions of Americans. Third, and perhaps least widely appreciated, the reaction to *Sutton* points out that federal courts—even the U.S. Supreme Court—do not necessarily have the last word on the meaning of statutes. Having lost in court, disgruntled litigants and their representatives may appeal to Congress for legislation that overturns unfavorable judicial decisions.

In fact, since the mid-1970s, Congress has passed hundreds of "overrides"—laws that explicitly seek to reverse or materially modify judicial interpretations of statutes and related administrative rules.[20] The Civil Rights Act of 1991,[21] the "Grove City" Bill,[22] and the Voting Rights Act of 1982[23] offer a few prominent examples, culminating high-profile efforts of congressional liberals and moderates to reverse conservative Supreme Court interpretations of civil rights laws. Of course, most overrides are less publicly visible than these bills, but they also concern important policy areas such as antitrust, intellectual property rights, immigration, federal criminal law, bankruptcy, taxes, and environmental law.

Whether front-page news or not, the passage of overrides potentially serves vital functions in American policy-making, functions that have heightened significance in the current "age of statutes."[24] After all, federal statutes—as well as administrative rules and judicial decisions interpreting them—often require revision. Some laws, such as the ADA, are ambiguous. Others may conflict, produce unintended consequences, or reflect antiquated technology, science, market conditions, or political values. Moreover, even if laws are skillfully drafted and reasonably construed, Congress, federal agencies, and courts represent distinct policy-making forums, which may conflict over the reading of statutes. Under these circumstances, passing overrides offers Congress a direct means to send follow-up signals to the courts that aim to repair flawed statutes, reconcile discordant statutory constructions, and reverse errant judicial decisions.

The passage of overrides promises another, more subtle function. It allows dissatisfied groups to revisit issues in a legislative forum, and raise concerns that courts—as adjudicators of discrete legal disputes—may either have overlooked or be poorly designed to consider.[25] As a result, the passage of overrides has the potential to broaden deliberation on contested issues as well as set the legislative record straight.

Of course, promising is one thing; delivering is quite another. Accordingly, this book asks: do overrides fulfill their promise? Specifically, does the passage of overrides effectively clarify the law, reverse objectionable judicial interpretation of statutes, and promote open policy-making? More broadly, what does the passage of overrides suggest about the nature of contemporary court-Congress interaction over the meaning of statutes?

The Debate

The answers to these questions are far from clear, because the major characterizations of American policy-making—pluralism, capture, and hyperpluralism—rest on competing assumptions about the nature of inter-branch relations in a fragmented lawmaking process. These assumptions, in turn, suggest three distinct views of the passage of overrides, which can be called the "pluralist," "capture," and "hyperpluralist" views.

To elaborate, pluralism assumes that the genius of American government lies in its fragmentation of power among overlapping political forums, which are designed to approach lawmaking differently and respond to distinct constituencies and resources. This dispersal of power provides multiple access points to diversely representative lawmakers, which should encourage a wide range of interests to participate in policy-making. It reduces opportunities for unilateral action by any single branch of government, or majority or minority faction, which should protect individual liberty. It promotes iterative policy-making among the branches of government, which in turn should serve several functions: the generation of inter-branch feedback; the revision of poorly drafted or outmoded laws; and, over time, the creation of policy consensus and, hence, legal certainty.[26]

Applying this logic to the passage of overrides, pluralists envision an open and effective policy dialogue among the branches. More specifically,

Congress initiates the dialogue by passing a statute, which agencies implement according to federal regulations. Competing interest groups then turn to courts, which resolve specific disputes arising under the statute and regulations. In the course of litigation, judges can fill gaps that inevitably appear when abstract rules are applied to concrete cases; they can alert Congress to unintended consequences of statutes and administrative rules; and, if needed, they can give voice to those who failed to participate in other policy-making forums. If litigation reveals statutory flaws, or produces objectionable judicial interpretations, interest groups can appeal to Congress, which can scrutinize the courts' decisions and revise the original statute in light of lessons learned from litigation.[27]

Capture theorists counter that the American system of separate institutions sharing power is not a formula for open, inter-branch dialogue; rather, it is a policy-making obstacle course that systematically favors well-organized interests, which alone have the necessary determination, resources, and allies to pursue their agendas in multiple political forums.[28] Classic versions of this argument envisage regulated industries dominating agencies. Over time, however, modern capture theory—which is sometimes called "public choice" theory—has been stretched in several ways. First, it has been applied to the passage of overrides as well as regulatory rule-making.[29] Second, and more controversially, it has been applied to governmental entities as well as regulated industries on the ground that governmental entities are well suited to obtain congressional reversals of unfavorable court rulings at the expense of politically weak groups, such as immigrants and criminal defendants.[30]

More specifically, as applied to the passage of overrides, capture theory has lawmaking and litigation components. In Congress and federal agencies, well-organized groups have the motive, means, and opportunity to control lawmaking at the expense of unorganized interests and uninformed voters. The motive is favorable legislation and regulations. The means are promises to support accommodating members of Congress in future campaigns and accommodating agencies in future budget battles. The opportunity stems from the costs of political participation, which fall disproportionately on diffuse or poorly organized interests because these groups are unlikely to mobilize for political action in the first place and, even if mobilized, are unlikely to have the connections, experience, and staying power to navigate Washington's lawmaking maze. The net results, it is contended, are skewed statutes and administrative rules that favor well-organized interests.

Enacting favorable laws and regulations is not enough, however, to capture a system of fragmented policy-making authority. Groups must win in the courts as well. Fortunately for them, well-organized interests are likely to be "repeat players": entities that litigate frequently and face a large number of similar claims.[31] As repeat players, they should be uniquely situated to use litigation as a policy-making tool. Why? Unlike "one-shotters," which litigate infrequently and face discrete claims, repeat players can litigate strategically, with an eye toward shaping the rules of the game. Thus, repeat players can settle unfavorable cases, and focus on cases that place their claims in the most sympathetic light (and before the most sympathetic judges). Over time, such selective litigation should shape legal precedents to their advantage. Moreover, if well-organized groups unexpectedly lose in court, they can appeal to Congress for corrective legislation. Then, armed with a new statute, they can return to court and pursue cases that are likely to lock in their legislative gains.

Hyperpluralists offer a different critique of fragmented power. Whereas contemporary capture theory suggests that the cost of competing in multiple policy-making arenas creates unfair barriers to political participation, hyperpluralists maintain that the American system of separate institutions sharing power is too fragmented and open to a fault.[32] In connection with the passage of overrides, the hyperpluralist argument has several steps. First, fragmented lawmaking authority creates political incentives for elected officials to enact vague or partial overrides, which send controversial aspects of override issues back to the courts. The reason is straightforward. Vague laws allow members of Congress to claim credit for enacting statutes, while avoiding tough choices that may alienate constituents or haunt them in future campaigns.[33] Second, even if members of Congress intend to enact clear overrides, it is difficult to pass coherent statutes on Capitol Hill because federal statutes are drafted piecemeal by specialized committees and individual members who serve different political constituents. As a result, American statutes tend to accrete layer upon layer, regardless of internal consistency or consistency with existing laws.[34] Third, if Congress manages to pass clear overrides, or agencies manage to promulgate rules that make sense of vague or flawed measures, no guarantee exists that the courts will apply the law consistently. To the contrary, federal judicial power is widely dispersed among politically selected—and ideologically diverse—judges, whose decisions are rarely reviewed by the Supreme Court.[35] Accordingly, American statutes may often be applied inconsistently, reflecting discordant conservative and liberal readings of the law.

The consequent legal uncertainty, hyperpluralists add, undermines the quality of American policy on several levels. Most obviously, in the absence of clear rules, substantively similar claims are more likely to be treated differently, which is patently unfair. After all, why should Cubans seeking asylum in Miami be treated differently than similarly situated Chinese seeking refuge in Los Angeles? Why should criminal defendants facing the same federal charges in Texas be treated differently than those in Massachusetts? Why should manufacturers in the South face different federal regulatory standards than those in other regions of the nation? Ideally, they should not, especially when courts apply federal laws that purport to create national standards.

In addition, persistent legal uncertainty reduces the efficiency of legal processes, which hurts *both* one-shotters and repeat players. With respect to one-shotters, if the governing law is unclear, parties must litigate both legal standards and underlying factual issues. At the margin, the expense of contesting legal questions on top of factual issues may discourage lawsuits that are legally meritorious but involve small stakes.

One might counter that deterring lawsuits poses little concern in the United States; indeed, some might welcome fewer lawsuits.[36] Contrary to popular belief, however, research typically shows that Americans are not litigation crazy.[37] For example, studies show that only 10 of every 100 Americans hurt in accidents file any type of claim, and only 2 of 100 file lawsuits.[38] Only 5 of every 100 Americans who believe that another's illegal conduct cost them over $1,000 file lawsuits.[39] Even in the area of medical malpractice, a perceived hotbed of litigation, a leading study shows that only 1 of every 8 patients injured by doctors' negligence file lawsuits.[40] Among those who do file claims, many give up when confronted with a long and unpredictable adversarial process.[41] If these studies are correct, and many ordinary Americans do forego legitimate claims, then deterring one-shotters from pursuing litigation would be troubling indeed.

At the same time, unclear rules are not a panacea for repeat players. Although repeat players may be in a better position to absorb litigation costs, legal uncertainty may drive them to engage in repetitive and wasteful litigation, which adds needless expense to doing business in the United States.[42] In addition, legal ambiguity limits the ability of repeat players to plan, which in extreme cases may cast a shadow on clearly beneficial activities. Consider the production of childhood vaccines. In the mid-1980s, lawmakers feared a national shortage of the vaccine for diphtheria, pertussis, and tetanus—the "DPT vaccine"—because some drug manufacturers claimed they could no longer obtain insurance against the unpredictable risk of massive jury verdicts. Eventually, Congress passed reforms that created obstacles to bringing tort claims related to vaccinations. Once Congress deterred families from filing such claims, production of the DPT vaccine stabilized, and research and innovation in vaccines flourished.[43]

In sum, the logic of pluralism, capture, and hyperpluralism paint very different pictures of the passage of overrides. Pluralism implies that the passage of overrides should be part of an inter-branch feedback loop that features open congressional deliberation, the passage of clear and comprehensive follow-up legislation, and judicial consensus after Congress acts. Capture theory suggests that the passage of overrides should be part of a one-sided policy-making process that produces clear override bills and

Table 1.1   The Pluralist, Capture, and Hyperpluralist Views of the Passage
of Overrides

Questions	Pluralist	Capture	Hyperpluralist
Does the passage of overrides typically feature diverse interest group participation?	Yes	No	Yes
Does Congress typically pass clear and comprehensive override statutes?	Yes	Yes	No
Does the passage of overrides typically promote legal certainty?	Yes	Yes	No

judicial consensus in favor of well-organized interests at the expense of
diffuse interests and one-shotters. Hyperpluralism implies that the passage
of overrides should be part of an ongoing process of inter-branch stalemate, which is open but fails to produce legal certainty because either
(1) Congress passes vague or partial overrides, or (2) politically selected,
independent, and ideologically diverse judges resist congressional oversight and read the law along partisan lines. Table 1.1 summarizes the main
points of contention.

Assessing the Debate

In the abstract, assessing the pluralist, capture, and hyperpluralist views is
difficult because each view has a ring of plausibility. Consistent with
pluralism, the passage of overrides may be open and effective. Consistent
with capture theory, it may involve one-sided lawmaking and litigation;
or, consistent with hyperpluralism, it may involve congressional passing-
the-buck or inter-branch stalemate, which results in persistent legal
uncertainty. Alternatively, each view might be partially correct, accurately
characterizing some—but not all—cases. Indeed, it is not difficult to find
examples of open and effective, one-sided and effective, and open but
ineffective override processes. Consider the following cases:

   *The Central Intelligence Information Act: An Open, Effective
Override Process.*   After Watergate, Congress passed a spate of "sunshine
acts": laws aimed at improving public access to governmental records. The
acts pitted individual citizens and public interest groups, which seek access
to governmental files, against governmental agencies that often seek to
protect their records' confidentiality.

Following the passage of these laws, the competing interests vigorously litigated the scope of public access to government files. Litigation, in turn, revealed a potential conflict between the Privacy Act, which provides a number of exceptions to government disclosure, and the Freedom of Information Act (FOIA), which provides broad access to governmental documents. Faced with this conflict, the D.C. and Third Circuits of the U.S. Court of Appeals construed the laws expansively, holding that exemptions under the Privacy Act should not thwart requests under the FOIA.[44] The Fifth and Seventh Circuits read them restrictively, holding that information exempt from disclosure under the Privacy Act should also be exempt under the FOIA.[45]

Stalemated in court, the competing interests appealed to Congress for clarification. In 1984, after hearing testimony from groups on both sides of the issue, including the Central Intelligence Agency (CIA), which advocated a narrow interpretation of the laws, and the American Civil Liberties Union (ACLU) and American Bar Association, which called for a broad interpretation, Congress enacted the Central Intelligence Information Act (the Information Act). The Information Act explicitly rejected the Fifth and Seventh Circuits' narrow interpretation of the laws, and directed courts to favor an individual's right of access to information about themselves over the government's interest in confidentiality.

In passing the act, Congress stated: "Whatever ambiguity exists will be removed."[46] Congress was right. After the act, judicial consensus emerged on the underlying issues that was consistent with the terms of the new law.[47] Indeed, according to the First Circuit, "The clarity of the statutory command [in the Information Act] is stunning."[48]

Court-Congress interactions surrounding the Information Act seem a textbook example of open and effective override processes. The process was open in that competing interests had the resources and willingness first to bring lawsuits and then to participate in congressional deliberations. In addition, the process engendered inter-branch feedback and policy consensus. Specifically, litigation revealed tension between statutes, which engendered controversy in the courts. This controversy spilled into the legislative arena when the litigants appealed to Congress for clarification. After hearing testimony from all sides, Congress passed a comprehensive override, which sought to eliminate the drafting errors exposed in litigation. After Congress acted, courts abandoned the overridden decisions and uniformly applied the new law.[49]

Criminal Fine Improvements Act of 1987: A One-Sided, Effective Override Process. Similar to the Information Act, the Criminal Fine Improvements Act of 1987 (Fine Improvements Act) addressed the interplay between separately enacted statutes: section 13 of the Assimilative Crimes Act (ACA) and section 3013 of the Comprehensive Crime Control Act of 1984 (the Crime Control Act). Overall, section 13 of the ACA seeks to avoid gaps in criminal law that governs federal enclaves, such as military bases and territories. It provides that violations of local laws on federal lands constitute federal offenses, and are subject to "like punishments."[50] Thus, the ACA "assimilates" local law into federal law. Section 3013 of the Crime Control Act provides that violators of federal criminal law must pay a special assessment into a federal fund for crime victims.

The question was somewhat complex: namely, are violators of the ACA required to pay under the Crime Control Act if local law does not require similar payments? The statutes sent mixed signals. On one hand, section 13 of the ACA states that violators should be held to "like punishments." This language suggests that violators of assimilated crimes should pay under the Crime Control Act only if local law provides an analogous victims' fund. On the other hand, section 3013 of the Crime Control Act does not distinguish between violations of the ACA and other federal criminal statutes. It simply states that violators of federal criminal law— whether assimilated from local law or not—must pay into the federal fund.

Courts struggled with this question. The Fourth and Tenth Circuits of the U.S. Court of Appeals held that violators under the ACA were exempt from section 3013 of the Crime Control Act, unless state law established a victims' fund. They reasoned that the ACA was intended to incorporate— not expand upon—local criminal law, and that any ambiguity in the statutory framework should be construed in favor of criminal defendants.[51] The Third and Eighth Circuits flatly disagreed. Applying the plain language of the Crime Control Act, they held that violators under the ACA must pay into the federal victims' fund, regardless of local law.[52]

Dissatisfied with the Fourth and Tenth Circuits' narrow construction of the statutes, prosecutors and law enforcement officials appealed to Congress. In 1987, Congress responded and passed the Fine Improvements Act, which explicitly reversed the Fourth and Tenth Circuits' decisions.[53] Following the override, courts have consistently held that violators under the ACA are liable under the Crime Control Act, even if local law fails to provide a victims' fund.[54]

Comparing the Information Act and the Fine Improvements Act illustrates the difference between open and effective versus one-sided and effective override processes. In both cases, the original statutes generated considerable litigation, which revealed an unintended flaw in the original statutory framework. In both cases, Congress passed an override that sought to fix the statutory glitch. And, in both cases, the override triggered judicial consensus. In the Information Act case, however, competing interests actively participated in each stage of the process, and Congress passed an override that favored the public's right of access over the objections of powerful governmental agencies. In the Fine Improvements Act, governmental interests appealed to Congress without opposition from groups with competing viewpoints, and Congress rewrote the law in their favor. Thus, the Fine Improvements Act produced judicial consensus, but the process seemed narrowly responsive to well-organized groups, such as prosecutors and law enforcement officials, at the expense of politically unpopular groups, such as convicted criminals.

The Civil Rights Act of 1991: An Open but Ineffective Override Process. The Civil Rights Act of 1991 illustrates another possibility: open but ineffective override processes. The Civil Rights Act of 1991 traces its roots to long-standing controversy over "disparate impact analysis": a judicial doctrine under Title VII of the Civil Rights Act of 1964, which prohibits discrimination in the workplace. Disparate impact analysis originated in the famous Supreme Court case *Griggs v. Duke Power Company.*[55] Under *Griggs,* the Court held that employment practices affecting minorities disproportionately create a presumption of discrimination, regardless of an employer's intent. To rebut this presumption, the employer must prove the practices are specifically related to job performance and a "business necessity."[56]

During the 1980s, the Rehnquist Court handed down a series of sharply divided cases that sought to limit employment discrimination law, in general, and disparate impact claims, in particular. The most prominent case—*Wards Cove Packing v. San Antonio*[57]—attacked disparate impact analysis on two fronts. First, the majority eroded the presumption of discrimination, holding that even striking statistical discrepancies among ethnic or racial groups within general job categories was insufficient to show discrimination. Instead, plaintiffs would be required to connect specific practices with specific discriminatory effects.[58] Second, even if plaintiffs linked specific practices to specific effects, plaintiffs could not shift the burden to employers to exonerate their practices. Instead, the majority ruled that plaintiffs would have to prove that the practices were not justified.[59]

Conservatives hailed *Wards Cove* and similar cases as a return, or at least a partial return, to the original spirit and language of Title VII, which they argued targeted intentional discrimination and explicitly rejected racial quotas.[60] Liberals decried them as rank judicial activism, which violated well-settled judicial precedent.[61] They added that, even if the Supreme Court initially misread Title VII under *Griggs,* Congress had ample opportunities to reject disparate impact analysis. Rather than reject it, however, Congress embraced it by extending disparate impact analysis to voting rights, fair housing, and age discrimination laws.[62]

Not satisfied with criticizing *Wards Cove* and its progeny, liberals quickly appealed to Congress to reverse these cases. Their efforts stalled in the 101st Congress, because President Bush vetoed the Civil Rights Act of 1990.[63] In the 102nd Congress, however, efforts to overturn the Court's decisions reportedly received a lift from two unexpected sources: the confirmation hearing of Justice Clarence Thomas, which erupted over Anita Hill's allegations of sexual harassment, and former Ku Klux Klan member David Duke's surprisingly strong showing in the Republican gubernatorial primary in Louisiana.[64] Specifically, after failing to torpedo Justice Thomas's nomination, Democrats wanted to pass a civil rights bill to regain a measure of face with their base. Following the unseemly rise of David Duke, and the often-distasteful spectacle of white, male GOP senators grilling Anita Hill about intimate details of her relationship with Clarence Thomas, moderate Republicans and President Bush wanted to blunt perceptions of racism and sexism prior to the upcoming 1992 elections.

Despite these political incentives to pass a bill, the competing interests could not reach a specific agreement. Instead, they crafted a compromise measure—the Civil Rights Act of 1991—which seems impressive at first glance but leaves many tough issues unresolved. Indeed, according to the *Congressional Quarterly*, "[V]agueness was part of the compromise" that enabled the 1991 act to pass.[65] For example, on the central issue of disparate impact analysis, the act provides that once a plaintiff shows that "a particular employment practice causes a disparate impact" on minorities, the employer must "demonstrate that the challenged practice is *job related* for the position in question and consistent with *business necessity*."[66] Congress, however, did not define *job related* and *business necessity* in the statute. This omission was crucial, because these terms were highly contested and subject to multiple interpretations.

The accompanying legislative history, moreover, offers little help in construing these key provisions. To their credit, leading lawmakers tried to provide courts with some guidance. They agreed that a brief memorandum from Senator John Danforth should furnish the exclusive legislative history on "job related" and "business necessity." The memo stated that the bill is "intended to reflect the concepts . . . of *Griggs v. Duke Power Co.,* . . . , and in other Supreme Court decisions prior to *Wards Cove Packing Co. v. Antonio*."[67] The deal quickly collapsed, however, as rank-and-file liberals and conservatives in Congress packed the legislative record with inconsistent, politically motivated statements.[68] Frustrated by efforts to "doctor the legislative history," Senator Danforth warned that courts should take the floor debates and statements in the *Congressional Record* "with a large grain of salt."[69]

On other issues, Congress did not even try to guide the courts. Consider "retroactivity," specifically whether the 1991 Civil Rights Act applied to lawsuits on the courts' dockets when the act was passed. The statute was silent on this issue and Senator Edward Kennedy explained as follows: "It will be up to the courts to determine the extent to which the bill will apply to cases and claims that are pending on the date of enactment."[70] Reflecting on these events, Shep Melnick, a keen observer of the American policy-making process, wrote, "What the federal courts will eventually make of all this is anybody's guess."[71]

Guess is the right word.[72] Following the passage of the Civil Rights Act of 1991, courts have developed at least four tests for "job related" and "business necessity."[73] Nor has confusion been limited to definitional issues. The issue of retroactivity split the circuits. The D.C. Circuit ruled that the act did not apply to cases filed before its passage, whereas the Ninth Circuit ruled the opposite.[74] In 1994, the Supreme Court granted certiorari to resolve the split, and held that the Civil Rights Act of 1991 did not apply retroactively.[75] However, as in so many civil rights cases, the Supreme Court was divided, and the majority and dissent offered contradictory readings of the statute.[76]

To make matters more confused, courts have added vague glosses to the Civil Rights Act of 1991. For example, the act allows for the recovery of punitive damages. In a 6 to 5 *en banc* decision, the U.S. Court of Appeals for the D.C. Circuit held that plaintiffs could recover punitive damages only if an employer's conduct was "egregious"—a term that does not appear in the statute.[77] In a 5 to 4 decision, the Supreme Court rejected the Circuit Court's interpretation in favor of its own innovation, ruling that the act bars punitive damages as long as employers try to comply with the law in "good faith." To reiterate, the Court acted unilaterally. The statute does not provide a good-faith exception and neither party to the lawsuit argued for one.[78] Moreover, the Court failed to define *good faith*, inviting yet another round of judicial policy-making by the lower courts.

This process seems a classic illustration of an open but ineffective override process. The process was clearly open; groups of every ideological and political stripe participated in litigation and congressional deliberations. Congress, meanwhile, struggled to pass *any* legislation. Indeed, without a political boost from the unlikely pair of Anita Hill and David Duke, stalemate on a civil rights bill may have persisted indefinitely. Moreover, despite political incentives to reach an accord, the factions could not enact specific legislation. Instead, members of Congress fudged; they passed a vague statute that allowed claiming credit on both sides of the aisle, but deliberately punted controversial matters to the courts.

Judges, in turn, continue to divide over the proper interpretation of the law, resulting in persistent legal uncertainty over important rules governing the American workplace.

Of course, these examples do not exhaust the range of plausible court-Congress relations underlying the passage of overrides. Congressional deference to the courts may not constitute passing the buck, as in the case of the Civil Rights Act of 1991; rather, it may reflect a broad consensus that judges should be given flexibility to refine legal standards on a case-by-case basis in dynamic policy areas. Alternatively, Congress may try and fail to resolve the underlying issue because it unintentionally passes unclear overrides or politically independent American judges resist congressional oversight.[79] Another possibility is that well-organized groups capture the lawmaking process, but not the judicial process, because judges use their power of statutory interpretation to temper the effects of one-sided congressional revisions.

Overview

The previous examples underscore the questions raised at the outset about the passage of overrides. Most fundamentally, do overrides matter? That is, does the passage of overrides clarify the law, as in the cases of the Information Act and the Fine Improvements Act, or does the controversy that produced litigation and congressional revision of the original statute spill into the courts after Congress acts, as in the case of the Civil Rights Act of 1991? Assuming that overrides matter, what patterns of court-Congress relations underlie the override process? Consistent with pluralism and the Information Act, are overrides part of open and effective inter-branch policy-making processes? Consistent with modern capture theory and the Fine Improvements Act, are they part of one-sided lawmaking and litigation processes? Or, consistent with hyperpluralism and the Civil Rights Act of 1991, are they part of open but ineffective inter-branch relations? If court-Congress interaction related to the passage of overrides varies, which patterns are most common? Which are least common? What factors account for this variation? Finally, what do the data suggest about the broader pluralist, capture, and hyperpluralist debate about the implications of fragmented lawmaking power?

Summary of Data

Exploring these questions requires data on interest group, congressional, and judicial behavior before, during, and after the passage of overrides.[80] Accordingly, I have collected original data related to 100 randomly selected overrides that were passed from 1974 to 1990, which encompass diverse issue, interest group, and institutional contexts that scholars have argued may affect court-Congress relations.[81] The cases can be visualized as 100 timelines,[82] which consist of the following stages: (1) Congress passes a statute (which I call the "original statute"); (2) agencies typically promulgate rules that implement the original statute; (3) courts interpret the original statute and related rules; (4) Congress passes an override; (5) agencies typically generate another round of rules; and, in most cases, (6) courts interpret the override and new rules. The data include detailed observations on the following: court decisions under the original statute, interest group activity related to the passage of the override, the content of the override as well as the content of the legislative record and expert commentary related to the override, and post-override activity up to January 2001, which includes any court decisions under the override as well as additional congressional action.[83]

Summary of Main Findings

Overall, the data suggest that the passage of overrides is *typically* pluralistic, *rarely* captured, and *sometimes* hyperpluralistic.

The Passage of Overrides Is Typically Pluralistic.   The majority of cases—59 of 100—involved some form of pluralism. The most common override scenario in the sample by far—representing 46 of 100 cases—was the pluralist ideal of "effective deliberative revision": cases in which congressional deliberation on the override bill is open; Congress passes a "prescriptive override," a bill that seeks to resolve the override issue; and the override triggers judicial consensus.

Closer analysis of the cases revealed four additional findings that support the pluralist view. First, contrary to hyperpluralism and consistent with pluralism, the passage of overrides seems to *increase significantly* levels of judicial consensus, as indicated by a variety of measures. For example, there was a marked increase in non-partisan, consistent rule application under the relevant statutes. Thus, the data show that about 10 percent of the original statutes triggered judicial consensus. Following the passage of overrides, the overall level of judicial consensus increased five-fold, to about 50 percent.

Second, contrary to capture theory and consistent with pluralism, the passage of overrides is *almost always open,* as indicated by a content analysis of the witness lists and testimony on the override bill. In every case, competing interests litigated under the original statute. In 95 of 100 cases, competing interests participated in congressional deliberation on the override bill. In 84 of 100 cases, these interests then returned to the courts and relitigated override issues. Thus, in the typical case, competing interests had the resources and determination to go to court and Congress, and back again, despite the undoubted cost of lobbying and litigating on the override issue.

Third, contrary to hyperpluralism, the overriding Congress did not typically delegate, even though the override issues were highly divisive. Specifically, about 90 percent of the original statutes produced judicial dissensus in the pre-override period, as indicated by explicit circuit splits, dissents, or reversals on statutory grounds. Faced with such divisive issues, hyperpluralists would expect members of Congress to enact vague or "partial overrides": bills that explicitly send significant aspects of the override issue to the courts. However, in 79 of 100 cases, Congress confronted the underlying policy matter and passed prescriptive overrides that sought to resolve the override issue.

Finally, when Congress did pass partial overrides, delegation did not appear to reflect a collective throwing up of hands, as in the case of the Civil Rights Act of 1991. Instead, in 19 of 21 partial overrides, Congress' decision to give courts discretion on significant aspects of the override issue was supported by a broad policy consensus, as indicated by a content analysis of the legislative record and expert commentary at the time of the override's passage.

The Passage of Overrides Is Rarely Captured.   As noted earlier, only 5 of 100 cases involved one-sided congressional deliberation, and none of these cases involved the classic capture override scenario of a regulated industry unilaterally reversing unfavorable court decisions. Instead, these cases were similar to the Fine Improvements Act, in which relatively autonomous governmental entities, such as the Justice Department, successfully overrode technical procedural rulings of the court without opposition. Moreover, there was little evidence that repeat players systematically "won" in Congress at the expense of one-shotters. In fact, in most cases, the overriding Congress *reversed* judicial decisions that favored repeat players. Thus, to find any examples of capture in the sample, the concept had to be stretched.

The Passage of Overrides Is Sometimes Hyperpluralistic. Although examples of capture theory were relatively rare in the sample, a significant minority—37 of 100—of cases involved one of three hyperpluralist scenarios. Twenty-eight cases involved "weak congressional signals," cases in which non-partisan judicial dissensus followed open congressional deliberation and the passage of prescriptive overrides; seven cases involved "partisan judicial resistance," cases in which partisan judicial dissensus followed open congressional deliberation and the passage of prescriptive overrides; and 2 cases involved "delegation by default," cases in which

Congress passed partial overrides that delegate significant aspects of the override issue to the courts, despite a broad policy consensus that Congress should have passed prescriptive overrides that try to resolve the override issue.

Taken together, these findings suggest that the passage of overrides is remarkably open, but open congressional deliberation produces diverse pluralist and hyperpluralist scenarios. This variation raises the question: when does open deliberation produce pluralist versus hyperpluralist patterns of court-Congress relations? The data point to two factors. First, if the override issue directly affects the federal budget, members of Congress—or, more precisely, members of prestige and re-election committees—tend to draft more comprehensive and effective overrides, especially when the override issue involves the collection of tax revenue. It is worth stressing that, contrary to capture theory, the crucial issue is whether Congress's money is at stake and not the resources of the contending interest groups. Indeed, in almost all tax cases in the sample, members of prestige committees passed overrides *over the objection* of well-organized business interests. Second, if the override issue split the courts along partisan lines in the pre-override period, federal judges seemed more likely to resist congressional oversight, especially when the issue involved the interpretation of the statutory rights of discrete, insular minorities, such as African Americans or immigrants. Thus, some issues seem impervious to congressional control, even when Congress sends follow-up signals.

Intended Contributions to the Literature

Beyond offering specific findings about the passage of overrides and insights into the long-standing pluralist, capture, and hyperpluralist debate, this book seeks to illustrate a new way of studying inter-branch relations that bridges competing approaches and suggests areas of further inquiry. Specifically, after more than a decade of innovative and fruitful scholarship by political scientists and legal scholars, the study of court-Congress relations seems to have reached an impasse. Scholars have divided into three camps: positive political theorists, policy analysts, and legal scholars. Positive political theorists, or game theorists, seek to identify the strategic dynamics governing inter-branch relations. To do so, they have predominantly used spatial models or signaling games to describe interactions among competing political actors, who seek to maximize their preferences in iterated processes with asymmetric information.

The great strengths of these approaches are parsimony and hypothesis generation. Indeed, in Chapters 3 and 7, I draw on this literature extensively when analyzing whether and under what conditions Congress will send effective override signals. However, the pluralist, capture, and hyperpluralist views on the passage of overrides concerns issues other than strategic equilibrium among competing actors or the effectiveness of overrides as signals. They concern the nature of the political processes that underlie court-Congress relations, especially the diversity of interests that participate in multiple policy-making forums. Simple spatial models and signaling games are not well suited to address these types of process-oriented issues, because these games tend to place a "black box" around the processes that produce stable policy outcomes or effective signals.

This characterization of spatial models and signaling games is not intended as a criticism. All models simplify to gain analytic leverage, and both approaches provide invaluable insights into inter-branch relations in a system of separation of powers.[84] It merely recognizes that, if we are interested in exploring other aspects of inter-branch relations, such as the nature of interest group participation during the passage of overrides, we must look beyond these standard game theoretic approaches.[85]

Policy analysts have taken a different tack. Instead of providing highly abstract, deductive models of inter-branch relations, they work from the bottom up, offering rich descriptions of a small number of inter-branch relations or a number of inter-branch relations in a single policy area. These studies provide indispensable insights into the complexity of American policy-making that underscore the importance of issue, institutional, and interest group contexts in shaping policy outcomes. However, these studies do not provide a systematic basis for generalizing about the political dynamics of court-Congress relations, leaving readers to speculate as to whether insights in one setting apply to others.

Legal scholars offer a third approach to studying inter-branch relations, an approach that places a premium on assessing the proper method for construing statutes and the proper role of courts in policy-making. These studies provide valuable prescriptions for the reading of statutes and normative evaluations of the quality of specific judicial decisions. However, they often gloss over explanatory questions, leaving readers to guess at the conditions under which courts satisfy the prescriptive and normative criteria that have been devised with such care.

Under these circumstances, we need an approach that attempts to look past the existing divisions and instead provides the following: a contextually richer and more process-oriented understanding of court-Congress relations than simple spatial models and signaling games; a more systematic basis for generating hypotheses about the dynamics of court-Congress relations than "small-N" case studies; and a framework for describing patterns of court-Congress relations, which remains attuned to broader normative issues, including whether inter-branch policy-making serves basic democratic values, such as broad political participation, and important policy goals, such as legal certainty.

This book offers a significant downpayment on this research agenda, seeking to make contributions on conceptual, empirical, theoretical, and methodological grounds. Conceptually, this book offers a new perspective on the passage of overrides. Specifically, as discussed in Chapter 2, the existing literature tends to examine overrides from the perspective of Congress, examining when Congress responds to Supreme Court statutory interpretation decisions. This study examines the passage of overrides through the lens of pluralist, capture, and hyperpluralist characterizations of inter-branch policy-making, and creates a new typology for describing patterns of court-Congress relations that underlie the passage of overrides. Empirically, this book uses original data to describe the relative frequency of pluralist, capture, and hyperpluralist override scenarios; to explore the conditions that tend to produce the pluralist versus hyperpluralist override scenarios; and, on a limited basis, to probe the validity of pluralist, capture, and hyperpluralist assumptions about inter-branch relations in a fragmented policy-making process. Theoretically, it generates new hypotheses about current court-Congress relations based on a relatively large number of cases that reflect different issue, interest group, and institutional contexts. Methodically, it illustrates what I call "large-N process tracing," a technique that details the unfolding of political processes in a relatively large sample of cases along a few, theoretically crucial dimensions. This approach allows the researcher to develop generalized descriptions of the relative frequency of political process patterns, which in turn can serve as a useful basis for further empirical analysis as well as building theory.

Of course, any time one seeks to break new ground and combine diverse approaches, the result will be neither fish nor fowl. Positive political theorists will surely find the approach too inductive and messy. Quantitative scholars will want more data and refined measures, which will allow greater generalizability and more sophisticated methods of testing. Policy experts will want more detail, especially more thorough consideration of the role of agencies in the process. Legal scholars will want a comprehensive prescriptive theory for when each branch should take the policy-making lead. Ultimately, I agree. But in my judgment, the first step toward better theory and empirical tests in this area is returning to basics and then rethinking the outcomes to be explained and evaluated. In that spirit, this book is best understood as a beginning, not a culmination, of inquiry.

Plan of Argument

The book develops these arguments in seven chapters. Chapter 2 lays the foundation, explaining the promise of overrides in contemporary

American policy-making and reviewing the override literature. The goals are to underscore why the passage of overrides merits careful consideration and to provide context for the following chapters.

Chapters 3 through 7 analyze the data in two parts. Part I, comprising Chapters 3 and 4, considers the threshold question raised by the pluralist, capture, and hyperpluralist views—namely, do overrides matter? That is, does the passage of overrides clarify the law by significantly increasing levels of judicial consensus? In addressing this question, Chapter 3 explains my assumptions about the nature of legal constraints and sets forth the competing hypotheses. Chapter 4 describes the data and methods for probing these hypotheses and discusses the findings.

Part II, consisting of Chapters 5, 6, and 7, takes a closer look at the cases and asks, what patterns of interest group, congressional, and judicial activity underlie the passage of overrides? To answer this question, Chapter 5 creates an original typology of the override scenarios that builds on the logic of the pluralist, capture, and hyperpluralist accounts of inter-branch policy-making. Chapter 6 operationalizes these scenarios, reports their distribution in the sample, and analyzes the findings. Chapter 7 then explores what conditions tend to produce the predominant patterns of court-Congress relations in the sample, and offers a general theory of the dynamics of court-Congress relations in connection with the passage of overrides.

Chapter 8 concludes the analysis. It considers the data's lessons for the broader pluralist, capture, and hyperpluralist debate, and charts avenues of future inquiry.

Notes

1. William O. Douglas, "Legal Institutions in America," in *Legal Institutions Today and Tomorrow: The Centennial Conference Volume of the Columbia Law School,* ed. Monrad Paulsen (New York: Columbia University Press, 1959), 292. Law Professors Michael Solimine and James Walker strike a similar chord. They state: "[C]ongressional response to Supreme Court decisions is healthy for both institutions and for democracy, as a whole" ("The Next Word: Congressional Response to Supreme Court Statutory Interpretation Decisions," *Temple Law Review* 65 [1992]: 453).

2. Quoted in James Q. Wilson, *Bureaucracy: What Government Agencies Do and Why They Do It* (New York: Basic Books, 1989), 300.

3. This means that, using their "good" eyes, the sisters could see objects from 20 feet as well as individuals with 20/20 vision could see the same objects from 200 feet.

4. See generally Adam C. Wit, "*Sutton* and *Murphy:* What it Means to be Disabled under the ADA," *Employee Relations Law Journal* 25, no. 3 (1999): 41.

5. 42 U.S.C. sec. 12102(2)(A).

6. See Justice Stevens' dissent in *Sutton et al v. United Airlines, Inc.,* 527 U.S. 471, 507 (1999) (citing National Center for Health Statistics).

7. See, for example, Senate Report No. 101–116 (1989), 23–24; H. R. Report No. 101-485 (1990), Part II 51–52 and Part III 28–29.

8. See 29 C.F.R. Part 1630, App. 1630.2(j) (1998) (EEOC rules); 28 C.F.R. Part 35, App. A, Sec. 35.104 (1998) (Justice Department rules); and 49 C.F.R. Part 37.3 (1998) (Department of Transportation rules).

9. See 42 U.S.C. sec. 12101(a)(1); see also Wit, "*Sutton* and *Murphy,*" 46.

10. *Sutton et al v. United Airlines,* 1996 U.S. Dist. LEXIS 15106 (1996).

11. *Sutton et al v. United Airlines, Inc.,* 130 F.3d 893, 895 (10th Cir. 1997); accord *Gilday v. Mecosta County,* 124 F.3d 760, 765 (6th Cir. 1997).

12. See, for example, *Bartlett v. New York Board of Law Examiners,* 156 F.3d 321, 329 (2d Cir. 1998); *Arnold v. United Parcel Service, Inc.,* 136 F.3d 854, 863 (1st Cir. 1998); *Baert v. Euclid Beverage, Ltd.,* 149 F.3d 626, 630–31 (7th Cir. 1998); *Washington v. HCA Health Services of Texas,* 152 F.3d 464, 470 (5th Cir. 1998); *Matcza v. Frankford Candy & Chocolate Co.,* 136 F.3d 933, 937 (3d Cir. 1997); *Doane v. Omaha,* 115 F.3d 624, 627–28 (8th Cir. 1997) certiorari denied 522 U.S. 1048 (1998); *Harris v. H. & W. Contracting Co.,* 102 F.3d 516, 521 (11th Cir. 1996); *Holihan v. Lucky Stores, Inc.,* 87 F.3d 362, 366 (9th Cir. 1996).

13. "Supreme Court Grapples with Application of Disability Law," *San Francisco Chronicle,* 29 April 1999, A8.

14. Linda Greenhouse, "Justices Wrestle with the Definition of Disability: Is it Glasses? False Teeth?" *The New York Times,* 28 April 1999, A20 (N).

15. *Sutton et al v. United Airlines, Inc.,* 527 U.S. 471 (1999).

16. 527 U.S. at 482.

17. Ibid., 499. See also Linda Greenhouse, "High Court Limits Who is Protected by Disability Law," *The New York Times,* 23 June 1999, A1, A16 (N).

18. Quoted in Robin Toner and Leslie Kaufman, "Ruling Upsets Advocates for the Disabled," *The New York Times,* 24 June 1999, A22 (N).

19. Ibid.

20. More precisely, overrides are bills that *explicitly* (1) overrule an interpretation of a statute, (2) modify the interpretation in some material way so that the same case would be decided differently and subsequent cases would be decided differently, or (3) modify the outcome of a decision such that a particular case would come out differently but would not necessarily change similar cases in the future (or, in effect, exempts the loser in court from an unfavorable decision). See William Eskridge Jr., "Overriding Supreme Court Statutory Interpretation Decisions," *The Yale Law Journal* 101 (1991): 331, 424–41 app. 1 (identifying about 340 overrides from 1967 to 1990 using this definition). Of course, Congress may pass laws that unwittingly modify existing judicial decisions. This study excludes such "accidental" overrides to focus on intentional court-Congress interaction. In addition, Congress may override judicial

decisions without explicitly identifying the cases. Implicit overrides were excluded on practical grounds; such overrides are extremely difficult—if not impossible—to identify systematically.

21. The Civil Rights Act of 1991 sought to reverse a series of conservative Supreme Court decisions that interpreted Title VII's ban on employment discrimination narrowly. For more on the Civil Rights Act of 1991, see pages 12–15 and accompanying notes.

22. The Grove City Bill sought to overturn *Grove City College v. Bell*, 465 U.S. 555 (1984), a Rehnquist Court decision that restrictively read Title IX's ban on sex discrimination in federally funded school programs. For a brief overview of the passage of the Grove City Bill, see "'Grove City' Rights Bill Shelved by Senate," *CQ Almanac* 40 (1984): 239; "'Grove City' Bill Enacted Over Reagan's Veto," *CQ Almanac* 44 (1988): 63.

23. The Voting Rights Act of 1982 targeted *City of Mobile v. Bolden*, 446 U.S. 55 (1980), which required proof of discriminatory intent when challenging election practices (as opposed to showing that election practices produced discriminatory results). For more on the passage of this override, see "Voting Rights Act Extended, Strengthened," *CQ Almanac* 38 (1982): 373.

24. The phrase "age of statutes" comes from the title of Guido Calabresi's *A Common Law for the Age of Statutes* (Cambridge, Mass.: Harvard University Press, 1982). For more on the promise of overrides in contemporary American policy-making, see Chapter 2 at pages 34–41 and accompanying notes; see also Richard Paschal, "The Continuing Colloquy: Congress and the Finality of the Supreme Court," *Journal of Law & Politics* VIII (1991): 195 (stating that overrides are "the most effective *and easily achieved* way for Congress to respond to judicial pronouncements"); Patrick Moynihan, "What Do You Do When the Supreme Court is Wrong?" *The Public Interest* 57 (1979): 23 (stating legislation is an "unequaled" means for addressing errant Supreme Court decisions).

25. For more on the potential limits on courts as a policy-making forum, see generally David Horowitz, *The Courts and Social Policy* (Washington, D.C.: Brookings Institution, 1977); Lon Fuller, "The Forms and Limits of Adjudication," *Harvard Law Review* 92 (1978): 353; see also Gerald Rosenberg, *The Hollow Hope: Can Courts Bring About Social Change?* (Chicago: University of Chicago Press, 1991).

26. See generally James Madison, "Federalist Paper Nos. 10 and 51," in *The Federalist Papers* (1788; reprint, New York: Penguin Books, 1987) (providing the fount of pluralist theory); Terri Jennings Peretti, *In Defense of a Political Court* (Princeton, NJ: Princeton University Press, 1999), 209–17 (providing an overview of the pluralist definition of democracy); Cass Sunstein, *The Partial Constitution* (Cambridge, Mass.: Harvard University Press, 1993), 133–45 (defining the concept of "deliberative democracy," which derives from pluralist accounts of American democracy); Robert Dahl, *A Preface to Democratic Theory* (Chicago: University of Chicago Press, 1956), 132–34 (describing the

concept of "minorities rule"); see also Aaron Wildavsky, *Dixon-Yates: A Study in Power Politics* (New Haven, Conn.: Yale University Press, 1962), 325 (concluding that "the TVA experience reinforces the conclusion that if the desired goal is the determination of policy outcomes most satisfactory to the widest range of interested parties, then the clash of interests may well be a more efficient process for achieving this end than calculation by any single hierarchy").

27. For a classic pluralist description of how court decisions can trigger interest group activity, which in turn triggers congressional statutory revisions, see David Truman, *The Governmental Process* (New York: Alfred A. Knopf, 1971), 496.

28. See generally George Stigler, "The Theory of Economic Regulation," *Bell Journal of Economics and Management Science* 2, no. 1 (1971): 3; see also Anthony Downs, *An Economic Theory of Democracy* (New York: Harper Collins, 1957); Mancur Olsen, *The Logic of Collective Action* (Cambridge, Mass.: Harvard University Press, 1971). Capture is not a particularly new concept in American politics. There is a long tradition of scholars who argue that the political system favors privileged groups. For example, "stratificationists"— such as C. Wright Mills—argue that a single "power elite" controls American politics (*The Power Elite* [Oxford: Oxford University Press, 1956]). Older versions of capture, however, were sharply criticized on both theoretical and empirical grounds, because they failed to provide a systematic account of how "elites" manage to gain control over the fragmented and dynamic American political landscape. See generally Robert Dahl, *Who Governs? Democracy and Power in an American City* (New Haven, Conn.: Yale University Press, 1961); Nelson Polsby, *Community Power and Political Theory* (New Haven, Conn.: Yale University Press, 1980) (providing classic pluralist accounts of political power in American politics). Public choice theory, which is central to this analysis and the override literature, claims to improve earlier versions of capture precisely because it offers a systematic explanation of the mechanisms of capture. For more on public choice theory, see Chapter 5 at 115–18 and accompanying notes.

29. See, for example, Michael Axline, "Forest Health and the Politics of Expediency," *Environmental Law* 26 (1996): 613 (criticizing the Salvage Logging Rider); Victor M. Sher and Carol Sue Hunting, "Eroding the Landscape, Eroding the Laws: Congressional Exemptions from Judicial Review of Environmental Laws," *Harvard Environmental Law Review* 15 (1991): 435 (discussing a string of congressional overrides of judicial environmental law decisions). See also Abner Mikva and Jeff Bleich, "When Congress Overrules the Court," *California Law Review* 79 (1991): 730 (suggesting that congressional overrides often represent an objectionable "politicization" of the statutory construction process). For a contrary view of the Salvage Logging Rider, see U.S. Senator Slade Gorton and Julie Kays, "Legislative History of the Timber and Salvage Amendments Enacted in the 104th Congress: A Small Victory for Timber Communities in the Pacific Northwest," *Environmental Law* 26 (1996): 641.

30. See generally Kevin R. Johnson, "*Los Olvidados:* Images of the Immigrant, Political Power of Noncitizens, and Immigration Law and Enforcement," *BYU Law Review* (1993): 1139.

31. See Marc Galanter, "Why the 'Haves' Come Out Ahead: Speculations on the Limits of Legal Change," *Law & Society Review* 9 (1974): 95; for more on Galanter's arguments, see the articles collected in *Law & Society Review* 33 (1999).

32. For classic statements of hyperpluralism, see Theodore Lowi, *The End of Liberalism: Ideology, Policy and the Crisis of Public Authority* (New York: Norton, 1979); Mancur Olsen, *The Rise and Decline of Nations* (New Haven, Conn.: Yale University Press, 1982). For a popularized version of these arguments, see Jonathan Rauch, *Demosclerosis: The Silent Killer of American Government* (New York: Random House, 1995). In addition, a large number of case studies show how the open, fragmented policy-making process on Capitol Hill waters down bold policy initiatives. See, for example, Eric Redman, *The Dance of Legislation* (New York: Simon and Schuster, 1973); Steven Waldman, *The Bill: How Legislation Really Becomes Law: A Case Study of the National Service Bill* (New York: Penguin Books, 1996); Jeb Barnes, "Bankrupt Bargain? Bankruptcy Reform and the Politics of Adversarial Legalism," *Journal of Law & Politics* XIII, no. 4 (1997): 893.

33. See generally Douglas R. Arnold, *The Logic of Congressional Action* (New Haven, Conn.: Yale University Press, 1990), 101; Terry Moe, "The Politics of Bureaucratic Structure," in *Can the Government Govern?* ed. John Chubb and Paul Patterson (Washington, D.C.: Brookings Institution, 1989), 278; Morris Fiorina, *Congress, Keystone of the Washington Establishment* (New Haven, Conn.: Yale University Press, 1989), 148. For an interesting theoretic critique of Moe's arguments, see Rui J. P. de Figueiredo Jr., "Electoral Competition, Political Uncertainty, and Policy Insulation," *American Political Science Review* 96, no. 2 (2002): 335.

34. Patrick S. Atiyah and Robert Summers, *Form and Substance in Anglo-American Law: A Comparative Study of Legal Theory, Legal Reasoning, and Legal Institutions* (Oxford: Clarendon Press, 1987), 315–23.

35. Peter L. Strauss, "One Hundred Fifty Cases Per Year: Some Implications of the Supreme Court's Resources for Judicial Review of Agency Action," *Columbia Law Review* 87, no. 6 (1987): 1098–99.

36. See, for example, Philip Howard, *The Death of Common Sense: How the Law is Suffocating America* (New York: Random House, 1994).

37. See generally Marc Galanter, "Reading the Landscape of Disputes," *UCLA Law Review* 31 (1983): 4. For a concise overview of the debate over whether Americans suffer from "hyperlexis," see Thomas Burke, *Lawyers, Lawsuits, and Legal Rights: The Battle Over Litigation in American Society* (Berkeley: University of California Press, 2002), 2–4.

38. See Deborah Hensler et al., *Compensation for Accidental Injuries in the United States* (Santa Monica, Calif.: RAND Institute for Civil Justice, 1991), 121–22, fig. 5.2.

39. See David Trubek et al., *Civil Litigation Research Project: Final Report, Part A* (Madison: University of Wisconsin Law School, 1983): 5–19, fig. 2.

40. See Paul C. Weiler et al., *A Measure of Malpractice: Medical Injury, Malpractice Litigation, and Patient Compensation* (Cambridge, Mass.: Harvard University Press, 1993), 69, 70 Table 4.1. See also Patricia Danzon, *Medical Malpractice: Theory, Evidence, and Public Policy* (Cambridge, Mass.: Harvard University Press, 1985), 24 (stating that "at most 1 in 10 negligent injuries resulted in a claim"); Peter Bell and Jeffrey O'Connell, *Accidental Justice: The Dilemmas of Tort Law* (New Haven, Conn.: Yale University Press, 1997), 58 (summarizing several studies).

41. Patricia Munch, *Costs and Benefits of the Tort System If Viewed as a System of Compensation* (Santa Monica, Calif.: RAND Institute for Civil Justice, 1977), 76.

42. See, for example, Barnes, "Bankrupt Bargain?" 906–7 (reviewing the administrative costs of consumer bankruptcy cases prior to the passage of the 1978 bankruptcy reforms).

43. Burke, *Lawyers, Lawsuits, and Legal Rights*, 163.

44. See, for example, *Greentree v. U.S. Customs Service*, 674 F.2d 74, 75 (D.C. Cir. 1982); *Porter v. Department of Justice*, 717 F.2d 787, 799 (3d Cir. 1983).

45. *Terkel v. Kelly*, 599 F.2d 214, 216 (7th Cir. 1979); *Painter v. FBI*, 615 F.2d 689, 691 (5th Cir. 1980).

46. United States Code Congressional and Administrative News (U.S.C.C.A.N.) (1984): 3788.

47. See, for example, *Ely v. FBI*, 781 F.2d 1487, 1489 n. 1 (11th Cir. 1986) (reversing on other grounds and noting that the government correctly dropped an argument under *Painter,* because it had "been implicitly overruled by statute, and explicitly rejected in the legislative history"); *Sullivan v. CIA*, 992 F.2d 1249, 1252 (1st Cir. 1993) (affirming the district court).

48. *Sullivan*, 992 F.2d at 1252 (1st Cir. 1993). The case itself involved an issue slightly different from the override issue. Specifically, a daughter sought government files about her father, who had died while purportedly on a mission for the CIA. The court unanimously denied her request because it fell outside the Information Act's right of access to files about oneself. The important point, from a pluralist perspective, is not that the Information Act provided universal public access to governmental files. It clearly did not. The point is that, after open congressional deliberation on the override issue, which featured competing viewpoints, the override resolved the override as Congress defined it.

49. It is worth stressing that, in Federalist Paper No. 10, Madison explicitly recognized that contending factions were inevitable in a large, diverse society. As

a result, from a pluralist perspective, it would be unreasonable to expect overrides to produce perfect harmony at the grassroots level. Instead, the test for effective overrides under pluralism is consensus among the branches of government. Given this test, as long as courts rule uniformly on the meaning of the law after Congress acts, post-override litigation should not be seen as evidence of hyperpluralism. Put differently, pluralism does not expect overrides to settle all conflict among contending interests; rather, it expects overrides to settle the law as read by the courts.

50. 18 U.S.C. sec. 13(a).

51. See, for example, *U.S. v. King,* 824 F.2d 313, 315–16 (4th Cir. 1987); *U.S. v. Mayberry,* 774 F.2d 1018, 1021–22 (10th Cir. 1985) (reversing the lower court's interpretation of the ACA).

52. *U.S. v. Donaldson,* 797 F.2d 125, 127 (3d Cir. 1986); *U.S. v. Dobbins,* 807 F.2d 130, 131 (8th Cir. 1986).

53. See U.S.C.C.A.N. (1987): 2140.

54. See *U.S. v. Heard,* 700 F.Supp. 12, 12–13 (S.D. Tex. 1988); see also *U.S. v. Davis,* 845 F.2d 94, 97, 97 n. 1 (5th Cir. 1988) (applying pre-1987 law but recognizing that the 1987 amendments had eliminated the "like punishments" requirement).

55. 401 U.S. 424 (1971).

56. In *Griggs,* African-American employees of a North Carolina power company challenged the use of standardized aptitude tests to screen transfers from lower-paying, unskilled "outside" jobs to better-paying "inside" positions. They argued that the testing requirements, whose implementation coincided with the date Title VII took effect, disproportionately disqualified minority applicants and were not proven "job related." The District Court and Court of Appeals rejected their claims, finding that the tests were fairly administered and not racially motivated. In reversing, the Supreme Court set forth disparate impact analysis for the first time (401 U.S. at 431–32).

57. 490 U.S. 642 (1989).

58. 490 U.S. at 657.

59. Ibid., 660.

60. Political conservatives typically decry *Griggs.* In their view, disparate impact analysis forces employers to choose between using quotas to balance their workforces' racial composition or facing costly and uncertain litigation—the precise dilemma that conservatives had fought so hard to avoid during the historic fight over the Civil Rights Act of 1964. See, for example, Roger Clegg, "Introduction: A Brief History of the Civil Rights Act of 1991," *Louisiana Law Review* 54 (1994): 1459–63.

61. For example, Justice Stevens' dissent in *Wards Cove,* which was joined by Justices Brennan, Marshall, and Blackmun, denounced the majority's "sojourn into judicial activism" and "casual—almost summary—rejection of the statutory construction that developed in the wake of *Griggs*" (490 U.S. at 642,

671–72). In a separate dissent in *Wards Cove,* Justice Blackmun lamented: "One wonders whether the majority still believes that race discrimination—or more accurately, race discrimination against non-whites—is a problem in our society, or even remembers that it ever was" (ibid., 662). On the Hill, Senator Edward Kennedy from Massachusetts warned that *Wards Cove* and similar cases represent "a serious threat to the 35 years of progress we have achieved toward a better and fairer society ("Court Narrows Reach of Anti-Bias Laws," *CQ Almanac* 45 [1989]: 316).

62. *Wards Cove,* 490 U.S. at 666 and accompanying notes (Stevens dissent).

63. "Bush Vetoes Job Bias Bill; Override Fails," *CQ Almanac* 46 (1990): 462.

64. "Compromise Civil Rights Bill Passed," *CQ Almanac* 47 (1991): 251, 256.

65. Ibid., 259.

66. 42 U.S.C. sec. 2000e-2(k)(1)(A)(ii) (emphasis added).

67. Quoted in "Compromise Civil Rights Bill Passed," 258–59 (citations omitted).

68. See R. Shep Melnick, *Between the Lines: Interpreting Welfare Rights* (Washington, D.C.: Brookings Institution, 1994), 5.

69. *Congressional Record, daily ed.,* S.15325 (29 October 1991).

70. 137 *Congressional Record* S.15485 (30 October 1991).

71. Melnick, *Between the Lines,* 6.

72. See generally Linda Lye, "Title VII's Tangled Web: The Erosion and Confusion of Disparate Impact and the Business Necessity Defense," *Berkeley Journal of Employment and Labor Law* 19, no. 2 (1998): 348–53.

73. Compare *Fitzpatrick v. City of Atlanta,* 2 F.3d 1112, 1119 (11th Cir. 1993) (employer must show practices having a disparate impact on minorities are demonstrably "necessary to meeting a goal that, as a matter of law, qualifies as an important business goal for Title VII purposes"); *Banks v. City of Albany,* 953 F.Supp. 28, 35 (N.D.N.Y. 1997) (adopting the same standard); *Bradley v. Pizzaco of Nebraska, Inc.,* 7 F.3d 795, 798 (8th Cir. 1993) (requiring the employer to show "a compelling need . . . to maintain [the] practice . . . and that there is no alternative to the challenged practice"); *Nash v. Consolidated City of Jacksonville,* 895 F.Supp. 1536, 1545 (M.D. Fla. 1995) (holding that "[t]he business purpose must be sufficiently compelling to overcome any racial impact; [and] the challenged practice must effectively carry out the business purpose it is alleged to serve"), affirmed by 85 F.3d 643 (11th Cir. 1996) (casting doubt on whether the *Fitzpatrick* or *Nash* standard applies in the Eleventh Circuit); *Donnelly v. Rhode Island Board of Governors for Higher Education,* 929 F.Supp. 583, 593 (D.R.I. 1996) (holding that employers must show only that the practice is "reasonably necessary to achieve an important business objective"), affirmed by 110 F.3d 2, 6 (1st Cir. 1997) (but expressly leaving open the proper standard for "business necessity").

74. Compare *Gersman v. Group Health Association Inc.*, 975 F.2d 886, 890 (D.C. Cir. 1992) with *Estate of Reynolds v. Martin*, 985 F.2d 470, 476 (9th Cir. 1993).

75. *Landgraf v. USI Film Products*, 511 U.S. 244 (1994).

76. Compare the majority's reasoning at 511 U.S. at 282–86 with Blackmun's dissent at 294–97.

77. See *Kolstad v. American Dental Association*, 139 F.3d, 958, 968–69 (D.C. Circuit 1998); Linda Greenhouse, "Ruling Raises Hurdle in Bias-Award Cases," *The New York Times*, 23 June 1999, A16 (N).

78. See *Kolstad v. American Dental Association*, 527 U.S. 526, 546 (1999).

79. See, for example, Daniel Bussel, "Textualism's Failures: A Study of Overruled Bankruptcy Decisions," *Vanderbilt Law Review* 53 (2000): 915.

80. It is worth stressing that the dependent variables of the study—or outcomes to be explained—are the openness of congressional deliberation, the comprehensiveness of congressional signals, and the levels of judicial consensus *given an override*. In light of these dependent variables, the universe of cases involves political activity before, during, and after the passage of overrides. Of course, by conditioning the sample on the passage of overrides, I have intentionally traded generalizability for greater depth of analysis. Such trade-offs are often unavoidable when doing data-intensive empirical work. As developed in later chapters, I believe that focusing on these cases is appropriate for several reasons: (1) the passage of overrides represents a critical, formal check on the courts; (2) the override literature overlooks the political activity surrounding the passage of overrides, which are central for assessing the practical and normative significance of overrides; and (3) the passage of overrides represent theoretically interesting "extreme cases" that provide a useful optic for viewing pluralist, capture, and hyperpluralist assumptions about the nature of inter-branch relations in a system of fragmented lawmaking power. For more on how extreme cases—even single case studies—can contribute to a given field, see Arend Lijphart, "Comparative Politics and Comparative Method," *American Political Science Review* 65 (1971): 691–93; David Collier, "The Comparative Method," in *Political Science: The State of the Discipline Volume II*, ed. Ada W. Finifter (Washington, D.C.: American Political Science Association, 1993), 105–19; see also Theda Skocpol and Margaret Somers, "The Uses of Comparative History in Macrosocial Inquiry," *Comparative Studies in Society and History* 12 (1980): 197 (discussing the concept of a "research cycle").

81. This literature is discussed in Chapter 7.

82. Alternatively, the data can be visualized as a spreadsheet. Each row represents a case of inter-branch statutory construction and each column represents observations about each process.

83. The construction of the sample and sampling issues are discussed more fully in Chapter 4.

84. It should be added that the predictive value of game theory is a matter of strong contention, as scholars are just beginning to test formal models rigorously. Compare Jeffrey A. Segal, "Separation-of-Powers Games in the Positive Political Theory of Congress and the Courts," *American Political Science Review* 91, no. 1 (March 1997): 28 (finding that formal models of Supreme Court relations with other branches do not perform as well as his attitudinal model), with Pablo T. Spiller and Rafael Gely, "Congressional Control or Judicial Independence: The Determinants of U.S. Supreme Court Labor-Relations Decisions, 1949–1988," *Rand Journal of Economics* 23, no. 4 (1992): 463; Rafael Gely and Pablo T. Spiller, "A Rational Choice Model of Supreme Court Statutory Interpretation Decisions with Applications to the *State Farm* and *Grove City* Cases," *Journal of Law, Economics, and Organization* 6, no. 2 (1990): 263 (finding empirical support for their formal models). For more on the distinction between prediction and explanation, see Lawrence Baum, *The Puzzle of Judicial Behavior* (Ann Arbor: University of Michigan Press, 1997), 5–6.

85. Of course, new applications of game theory might be used to study a variety of aspects of the override process, including how different decision-making rules may affect political participation. Indeed, I hope that this work will stimulate further formal analyses of court-Congress interaction by offering more refined descriptions of the passage of overrides and the nature of congressional follow-up signals.

2 Overrides in Contemporary
U.S. Policy-Making: Promise
and Current Understanding

Before turning to the data, this chapter provides background for the argument, explaining the promise of overrides in contemporary American policy-making and the current understanding of the override process. It opens by exploring the formal role of overrides within the U.S. system of checks and balances, arguing that overrides represent Congress's most promising formal tool for clarifying statutes and reining in errant statutory interpretation decisions.[1] Indeed, as a formal matter, other checks—such as impeachment, constitutional amendments, the power of the purse, and judicial appointments—pale in comparison. Moreover, in an age of statutes and an era of heightened judicial policy-making, overrides' core functions of clarifying the law and checking the courts are more important than ever.

Having laid out the formal promise of overrides in American policy-making, the chapter then turns to the override literature. Despite the potential significance of overrides, our current understanding of their practical significance remains incomplete. Most important, the literature neglects the fundamental question of whether the passage of overrides serves important democratic values, such as promoting broad political participation, and policy goals, such as enhancing legal certainty. Subsequent chapters address this question, exploring whether the passage of overrides, in fact, clarifies the law, reverses objectionable judicial statutory interpretations, and involves broad political participation.

Overrides and the American System of Checks and Balances

As a general matter, statutory construction—the process by which the meaning of laws is defined and refined—can be problematic for a variety of reasons. Congress may pass flawed statutes, courts may hand down

inconsistent or controversial decisions, or as distinct branches of government with different constituencies and approaches to lawmaking, Congress
and the courts may simply disagree over the proper reading of statutes.

Fortunately, the constitution provides Congress with several methods
for sending follow-up signals to the courts and reining in errant decisions,
such as impeachment, constitutional amendments, the power of the purse,
judicial appointments, and the passage of overrides. Each of these powers
has an important role in the American system of checks and balances;
however, as a formal matter, overrides promise Congress an unmatched
tool for clarifying statutes and reversing objectionable judicial decisions.
Consider Congress's four alternatives to overrides listed earlier.

Impeachment

Somewhat surprisingly, judicial impeachments were probably intended as a
means to reverse questionable court decisions. In Federalist Paper No. 81,
Alexander Hamilton argues that Congress's power to impeach judges will
provide "complete security" against the "[p]articular misconstructions
and contraventions of the will of the legislature [that] may now and then
happen."[2] Constitutional powers are not etched in legal stone, however;
they are politically constructed over time.[3] Thus, despite recent rumblings
by House Republicans, such as Representative Tom Delay, who favors
impeaching judges for failing to toe the majority party's line, the Senate
established an enduring historical precedent in 1805 when it refused to
impeach Justice Samuel Chase for politically unpopular decisions.[4] As a
result, impeachment is generally reserved for judicial breaches of ethical
conduct, as opposed to judicial violations of legislative bargains.

Constitutional Amendments

Amending the constitution offers another potential tool for reversing
objectionable court rulings. However, it is far more cumbersome than
enacting an override and is rarely used. Compare the track records.
Overrides are ordinary statutes that must pass the House and Senate by a
majority vote and be signed by the president. Moreover, if Congress
objects to judicial interpretations of an override, it can reverse them by
passing another statute. Although enacting new laws on Capitol Hill is not
easy, Congress manages to pass dozens of overrides per session.[5]

Constitutional amendments, by contrast, are not ordinary statutes.
They must pass both chambers of Congress by a two-thirds vote and be
ratified by three-fourths of the states. Moreover, Congress cannot directly
reverse objectionable judicial interpretations of constitutional amendments by passing statutes; it must re-run the gauntlet of amending the

Constitution. The bottom line? Whereas the override process has produced hundreds of court reversals since the 1970s, the constitutional amendment process has produced only a handful of court reversals since 1789.[6]

The Power of the Purse

Although often overlooked, Congress can use its budgetary powers to send policy signals to the courts. Specifically, although Congress cannot *cut* federal judges' salaries under Article III, it can set the courts' administrative budgets and *refuse to raise* judges' pay.[7] Congress has used this power creatively. For example, following the landmark Warren Court decision of *Reynolds v. Sims,*[8] which established the principle of one person–one vote in drawing electoral districts, the Senate amended a House bill that proposed to raise all federal judges' salaries by $7,500 annually. The Senate's amendment limited the raise of Supreme Court justices to only $2,500 per year, $5,000 less than other judges. In support of this differential treatment, Senator John Tower explained as follows: "Since the Supreme Court seems to reason it should legislate and amend the Constitution, perhaps members of the Supreme Court should receive a salary no higher than received by legislators."[9]

It should be added that Congress's budgetary bullying did not work in this case. The Warren Court did not abandon *Reynolds,* despite the Senate's obvious disapproval, and Congress soon backed down.[10] Nor does it seem likely that such tactics would succeed.[11] In sum, the power of the purse is a blunt instrument when compared to the passage of overrides; it can punish judges for objectionable decisions but does not require judges to change their rulings as a formal matter, and it seems unlikely to affect judges' decisions significantly as a practical matter.

Judicial Appointments

The appointment power is the most visible check on the courts, and it can significantly affect doctrine, especially Supreme Court doctrine. However, even the appointment power cannot match the promise of overrides as a formal means to overturn specific decisions and clarify the law. First, and most obviously, unlike passing overrides, appointing judges does not directly reverse existing judicial decisions; it places new judges on the bench. As a result, the appointment power affects judicial outcomes indirectly. Moreover, although judges typically act in accordance with the preferences of their appointers, there are striking exceptions to the rule, such as Supreme Court Justices Earl Warren and William Brennan, who were appointed by President Dwight Eisenhower, a Republican, and later became leading liberals on the Court.[12]

Second, unlike enacting overrides, the elected branches cannot appoint new judges whenever they choose. They must either create a new judgeship or await a vacancy. If the elected branches create a new judgeship, they in some sense dilute the influence of their new appointee. If they await a vacancy, their appointment may only marginally influence judicial outcomes, even if the elected branches accurately assess their candidate's preferences. The reason is that the doctrinal impact of judicial appointments depends on the preferences of the vacating judges as well as the appointed judges. Thus, as Jesse Choper argues, President Ronald Reagan's appointments of Justices Sandra Day O'Connor, Antonin Scalia, and Anthony Kennedy made only modest differences as a policy matter because they replaced justices Potter Stewart, Warren Burger, and Lewis Powell, who held similar conservative views.[13] An analogous logic applies to lower court appointees. In short, although the appointment power represents a formidable check on the courts, it cannot match the promised precision of overrides in reversing specific decisions and sending courts marching orders.

The Heightened Promise of Overrides in Contemporary U.S. Policy-Making

In today's policy-making environment, the potential significance of overrides may be greater than ever. Why? As will be discussed in the following sections, more than ever, Congress may need to revise statutes because today's statutes may be increasingly prone to obsolescence and inconsistency; today's Supreme Court is increasingly overwhelmed and less likely to harmonize conflicting lower court statutory interpretations; and today's federal judges have greater opportunities to overreach—from the right or the left—under the guise of statutory interpretation.

Congressional Revision of Statutes

Congress may need to revise and update statutes more than ever because rapid changes in technology, markets, and science are constantly rendering statutes obsolete in unsettled or dynamic policy areas, such as intellectual property rights, antitrust, and environmental law. Consider copyright law. In the early 1900s, copyright law did not apply to reproductions that were unintelligible without the aid of a machine. At the time, this meant that federal copyright laws did not apply to devices such as piano rolls used in player pianos.[14] The advent of phonograph records, tape cassettes, and other recording devices, however, meant that federal copyright law provided almost no protection against piracy. As a result, Congress was forced to update copyright law to include electronic copies.[15] Nor was this an isolated event. Congress has been forced to revise aspects of copyright law in light of other new technologies, such as photocopiers,[16] as well as new forms of written expression, such as computer programs.[17]

In addition, the growing number, complexity, and interdependence of federal laws have likely increased conflicts among statutes.[18] Recall the messy interplay between the Privacy Act and FOIA as well as the ACA and Crime Control Act, which were discussed in Chapter 1.[19] In those cases, Congress enacted separate laws that inadvertently conflicted. Similar drafting errors can be found in the tax code and other statutes.[20] Surely these instances are not alone; statutes are bound to collide as federal law continues to expand.

Congressional Harmonization of Judicial Decisions

Congress may currently need to harmonize judicial interpretations of statutes because it is increasingly doubtful that the Supreme Court meaningfully serves as a "court of errors" that monitors lower court dockets and promptly weeds out inconsistent decisions.[21] This argument rests on the confluence of two factors: (1) the American statutory construction process is a virtual recipe for inconsistent rule application, and (2) the U.S. Supreme Court is now swamped.

The American statutory construction process seems likely to produce discordant statutory interpretations, because it combines ad hoc statutory drafting procedures, decentralized judicial authority, and politically selected and ideologically diverse judges. First, as will be discussed more fully in Chapter 3, American statutes are notoriously ambiguous and prone to technical error. American political scientists trace this propensity to electoral incentives. In order to maximize their chances of re-election, elected officials will tend to pass vague laws, which allow them to claim credit for taking action, while leaving tough policy choices to unelected judges and bureaucrats.[22]

Comparativists, such as Professors Patrick S. Atiyah and Robert Summers, focus on the American legislative drafting process itself.[23] They argue that, unlike Great Britain, which features a centralized, professional staff of legislative draftsmen, American statutes are subject to multiple rounds of mark-ups and amendments by specialized committees and subcommittees, each of which has different constituencies and areas of technical expertise. Under these circumstances, U.S. statutes are drafted piecemeal. The resulting patchwork is often confusing, providing neither clear legal guidance nor effective constraints on judicial decision-making.

Second, even if statutes are clear, or agencies promulgate rules that make sense of unclear statutes, the American "coordinate" system of justice encourages flexible rule application, as opposed to European hierarchical systems that emphasize consistent rule application.[24] So, for example, decision-making authority in American courts is decentralized, which protects the discretion of trial court judges, who are closest to the facts of each case, and limits top-down control by appellate courts. In addition, U.S. federal judges are selected for their political experience and problem-solving skills, as opposed to professional reputation and legal skills. As a result, they tend to approach statutory interpretation less formally than their European counterparts, asking not only what the rules say but also whether rules are fair given the facts of each case.[25]

Decentralized judicial authority and flexible rule application alone do not ensure inconsistent statutory interpretation decisions; ideologically homogenous judges might agree on what is fair and uniformly decide cases irrespective of the formal rules. However, American lower court judges are not ideologically homogeneous, as indicated by the political party of the president who appointed them.[26] As seen in Table 2.1, the U.S. District Courts and Court of Appeals are roughly divided between Republican and Democratic appointees, with slightly more than half of all active federal

Table 2.1   Composition of Federal Bench by Appointing President, 01/01/2001

	District Courts				Court of Appeals			
	Active		Senior		Active		Senior	
	%	(N)	%	(N)	%	(N)	%	(N)
Clinton	44.7%	(297)	–	–	35.9%	(60)	–	–
Bush	20.0%	(133)	1.2%	(4)	18.6%	(31)	3.3%	(3)
Reagan	19.7%	(131)	26.8%	(91)	21.6%	(36)	34.1%	(31)
Carter	5.4%	(36)	29.4%	(100)	7.8%	(13)	25.3%	(23)
Ford	.5%	(3)	7.1%	(24)	.6%	(1)	6.6%	(6)
Nixon	.9%	(6)	18.8%	(64)	.6%	(1)	16.5%	(15)
Johnson	.2%	(1)	10.6%	(36)	–	–	13.2%	(12)
Kennedy	–	–	3.8%	(13)	–	–	1.1%	(1)
Eisenhower	–	–	2.3%	(8)	–	–	–	–
Democratic appointees	50.3%	(334)	43.8%	(149)	43.7%	(73)	39.6%	(36)
Republican appointees	41.1%	(273)	56.2%	(191)	41.4%	(69)	60.5%	(55)
Vacancies	8.6%	(57)	–	–	14.9%	(25)	–	–
Totals	100.0%	(664)	100.0%	(340)	100.0%	(167)	100.0%	(91)

Source: Sheldon Goldman, Elliot Slotnick, Gerard Grynski, and Gary Zuk, "Make-up of the Federal Bench," *Judicature* 84 (2001): 253, table 8.

judges being GOP appointments. Even after twelve years of Republican administrations under Presidents Reagan and George Bush, Democratic appointees constituted a significant minority on the bench, representing more than a quarter of all active judges on the federal district and circuit courts. President Jimmy Carter appointed most of these Democratic judges, who are reputed to be as liberal as Reagan–Bush appointees are conservative.[27] As a result, we would not expect American lower court judges to construe the law consistently as they decide what is fair on a case-by-case basis.

In theory, the Supreme Court could monitor lower court interpretations of statutes and harmonize inconsistent rulings. Today, however, it seems doubtful the Court meaningfully fulfills this function, because there are simply too many appellate court decisions. Consider the following numbers: in 1925, the ratio of Supreme Court justices to circuit court judges was 1 to 4.7; in 1995, it was 1 to 27.2; in 1925, the Supreme Court reviewed about 1 in 10 circuit court decisions; in the 1984 term, the Court reviewed about 1 in 200—or .005—circuit court decisions. At this rate, the average circuit court judge's opinions "will come under scrutiny only two or three times in a decade."[28]

Of course, not all appellate court decisions warrant Supreme Court review, and not all cases involve issues of statutory interpretation. Nevertheless, the drop from a 10-percent review rate to a 0.5-percent review rate suggests that significant numbers of important cases escape Supreme Court review. Admittedly, Congress cannot review all the cases missed by the Court. But passing overrides can supplement Supreme Court review, which promises greater clarity and more frequent refinements of federal laws.[29]

Congressional Supervision of the Courts' Statutory Interpretation

Congress may need to check courts more than ever because the current age of statutes affords unprecedented opportunities for judicial policy-making. Of course, policy-making from the bench is nothing new in the United States. Many traditional features of American government—fragmented political authority, the doctrine of judicial review, the common law tradition—have placed courts deeply in the "political thicket" almost since its founding.[30] Hence Alexis de Tocqueville's observation in the 1830s that important political questions in the United States often become judicial questions,[31] and Stephen Skowronek's characterization of early American government as a "state of courts and parties."[32] Indeed, when compared cross-nationally, the United States has always featured greater levels of "adversarial legalism": a mode of dispute resolution and policy-making characterized by high levels of "formal legal contestation," in which

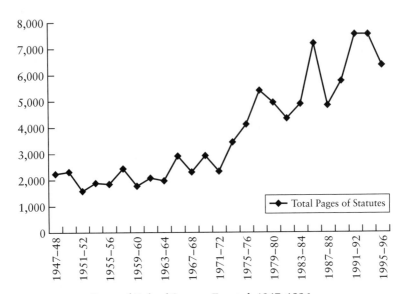

FIGURE 2.1   Pages of Federal Statutes Enacted, 1947–1996.

Source: Norman Ornstein, Thomas Mann, and Michael Malbin, *Vital Statistics on Congress 1997–1998* (Washington, D.C.: CQ Quarterly 1998), 167, table 6-4.

contending interests invoke preexisting legal rights and procedures backed by the threat of litigation.[33]

The pervasiveness and intensity of contemporary judicial policy-making, however, marks a significant departure from earlier eras. The most obvious explanation for this shift lies in the sheer volume and scope of today's federal statutes and statutory lawsuits. As seen in Figures 2.1 and 2.2, the patterns are striking. In the 1950s, the average Congress passed about 1900 pages of new laws each session. In the 1990s, the typical Congress more than tripled that amount, enacting an average of about 7000 pages of statutes per session. Not surprisingly, a rising tide of litigation has coincided with this flood of statutes. In 1961, about 13,500 statutory claims were filed in U.S. District Courts. In 1980, that figure climbed to more than 75,000. In 1997, nearly 168,000 statutory claims were filed, an increase of more than twelve-fold from 1961. Equally important, these laws and lawsuits touch nearly every aspect of ordinary citizens' lives, including the way they work, how they vote, the schooling of their children, even the air they breathe.

Admittedly, not all statutory lawsuits offer opportunities for judicial policy-making. Many cases turn on factual rather than legal issues, and even if cases potentially raise far-reaching policy issues, many lawsuits

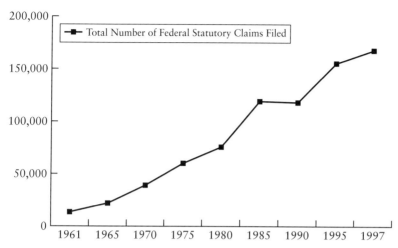

FIGURE 2.2   Number of Statutory Claims Filed in U.S. District Court, 1961–1997.

Source: Compiled from *Statistical Abstract of the United States* (Washington, D.C.: U.S. Department of Commerce, 1962–1967, 1993, 1996, and 1998).

settle prior to adjudication.[34] At the same time, statutory lawsuits often *require* policy-making from the bench, because formal rules tend to connote simple scenarios that fail to anticipate the complexity of actual disputes. Accordingly, even if judges are inclined to follow the letter of the law—an assumption many would contest about politically selected American judges—they often must legislate "interstitially," filling gaps that unavoidably appear when general rules are applied to specific cases.[35] Filling ostensibly small gaps in statutory language can require leaps in policy. Recall *Sutton v. United Airlines.*[36] *Sutton* addressed a seemingly technical ambiguity in the definition of disability under the ADA. However, in resolving this ambiguity, the Supreme Court established that millions of Americans are disabled enough to be fired (or not hired at all), but not disabled enough to seek redress under the ADA.

Moreover, there is good reason to suspect that federal judges will have ample opportunity to address high-stakes policy issues in contemporary American policy-making. Why? Many distinctive features of the modern U.S. administrative state place federal courts at the center of significant, and highly contested, regulatory matters.[37] More specifically, beginning in the late 1960s, Congress passed laws that sought to address widespread social problems, such as discrimination, consumer safety, and environment degradation. However, unlike European and Japanese lawmakers and reformers, who expanded existing national bureaucracies to implement their ambitious programs, members of Congress and American reformers distrusted centralized authority and built their programs on fragmented policy-making structures. As a result, the American administrative state is relatively decentralized, featuring an alphabet soup of overlapping—and often competing—federal and state agencies as well as procedural mechanisms, such as "private attorneys general" provisions that allow public interest groups to bypass agencies and bring lawsuits to enforce regulatory rules themselves.[38] In this fragmented regulatory framework, courts play a special role in resolving turf wars among contending agencies and weighing public interest groups' efforts to enforce regulatory mandates.

During the same period, federal judges created new legal doctrines that further enhanced their role in reviewing administrative procedures and rulemaking. For example, the landmark Supreme Court decision of *Goldberg v. Kelly*,[39] which required hearings for those facing the loss of welfare benefits, touched off the modern "due process revolution." The due process revolution, in turn, created panoply of administrative hearings that could be appealed to the courts as well as a constitutional basis for objecting to the fairness of agency procedures.[40] Meanwhile, federal judges relaxed traditional limitations to bringing private actions against agencies, which has facilitated public interest group litigation.[41]

Beyond expanding the formal role of courts in regulatory decisions, the creation of a decentralized welfare state and innovations in administrative law had another, more subtle effect. These changes helped spawn a class of entrepreneurial lawyers and public interest groups. These groups have proven both resourceful litigants, who find new ways to use lawsuits to pursue their political agendas, and powerful lobbyists, who reinforce and expand the role of courts and litigation in American policy-making.[42]

Standing alone, creating new rights, widening courtroom doors, and energizing public interest lawyers did not ensure extensive judicial influence over regulatory procedures or outcomes. It is conceivable that federal judges could have entertained these lawsuits, but generally deferred to agencies. As a general matter, however, American judges do not always rubber-stamp agency rule-making. Instead, they often scrutinize agency decisions under the "hard look" doctrine, which can serve as a doctrine of judicial second-guessing.[43]

This pincer movement by Congress and the courts, as well as the resulting changes in the American administrative state, has had a predictable and profound effect on judicial power in the United States. Put simply, today's federal judges not only serve their traditional role of resolving politically important legal disputes but also play a significant role in administering a rights-based regulatory state by arbitrating conflicts among competing agencies as well as adjudicating public challenges to agency procedures and decisions.[44] As a consequence, American judges currently shape issues far beyond the reach of their counterparts abroad, such as the improvement of coal mine safety,[45] the quality of nursing home care,[46] the oversight of large corporate insolvencies,[47] the creation of educational opportunity,[48] the mediation of labor relations,[49] the approval of new drugs,[50] the regulation of air quality,[51] the use of polyvinyl chlorides,[52] and the list goes on and on.[53]

The point is *not* that innovative or even highly politicized judicial policy-making is always objectionable. To the contrary, a flexible and politically responsive federal bench can promote democratic values, such as giving voice to interests that fail to participate in legislative or executive decision-making. In the 1960s and 1970s, for example, shocking stories emerged about overcrowding, squalor, and violence in American prisons, especially in the South. Not surprisingly, state and federal elected officials were slow to champion the rights of convicted criminals. Fortunately, prisoners and their advocates could turn to federal judges, who were free from electoral constraints and willing to tackle politically sensitive issues. As a result, instead of acquiescing to an appalling status quo, they constructed novel legal theories to take over prisons and implement much-needed reform.[54]

The point is that increased judicial policy-making, whether from the right or the left, automatically heightens the significance of political checks on the courts. Why? Unchecked policy-making by *any* branch of government undermines a central bulwark against arbitrary state action in the American system of separate institutions sharing powers, namely, mutual supervision and redundant policy-making by diversely representative forums.[55] Accordingly, as the volume, scope, and intensity of policy-making from the bench has increased during an age of statutes and an era of revved-up adversarial legalism, the potential significance of the override process—as Congress's most direct and credible means to reverse controversial judicial constructions of statutes—has also increased.

The Override Literature

Current Understanding of the Override Process

Despite the *potential* significance of overrides, the *practical* significance of overrides remains imperfectly understood. In order to summarize the current understanding of overrides, both its strengths and weaknesses, it is useful to conceptualize overrides as part of a multi-tiered process, called here the "pyramid of statutory construction." As shown in Figure 2.3, the bottom tier consists of all original statutes passed by the elected branches of government. The next tier includes statutory interpretation decisions. The penultimate tier consists of decisions that trigger a congressional

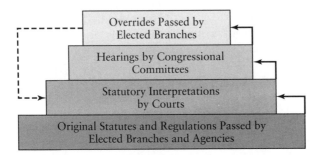

FIGURE 2.3   The Pyramid of Statutory Construction

oversight hearing, and the top tier includes all overrides enacted into law. The arrows represent the political processes by which issues move between tiers.

Overall, scholars have concentrated on the pyramid's upper reaches. Most studies focus on the top of the pyramid, examining the conditions under which Congress seeks to reverse Supreme Court decisions. These studies include the following: case histories of single overrides and studies of overrides in a small number of policy areas;[56] a handful of more comprehensive studies, which seek to track a larger number of overrides across a range of policy areas and over time;[57] and, most recently, game theoretic studies, which model the strategic logic of congressional oversight of the courts and statutory interpretation.[58] Others explore the politics of overrides on the floor of Congress, testing whether members of Congress defer to judges on matters of statutory interpretation.[59] A final group analyzes placement of statutory interpretation decisions on congressional committees' agendas in a small number of issue areas, such as labor or antitrust, or single committees, such as the Judiciary Committees.[60]

Although far from definitive, these studies converge on at least four key insights about the override process:

- *The passage of overrides faces daunting political obstacles.* There are a number of obstacles to passing overrides. Inertia is one. Passing any law through the complex American lawmaking process is notoriously difficult,[61] and overrides are no exception.[62] Game theorists suggest another: statutory interpretation decisions may break apart legislative coalitions. Specifically, if part of the original lawmaking coalition prefers a judge's statutory construction to the initial legislative bargain—and their votes cannot be replaced—the judge's interpretation will stand, even if it flatly contradicts the letter or spirit of the original statute.[63] Finally, override opponents may enjoy a natural advantage over override proponents, because the open, fragmented American policy-making process features "multiple veto points," which on Capitol Hill make it easier to play defense by blocking legislation, than to play offense by passing new laws.[64]

- *Despite obstacles, absolute levels of congressional override activity have increased.* Following Watergate and the growth of congressional staffs and inter-branch mistrust, absolute levels of congressional scrutiny of the courts has increased, notwithstanding the difficulty of placing issues on crowded legislative agendas and passing statutes. For example, William Eskridge's data suggest the average number of overrides passed every session from 1974 to 1991 nearly tripled the average number passed per session from 1967 to 1974.[65] Equally important, Congress conducts frequent hearings on statutory interpretation decisions, especially Supreme Court decisions. One study shows that in the period from 1979 to 1987, the Judiciary Committees held hearings on an estimated 40 percent of all Supreme Court decisions handed down from 1977 to 1983, which fell within their jurisdiction.[66]

- *Governmental entities seem particularly adept at obtaining overrides.* Available data suggest that a wide range of groups is able to secure overrides. However, federal, state, and local governmental agencies seem to outstrip other groups—including business interests—at placing decisions on Congress's agenda. Interestingly, the available evidence implies that business groups are better at obtaining oversight hearings than securing the passage of overrides.[67]

- *Congress does not "revere" Supreme Court's interpretation of statutes.* For years, leading public law scholars assumed Congress deferred to Supreme Court interpretations of statutes.[68] As Glendon Schubert once wrote, "Many congressmen are lawyers; and the argument that proponents of an amendatory bill are showing disrespect for the highest court in the land is an effective one."[69] Data suggest otherwise. In a widely cited study, Harry Stumpf examined the content of legislative debates on a number of legislative responses to Supreme Court decisions. He found the judicial "reverence" argument was rarely made in connection with overrides and when used was "almost totally ineffective."[70] John R. Schmidhauser et al.'s analysis of roll call votes on override measures in the 79th through 90th Congresses generally confirms Stumpf's findings.[71]

Collectively, these findings have two broader implications. First, Congress takes statutory interpretation seriously, especially Supreme Court statutory interpretation decisions. That is not to say Congress now patrols the extensive federal court dockets like the police, searching court reports for offending decisions. Surely, many important statutory interpretation decisions slip through the cracks of congressional scrutiny.[72] Nevertheless, the increase in the number of overrides, frequency of oversight hearings, and absence of congressional deference to judicial statutory construction suggest that Congress engages in significant "fire alarm" oversight of the courts, responding to concerns of groups, especially governmental entities, that seek legislative relief from objectionable judicial decisions.[73]

Second, in addition to being Congress's best *formal* tool for clarifying statutes and reining in objectionable statutory interpretation decisions, Congress is increasingly relying on the passage of overrides as a check on the courts. Compare the frequency of the passage of overrides to other checks on the courts. The passage of overrides is far more common than judicial impeachments and constitutional amendments. Moreover, override activity seems to be gaining on judicial appointments, which is the most prevalent and publicly visible check on the courts. During the Kennedy-Johnson years, for example, the president appointed and the Senate approved an average of about 180 federal judges per term. The best available data indicate that Congress passed an average of 28 overrides every four years for that period. After the mid-1970s, the president has appointed and the Senate has approved an average of about 210 federal judges per term. During the same period, the best available data suggest that Congress passed an average of 72 overrides per four years. Thus, following the mid-1970s, the ratio of overrides to appointments has increased from 1 to 6.5 to about 1 to 3. Of course, these numbers are rough, but they indicate that overrides represent an increasingly important part of Congress's tool kit for repairing objectionable judicial behavior.

Gaps in the Literature

Although the override literature offers a number of important insights, it suffers at least two major limitations. First, the literature is largely silent on what happens after Congress acts: namely, do independent, politically selected judges acquiesce to congressional reversals of their statutory interpretations, or do they resist congressional oversight?[74] Rather than confront these issues, most studies, consistent with either pluralist or capture conceptions of court-Congress relations, simply assume that overrides will effectively clarify the law and constrain judicial discretion.[75]

The validity of this assumption is not self-evident. As seen in Chapter 1, the effectiveness of overrides seems to vary. Some overrides, such as the Information Act and the Fine Improvements Act, do clarify the law, marking a clear shift from discordant to consensual rule application. Other overrides, such as the Civil Rights Act of 1991, fail to produce judicial consensus. Indeed, that override seemed to spur litigation and bring about confusion.

Second, the central normative question—does the passage of overrides enrich American democracy and policy-making?—has been given short shrift. To the extent the issue is addressed at all, the debate is far too simplified. Some, consistent with pluralism, insist that the passage of overrides is always "healthy" for American policy-making and democracy, representing a salutary form of inter-branch feedback that reflects input from diverse interest groups and revises statutes in light of lessons learned from litigation.[76] Others, consistent with modern capture theory, suggest that industry groups and governmental agencies use the passage of overrides to thwart groups that initially won in court but lack the political resources to participate in congressional deliberations on the override bill.[77]

Even a cursory review of cases suggests these standard characterizations are incomplete at best. Most obviously, they overlook plausible hyperpluralist override scenarios, in which the passage of overrides is open but ineffective. The Civil Rights Act of 1991 leaps to mind. In that case, members of Congress were faced with highly contentious issues concerning race and sexual harassment in the American workplace and found it difficult to enact a clear override. The result was a vague compromise that intentionally papered over differences among competing factions and sent controversial issues back to the courts, which continued to apply the law inconsistently. Thus, instead of effective congressional revision or capture, the Civil Rights Act seemed to involve partisan judicial policy-making and congressional passing-the-buck.

As noted in Chapter 1, open and effective congressional revision, effective interest group capture, and congressional passing-the-buck are not the only plausible alternatives. For example, Congress may delegate to courts based on a good-faith policy consensus that judges should refine the law on a case-by-case basis in dynamic policy areas. Alternatively, Congress may try and fail to send clear follow-up signals to the court on override issues. Another possibility is that the overriding Congress passes reasonably clear overrides, but the courts may find ways to resist congressional oversight and apply the law along partisan lines. Finally, there may be cases in which well-organized groups manage to dominate the rule-making process but lose in court because federal judges use their power of statutory interpretation to check one-sided congressional deliberations.

In short, we still do not fully understand the practical and normative significance of the passage of overrides. Given the promise of overrides in contemporary American policy-making, as well as their theoretical interest as cases of explicit inter-branch interaction, the time is ripe to take a closer look.

Notes

1. Accord Richard Paschal, "The Continuing Colloquy: Congress and the Finality of Supreme Court," *Journal of Law & Politics* VIII (1991): 195; see also Daniel Patrick Moynihan, "What Do You Do When the Supreme Court is Wrong?" *The Public Interest* 57 (1979): 23.

2. Alexander Hamilton, *The Federalist Papers* (1788; reprint, New York: Penguin Books 1987): 453.

3. See generally Keith E. Whittington, *Constitutional Construction: Divided Powers and Constitutional Meaning* (Cambridge, Mass.: Harvard University Press, 1999); Jack N. Rakove, *Original Meanings: Politics and Ideas in the Making of the Constitution* (New York: Alfred A. Knopf, 1996).

4. Whittington, *Constitutional Construction,* 20–71 (discussing the attempted impeachment of Samuel Chase in some detail); see also Lawrence Friedmann, *A History of American Law* (New York: Simon and Schuster, 1973), 129–31. For more on Delay's call for a revival of political impeachment, see Anthony Lewis, "Destroy the Guardians," *The New York Times,* 7 April 1997, A13 (N); Bruce Fein, "Judge Not," *The New York Times,* 8 May 1997, A23 (N).

5. See William Eskridge Jr., "Overriding Supreme Court Statutory Interpretation Decisions," *The Yale Law Journal* 101 (1991): 338, table 1, 424–41 app. 1.

6. See Paschal, "Continuing Colloquy," 183. Of course, Congress is not helpless when confronted with objectionable constitutional interpretation decisions. For example, sometimes Congress can make minor adjustments to laws in order to satisfy the courts' constitutional objections and thus pursue the same broad policy objectives. Alternatively, sometimes Congress can blunt the practical effect of constitutional decisions by using its budgetary powers to eliminate programs or its statutory powers to strip courts of jurisdiction. In addition, Congress has been known to ignore constitutional decisions. Perhaps most famously, Congress continued to enact legislative vetoes after the Court had ruled them unconstitutional in *INS v. Chadha,* 919 (1983). See Louis Fisher, "Judicial Misjudgments about the Legislative Process: The Legislative Veto Case," *Public Administration Review* 45 (November 1985): 705; see also Janet Lindgren, "Beyond Cases: Reconsidering Judicial Review," *Wisconsin Law Review* (1983): 591–634 (providing an excellent account of how state legislatures can respond to objectionable constitutional decisions). The basic point, however, remains. The constitutional amendment process is far more cumbersome and less frequently used than the override process.

7. Article III states that judges shall "receive for their Services, a Compensation, which shall not be diminished during their Continuance in Office." Article III is silent, however, on Congress's power to *raise* judges' salaries or cut courts' administrative budgets.

8. 377 U.S. 533 (1964).

9. 110 *Congressional Record* 15844 (1964). Of course, instead of using the power of the purse affirmatively, Congress is far more likely to use this power negatively, meaning it will fail to act and thus not approve increases in judges' salaries or courts' administrative budgets. Indeed, Congress's repeated refusal to raise federal judges' salaries during the 1970s led a group of judges to sue, claiming inflation had impermissibly reduced their compensation under Article III. (The U.S. Court of Claims ultimately rejected their argument. See *Atkins v. United States,* 556 F.2d 1028 (1977), certiorari denied 434 U.S. 1009 [1978].) For more on these and other examples of Congress using its budgetary powers to check the courts, see Paschal, "Continuing Colloquy," 174 and accompanying notes.

10. Specifically, the conference committee that reconciled the House and Senate bills softened the blow, providing the Supreme Court justices with an annual raise of $4,500, $3,000 less than other judges. In the following year, a bill was introduced to give members of the Court the full $7,500 pay increase. However, the idea that Congress should use its budgetary power to pressure the Supreme Court to change its reapportionment decisions did not die. During the debate over the bill to restore the Supreme Court's pay increase, for example, Representative Robert Dole argued that the Court's raise should be contingent on reversing *Reynolds v. Sims,* 111 *Congressional Record* 5275 (1965).

11. The point is not that judges are immune to professional incentives. For example, Mark A. Cohen finds some evidence that, all things being equal, U.S. District Court judges were more likely to reject constitutional challenges to the U.S. Sentencing Commission in order to curry favor with Congress and the Justice Department. The reason, Cohen argues, is not that Congress holds the purse strings; rather, it is that members of Congress play an important role in the appointment process and hence may help promote them to the U.S. Court of Appeals ("Explaining Judicial Behavior or What's 'Unconstitutional' about the Sentencing Commission," *The Journal of Law, Economics, and Organization* 7, no. 1 [1991]: 188–89). However, even Cohen concedes that such professional considerations will affect judges only *"at the margin"* and that his sample is too small to draw any firm conclusions (ibid., 184 [emphasis in the original], 189). The point is that, when compared to overrides, congressional threats to freeze judicial salaries and court budgets seem relatively unpromising as a means to shape judicial behavior.

12. The impact of appointments on judicial behavior, especially Supreme Court decision-making, is the subject of a vast literature. In a seminal article, Robert Dahl argues that Supreme Court justices are unlikely to disagree with— much less challenge—the preferences of the "dominant lawmaking coalition" ("Decision-Making in a Democracy: The Supreme Court as a National Policy-Maker," *Journal of Public Law* 6 [1957]: 279). For a famous critique of Dahl's article, see Jonathan Casper, "The Supreme Court and National Policy-Making," *American Political Science Review* 70 (1976): 50. To the extent that the Court does take on the elected branches, Dahl insists clashes will be only

temporary, because presidents average two Supreme Court appointments per term, which usually tips the balance on divisive issues. Subsequent behavioral literature extends Dahl's argument to the lower courts, finding that the "effects of appointing-president cohorts are much stronger than the effects of maturation or time period on the district judges' . . . policy decisions" (C. K. Rowland and Robert Carp, "The Relative Effects of Maturation, Time Period, and Appointing President on Judges' Policy Choices: A Cohort Analysis," *Political Behavior* 5 [1983]: 119–22). See also Craig Ducat and Robert Dudley, "Presidential Power in the Federal Courts During the Post-War Era," American Political Science Association paper (August 1985); Robert Dudley and Craig Ducat, "Federal District Judges and Presidential Power: A Multivariate Analysis," American Political Science Association paper (August 1986) (both of which trace the tremendous access and persuasiveness of the federal government on the Supreme Court). For further discussion of appointees who surprise their appointers, see David O'Brien, *Storm Center: The Supreme Court in American Politics* (New York: W. W. Norton, 2003), 84–90.

13. Jesse Chopper, "The Current Justices of the U.S. Supreme Court: Their Philosophies, Ideologies, and Values," *Bulletin of the American Academy of Arts and Sciences* (Sept./Oct. 1997): 54.

14. See *White-Smith Music Publishing Company v. Apollo Company,* 209 U.S. 1, 8 (1909).

15. See generally Bruce J. McGiverin, "Digital Sound Sampling, Copyright and Publicity: Protecting Against the Electronic Appropriation of Sounds," *Columbia Law Review* 87 (1987): 1723.

16. See generally Randall Coyne, "Rights of Reproduction and the Provision of Library Services," *UALR Law Review* 13 (1991): 485.

17. See generally "Copyright Protection of Computer Programs under Federal Copyright Law," *ALR-Federal* 70 (1980 and Supplements): 178–79.

18. Peter Schuck, "The Limits of Law," in *The Limits of Law: Essays as Democratic Governance,* ed. Peter Schuck (Boulder, Colo.: Westview Press, 2000).

19. See Chapter 1 at pages 9–10, 10–12, and accompanying notes.

20. For a case involving tension between the tax code and the Employee Retirement Income Security Act (ERISA), the federal statute governing pensions, see *Calfee, Halter & Griswold et al. v. Commissioner,* 88 T.Ct. 641, 650–51 (1987) (arguing that these statutes conflicted over the tax-exempt status of employer contributions to pension funds).

21. Peter L. Strauss, "One Hundred and Fifty Cases Per Year: Some Implications of the Supreme Court's Limited Resources for Judicial Review of Agency Action," *Columbia Law Review* 87, no. 6 (1987): 1093; see also Matthew McCubbins, Roger Noll, and Barry Weingast, "Politics and the Courts: A Positive Theory of Judicial Doctrine and the Rule of Law," *Southern California Law Review* 68 (1995): 1634.

22. See generally Douglas R. Arnold, *The Logic of Congressional Action* (New Haven, Conn.: Yale University Press, 1990), 101; Morris Fiorina, *Congress, Keystone of the Washington Establishment,* 2d ed. (New Haven, Conn.: Yale University Press, 1989), 48. See also Terry Moe, "The Politics of Bureaucratic Structure," in *Can the Government Govern?* ed. John Chubb and Paul Patterson (Washington, D.C.: Brookings Institution, 1989), 277–79 (arguing that members of Congress will write statutes that combine general substantive provisions, which allow agencies broad discretion, with detailed procedural controls, which allows members of Congress to intervene of behalf of favored constituents).

23. See Patrick S. Atiyah and Robert Summers, *Form and Substance in Anglo-American Law: A Comparative Study of Legal Reasoning, Legal Theory, and Legal Institutions* (Oxford: Clarendon Press, 1987), 298–335.

24. See Mirjan Damaska, "Structures of Authority and Comparative Criminal Procedure," *The Yale Law Journal* 84 (1975): 519–20.

25. Robert Summers and Michele Taruffo, "Interpretation and Comparative Analysis," in *Interpreting Statutes: A Comparative Study,* ed. D. Neil MacCormick and Robert Summers (Brookfield, Vt.: Dartmouth University Press, 1991), 472–73 (finding that statutory construction in the U.S. is "less logical" and relies more heavily on arguments about the law's purpose and substantive policy arguments than other countries).

26. Numerous studies document the relationship between the party and ideology of the appointing president and judicial decision-making, especially in controversial policy areas. See generally Terri Jennings Peretti, *In Defense of a Political Court* (Princeton, NJ: Princeton University Press, 1999), 117–18 and accompanying notes (offering a concise summary of these studies and collecting authority). For studies involving the U.S. Supreme Court, see, for example, Thomas R. Marshall and Joseph Ignagni, "Supreme Court and Public Support for Rights Claims," *Judicature* 78 (1994): 146; Robert A. Carp, Donald Songer, C. K. Rowland, Ronald Stidham, and Lisa Richey-Tracy, "The Voting Behavior of Judges Appointed by President Bush," *Judicature* 76 (1993): 302; Neal C. Tate and Roger Handberg, "Time Binding and Theory Building in Personal Attribute Models of Supreme Court Voting Behavior, 1916–1988," *American Journal of Political Science* 35 (1991): 460; Neal C. Tate, "Personal Attribute Models of the Voting Behavior of U.S. Supreme Court Justices' Liberalism in Civil Liberties and Economic Decisions, 1946–1978," *American Political Science Review* 75 (1981): 355. For studies involving the lower federal courts, see, for example, Steve Alumbaugh and C. K. Rowland, "The Links Between Platform-Based Appointment Criteria and Trial Judges' Abortion Judgments," *Judicature* 74 (1990): 153; Ronald Stidham and Robert A. Carp, "Support for Labor and Economic Regulation among Reagan and Carter Appointees to the Federal Courts," *Social Science Journal* 26 (1989): 433; C. K. Rowland, Donald Songer, and Robert Carp, "Presidential Effects on

Criminal Justice Policy in the Lower Federal Courts: The Reagan Judges," *Law & Society Review* 22 (1988): 191; Jon Gottshall, "Reagan's Appointments to the U.S. Court of Appeals: The Continuation of a Judicial Revolution," *Judicature* 70 (1986): 49–50; Rowland and Carp, "Relative Effects of Maturation," 119–21.

27. See Rowland, Songer, and Carp, "Presidential Effects on Criminal Justice Policy," 191 (comparing the voting records of Carter and Reagan appointees in the lower courts on criminal defendant rights and finding that the differences "resemble differences one would expect if Presidents Carter and Reagan were Judges Carter and Reagan"). By contrast, it is argued that President Clinton, who faced a hostile Republican majority and Judiciary Committee, was forced to appoint more moderate judges, especially in his second term after the Monica Lewinsky scandal made the headlines. Sheldon Goldman, "Judicial Selection Under Clinton: A Midterm Examination," *Judicature* 78 (1995): 276; Sheldon Goldman and Elliot Slotnick, "Picking Judges Under Fire," *Judicature* 86 (1999): 265.

28. Strauss, "One Hundred Fifty Cases Per Year," 1099.

29. A rational choice argument can be made that the explosion of lower court decisions will affect not only the percentage of cases reviewed but also the content of Supreme Court doctrine. Specifically, facing an onslaught of lower court cases, a strategic Supreme Court will relax its precedents to maximize limited monitoring resources. See McCubbins et al., "Politics and the Courts," 1647.

30. The phrase "political thicket" comes from Justice Frankfurter's plurality opinion in *Colgrove v. Greene*, 328 U.S. 549, 556 (1946), which refused to adjudicate claims concerning legislative apportionment under the so-called political question doctrine and warned the courts to avoid this policy area. Sixteen years later, the Warren Court entered the thicket over Frankfurter's vehement dissent, handing down *Baker v. Carr*, 369 U.S. 186 (1962), which rejected the political question argument for the first time in a reapportionment case and marked the beginning of the Court's controversial role in drawing the political maps of the United States. For a lively debate on reapportionment decisions, particularly on the more recent cases, compare J. Morgan Kousser, *Colorblind Injustice: Minority Voting Rights and the Undoing of the Second Reconstruction* (Chapel Hill: University of North Carolina Press, 1999) with Abigail Thernstrom, *Whose Vote Counts? Affirmative Action and Minority Voting Rights* (Cambridge, Mass.: Harvard University Press, 1987).

31. Alexis de Tocqueville, *Democracy in America Vol. I* (1835; reprint, New York: Vintage Books, 1945): 290.

32. Stephen Skowronek, *Building a New American State: The Expansion of National Administrative Capacities, 1877–1920* (Cambridge: Cambridge University Press, 1982): 24–35 (elaborating the role of courts and parties in providing coherence to a system of fragmented political authority).

33. See Robert A. Kagan, *Adversarial Legalism: The American Way of Law* (Cambridge, Mass.: Harvard University Press, 2001): 1–17 (defining the concept of "adversarial legalism"). See also Kagan's earlier formulations in "Adversarial Legalism and American Government," *Policy Analysis & Management* 10 (1991): 372; "Do Lawyers Cause Adversarial Legalism? A Preliminary Inquiry," *Law & Social Inquiry* 19, no. 1 (1994): 1. For a critical assessment of Kagan's argument, see Frank B. Cross, "Adversarial Legalism: The American Way of Law," *Virginia Law Review* 89, no. 1 (2003): 189 (book review).

34. See Herbert M. Kritzer, "Adjudication to Settlement: Shading in the Grey," *Judicature* 70 (1986): 163 (studying the disposition of over 1600 state and federal cases).

35. See generally Benjamin Cardozo, *The Nature of the Judicial Process* (1921; reprint, New Haven, Conn.: Yale University Press, 1978), 113; William O. Douglas, "Legal Institutions in America," in *Legal Institutions Today and Tomorrow: The Centennial Conference Volume of the Columbia Law School,* ed. Monrad Paulsen (New York: Columbia University Press, 1959), 292; Martin Shapiro, *The Supreme Court and Administrative Agencies* (New York: The Free Press, 1968), 240–42 (discussing how agencies and courts inevitably fill loopholes in the law).

36. *Sutton et al. v. United Airlines, Inc.,* 527 U.S. 471 (1999). For more on *Sutton,* see Chapter 1 at pages 2–4 and accompanying notes.

37. Kagan, *Adversarial Legalism,* 40–58; see also Thomas F. Burke, *Lawyers, Lawsuits, and Legal Rights: The Battle Over Litigation in American Society* (Berkeley: University of California Press, 2002), 11–13.

38. Such provisions are common in environmental statutes, such as the Clean Air Act, the 1986 Superfund Act, the Endangered Species Act, and others.

39. 397 U.S. 254 (1970).

40. Burke, *Lawyers, Lawsuits, and Legal Rights,* 11.

41. See Richard B. Stewart and Cass Sunstein, "Public Programs and Private Rights," *Harvard Law Review* 95 (1982): 1195.

42. See generally Kagan, "Do Lawyers Cause Adversarial Legalism?" 38–59; Burke, *Lawyers, Lawsuits, and Legal Rights,* 45–51. For interesting glimpses into the world of public interest lawyers, see Susan Seager, "Saving the Earth," *California Lawyer* (April 1991): 39–43; Martha Derthick, *Up in Smoke: From Legislation to Litigation in Tobacco Politics* (Washington, D.C.: CQ Press, 2002).

43. Circuit judge Harold Leventhal coined this phrase in *Greater Boston Television Corp. v. FCC,* 444 F.2d 841, 851 (D.C. Cir. 1970). For more on the changing role of the federal courts in the administrative process, see Martin Shapiro, *Who Guards the Guardians: Judicial Control of Administration* (Athens: University of Georgia Press, 1988); Jeremy Rabkin, *Judicial Compulsions: How Public Law Distorts Public Policy* (New York: Basic Books, 1989); R. Shep Melnick, *Regulation and the Courts: The Case of the Clean Air Act* (Washington, D.C.: Brookings Institution, 1983).

44. Of course, this discussion of federal courts puts aside the enormous role of state courts in stretching traditional legal doctrines, such as tort and family law, to address complex policy issues. These innovations have provided public and private interests an avenue to bypass federal legislative and regulatory processes altogether and have given the courts another powerful platform for affecting issues beyond the reach of judges abroad. For more on the comparative role of judges in tort and family law, see Gary Schwartz, "Product Liability and Medical Malpractice," in *The Liability Maze: The Impact of Liability Law on Safety and Innovation,* ed. Peter Huber and Robert Litan (Washington, D.C.: Brookings Institution, 1991); Mary Ann Glendon, *Abortion and Divorce in Western Law* (Cambridge, Mass.: Harvard University Press, 1987).

45. John Braithwaite, *To Punish or Persuade: Enforcement of Coal Mine Safety* (Albany: SUNY Press, 1985).

46. Patricia Day and Rudolf Klein, "The Regulation of Nursing Homes: A Comparative Perspective," *Milbank Quarterly* 65, no. 3 (1987): 303.

47. Robert Reich, "Bailout: A Comparative Law Study in Law and Industrial Structure," *Yale Journal of Regulation* 2 (1985): 163.

48. David Kirp, *Doing Good by Doing Little: Race and Schooling in Britain* (Berkeley: University of California Press, 1979).

49. Derek Bok, "Reflections on the Distinctive Character of American Labor Laws," *Harvard Law Review* 84 (1971): 1394.

50. Harvey Teff, "Drug Approval in England and the United States," *American Journal of Comparative Law* 33 (1987): 567.

51. Lennart J. Lundqvist, *The Hare and the Tortoise: Clean Air Policies in the United States and Sweden* (Ann Arbor: University of Michigan Press, 1980).

52. Joseph Badaracco Jr., *Loading the Dice: A Five Country Study of Vinyl Chloride Regulation* (Cambridge, Mass.: Harvard Business School Press, 1985).

53. See Kagan, *Adversarial Legalism,* 8, table 1 (collecting authority).

54. For a scholarly analysis of court-led prison reform, see Malcom M. Feeley and Edward Rubin, *Judicial Policy-Making and the Modern State: How the Court Reformed America's Prisons* (Cambridge: Cambridge University Press, 1998). For a more journalistic account, see Jack Bass, *Taming the Storm: The Life and Times of Judge Frank M. Johnson and the South's Fight for Civil Rights* (New York: Doubleday, 1993), 323–46.

55. Peretti, *In Defense of a Political Court,* 78; see also Feeley and Rubin, *Judicial Policy-Making and the Modern State,* 345–46.

56. See R. Shep Melnick, *Between the Lines: Interpreting Welfare Rights* (Washington, D.C.: Brookings Institution, 1994); William Eskridge Jr., "Reneging on History? Playing the Court/Congress/President Civil Rights Game," *California Law Review* 79 (1991): 613; Carol F. Lee, "The Political Safeguards of Federalism? Congressional Responses to Supreme Court Decisions on State and Local Liability," *The Urban Lawyer* 20, no. 2 (1988): 301; Kevin R. Johnson, "*Los Olvidados:* Images of the Immigrant, Political Power of

Noncitizens, and Immigration Law and Enforcement," *Brigham Young University Law Review* (1993): 139; Victor M. Sher and Carol Sue Hunting, "Eroding the Landscape, Eroding the Laws: Congressional Exemptions from Judicial Review of Environmental Laws," *Harvard Environmental Law Review* 15 (1991): 435; Victor M. Sher, "Travels with Strix: The Spotted Owl's Journey Through the Federal Courts," *Public Land Law Review* 14 (1993): 41; Brian Marks, "A Model of Judicial Influence on Congressional Policy-Making: *Grove City College v. Bell,*" (Ph.D. diss., Washington University, St. Louis, Mo. 1984). For an econometric analysis of court-Congress relations in the field of labor relations, see Pablo T. Spiller and Rafael Gely, "Congressional Control or Judicial Independence: The Determinants of U.S. Supreme Court Labor-Relations Decisions, 1949–1988," *RAND Journal of Economics* 23, no. 4 (1992): 463.

57. See Joseph Ignagni and James Meernik, "Explaining Congressional Attempts to Reverse Supreme Court Decisions," *Political Research Quarterly* 47 (1994): 353; Eskridge, "Overriding Supreme Court Statutory Interpretation Decisions," 331; see also Paschal, "Continuing Colloquy," 195; Abner Mikva and Jeff Bleich, "When Congress Overrules the Court," *California Law Review* 79 (1991): 729; Michael Solimine and James Walker, "The Next Word: Congressional Response to Supreme Court Statutory Interpretation Decisions," *Temple Law Review* 65 (1992): 425; "Congressional Reversals of Supreme Court Decisions: 1945–1957," *Harvard Law Review* 71 (1958): 1324.

58. Of particular note are signaling models that take into account Congress's uncertainty about the future costs of passing overrides and the courts' uncertainty about the intensity of Congress's preferences. See, for example, Edward P. Schwartz, Pablo T. Spiller, and Santiago Urbiztondo, "A Positive Theory of Legislative Intent," *Law and Contemporary Problems* 57 (Winter 1994): 51. Other relevant game theoretic studies include Matthew McCubbins, Roger Noll, and Barry Weingast, "Structure and Process, Politics and Policy: Administrative Arrangements and the Political Control of Agencies," *Virginia Law Review* 75 (1989): 431; Eskridge, "Overriding Supreme Court Statutory Interpretation Decisions," 372–87; and Rafael Gely and Pablo T. Spiller, "A Rational Choice Model of Supreme Court Statutory Interpretation Decisions with Applications to the *State Farm* and *Grove City* Cases," *Journal of Law, Economics, and Organization* VI, no. 2 (1990): 263–84; see also John Ferejohn and Charles Shipan, "Congressional Influence on Bureaucracy," *Journal of Law, Economics, and Organization* 6 (1990): 1–17.

59. See, for example, Harry Stumpf, "Congressional Reaction to Supreme Court Rulings: The Interaction of Law and Politics," *Journal of Public Law* 14 (1965): 394; John R. Schmidhauser, Larry Berg, and Albert Melone, "The Impact of Judicial Decisions: New Dimensions in Supreme Court-Congressional Relations, 1945–1968," *Washington University Law Quarterly* (1971): 214–15.

60. See Eskridge, "Overriding Supreme Court Statutory Interpretation Decisions," 341–43 (reviewing Judiciary Committee responses to Supreme Court

decisions from 1979 to 1988); Beth Henschen, "Statutory Interpretations of the Supreme Court: Congressional Response," *American Politics Quarterly* 11, no. 4 (1983): 441 (examining congressional response to Supreme Court labor and antitrust decisions); Beth Henschen and Edward Sidlow, "The Supreme Court and the Congressional Agenda-Setting Process," *Journal of Law & Politics* V (1985): 685 (same).

61. Numerous case studies detail the rigors of passing legislation in Washington. See Eric Redman, *The Dance of Legislation* (New York: Simon and Schuster, 1973) (chronicling the passage of the National Health Service Corps bill); Steven Waldman, *The Bill: How Legislation Really Becomes Law: A Case Study of the National Service Bill* (New York: Penguin Books, 1996) (describing the passage of the National Service Bill); David Maranis and Michael Weisskopf, *"Tell Newt to Shut Up!"* (New York: Simon and Schuster, 1996) (describing how the Republican "Contract with America" largely foundered in Congress).

62. For a flavor of the potential political complexity of passing overrides, see Melnick, *Between the Lines* (detailing court-Congress interactions over the interpretation of statutes governing Aid to Families with Dependent Children, special education, and the food stamp programs).

63. For an elegant theoretical presentation of this argument, see McCubbins, Noll, and Weingast, "Structure and Process, Politics and Policy," 433–40. For very brief summary and critique of positive political theory, see Robert Katzmann, *Courts and Congress* (Washington, D.C.: Brookings Institution, 1997), 56–59. For excellent empirical accounts of how court decisions can affect coalition-building, see Michael W. McCann, *Rights at Work: Pay Equity and the Politics of Legal Mobilization* (Chicago: University of Chicago Press, 1994); R. Shep Melnick, "Separation of Powers and the Strategy of Rights: The Expansion of Special Education," in *The New Politics of Public Policy,* ed. Marc Landy and Martin Levin (Baltimore, Md.: Johns Hopkins University Press, 1995) (describing the instrumental role of court rulings in cementing a diverse coalition in favor of special education programs, including parents of handicapped children and the states); see also William K. Muir, *Law and Attitude Change* (Chicago: University of Chicago Press, 1973) (showing how a prominent lawyer used the Supreme Court school prayer cases as a political resource to persuade local school administrators to follow the law).

64. See generally Sven Steinmo, "American Exceptionalism Reconsidered: Culture or Institutions," in *The Dynamics of American Politics: Approaches and Interpretations,* ed. Lawrence Dodd and Calvin Jillison (Boulder, Colo.: Westview Press 1994), 126.

65. Eskridge, "Overriding Supreme Court Statutory Interpretation Decisions," 338, table 1. Further study is needed to assess the crucial issue of whether this increase is significant *relative* to increased judicial activity.

66. Ibid., 342; see also Lori Hausegger and Lawrence Baum, "Behind the Scenes: The Supreme Court and Congress in Statutory Interpretation," in *Great*

Theatre: The American Congress in the 1990s, ed. Herbert Weisberg and Samuel Patterson (New York: Cambridge University Press 1988): 224–47 (finding that Congress overturned a minimum 5.6 percent of Supreme Court decisions from the 1978 to 1989 terms, which is an even higher rate of override activity than suggested by Eskridge's data).

67. Eskridge, "Overriding Supreme Court Statutory Interpretation Decisions," 348–53.

68. Walter Murphy and Hermann Pritchett, *Courts, Judges, and Politics: An Introduction to the Judicial Process* (New York: McGraw-Hill, 1961), 554–55 (writing that "[c]ourts are protected by their magic; only rarely can a hand be laid on a judge without a public outcry of sacrilege").

69. Glendon Schubert, *Constitutional Politics* (Boston: Boston University Press, 1960), 257–58.

70. Stumpf, "Congressional Reaction to Supreme Court Rulings," 394.

71. Schmidhauser et al., "Impact of Judicial Decisions," 214–15 (finding that, although some evidence shows Republicans and Democrats coalesce to block court-curbing measures, which seek to strip the Court's jurisdiction or otherwise curtail its institutional powers, little bipartisan resistance was found to overrides, which target specific decisions).

72. Katzmann, *Courts and Congress,* 73–74. See also Abner Mikva, "How Well Does the Supreme Court Defend the Constitution?" *North Carolina Law Review* 61 (1983): 609 (asserting that "most Supreme Court cases never come to the attention of Congress"). For an interesting account of how ostensibly technical rulings can change policy, see Angus MacIntyre, "A Court Quietly Rewrote the Federal Pesticides Statute: How Prevalent is Judicial Statutory Revision," *Law & Policy* 7 (1985): 245.

73. For more on the distinction between police patrol and fire alarm oversight, see Matthew McCubbins and Thomas Schwartz, "Congressional Oversight Overlooked: Police Patrols versus Fire Alarms," *American Journal of Political Science* 28 (1984): 165–66.

74. Overall, to the extent studies focus on judicial aspects of the override process, they tend to look at Supreme Court decisions that invite overrides as opposed to judicial reactions to overrides. See, for example, Lori Hausegger and Lawrence Baum, "Inviting Congressional Action: A Study of Supreme Court Motivations in Statutory Interpretation," *American Journal of Political Science* 43, no. 1 (1999): 162; Pablo T. Spiller and Emerson Tiller, "Invitations to Override: Congressional Reversals of Supreme Court Decisions," *International Review of Law and Economics* 16 (1996): 503. There are a few exceptions. See James Brudney, "Congressional Commentary on Judicial Interpretations of Statutes: Idle Chatter or Telling Response?" *Michigan Law Review* 93 (1994): 1 (offering some excellent case studies on congressional signaling); Daniel Bussel, "Textualism's Failures: A Study of Overruled Bankruptcy Decisions," *Vanderbilt Law Review* 53 (2000): 887.

75. In most studies, the assumption that overrides matter is implicit. In others, it is simply asserted. For example, in his overview of Congress's formal powers over courts, Richard Paschal baldly states: "The most effective (and easily achieved) way for Congress to respond to judicial pronouncements is through its power to enact laws which overturn or modify the results embodied in the Court's decisions" ("Continuing Colloquy," 195). Former Senator Patrick Moynihan similarly concludes, without a scintilla of evidence, that legislation is an "unequaled" means for addressing errant Supreme Court decisions ("What Do You Do When the Supreme Court is Wrong?" 23). It should be noted that Stuart Nagel, in *The Legal Process from a Behavioral Perspective,* does consider the aftermath of what he calls "court-curbing" measures on the Supreme Court's behavior: bills that seek to curtail the Court's institutional powers. But Nagel *expressly* excludes overrides from his study ([Homewood, Ill.: The Dorsey Press, 1969], 261); see also Roger Handberg and Harold Hill, "Court Curbing, Court Reversals, and Judicial Review: The Supreme Court versus Congress," *Law & Society Review* 14 (1980): 309 (reanalyzing Nagel's data).

76. Douglas, "Legal Institutions in America," 292; Solomine and Walker, "The Next Word," 453.

77. See, for example, Michael Axline, "Forest Health and the Politics of Expediency," *Environmental Law* 26 (1996): 613; Sher and Hunting, "Eroding the Landscape, Eroding the Laws," 435 (discussing a string of congressional overrides of judicial environmental law decisions that favored the timber industry). See also Johnson, "*Los Olvidados,*" 139 (analyzing overrides in immigration law and suggesting immigrants have been forgotten in the override process).

Part I Do Overrides Matter?

3 Assumptions and Hypotheses

Because the override literature largely overlooks what happens after Congress acts, the analysis must address the threshold issue of whether overrides matter. More specifically, does the passage of overrides significantly increase levels of judicial consensus and hence legal certainty, or do independent federal judges find ways to circumvent overrides? This question is deceptively complex. In parsing its complexity, this chapter divides the analysis into two parts. First, it sets forth my assumptions about the nature of legal constraints and judicial decision-making, and explains why it is reasonable to assume that overrides are *capable* of significantly increasing levels of judicial consensus. Second, the chapter develops competing hypotheses about whether the passage of overrides, in fact, significantly increases levels of judicial consensus. With these assumptions and hypotheses in place, Chapter 4 discusses the data, methods, and findings.

Are Overrides Capable of Significantly Increasing Judicial Consensus?

This question of whether overrides matter raises issues about the nature of legal constraints and judicial decision-making that have divided scholars for more than a century. As will be discussed, this chapter does not seek to resolve controversy over these issues or prove anything counterintuitive about the nature of decision-making according to rules. Indeed, it is unclear whether we can resolve the long-standing debate between legalists, who assert that law—or at least a sense of professional obligation to apply the law in good faith—significantly constrains judicial decision-making, and behavioralists, who argue that formal rules merely provide cover for judicial policy-making. We can, however, identify the competing schools of thought and make assumptions explicit. Accordingly, this chapter opens by characterizing the main styles of argument about the nature of legal constraints and judicial decision-making (the legal model, the behavioralist model, and the institutionalist model), and why it is assumed that overrides, in the context of the broader override process, can send to the court effective signals that significantly increase levels of judicial consensus.[1]

The "Legal Model": Positivism, the Realist Critique, and Post-Positivism

The classic American conception of law and judicial decision-making is "legal formalism," which enjoyed its heyday among scholars in the late-nineteenth and early-twentieth centuries, when the academic study of law was introduced in American universities.[2] It recalls Max Weber's concept of "formal-rational" law, which envisages law as a set of mutually exclusive and exhaustive dispositional categories,[3] and it found new life under H. L. A. Hart's reformation of legal positivism, which holds that legal rules have clear, determinate meaning in routine cases.[4] Under this view, legal rules take the following form: "if condition X exists, legal status Y applies, and consequence Z shall be imposed."

Formalists imply that judicial decision-making under rules is mechanical: judges ascertain the facts, find the law, and deduce the result. Consider a speed limit, which fines drivers who exceed 35 miles per hour along a stretch of road. If drivers are caught exceeding the limit, they are speeders, and a judge will impose the prescribed fine; if drivers do not exceed 35 miles per hour, they are not speeders, and no fine will be imposed.

From this perspective, the issue of whether overrides can increase judicial consensus is axiomatic. By definition, formal rules provide the major premise of a syllogism that controls judicial decision-making. Hence, clearer rules mean more consistent rule application. Surely overrides hold the promise of clarifying the underlying rules. They offer Congress a direct means to refine the meaning of ambiguous laws and correct drafting errors that may have produced conflicting or confusing laws.

Few, if any, legal scholars currently adhere to legal formalism in its simplest form. The problem lies in its ideal of syllogistic legal reasoning. Linguists and legal philosophers have long argued that general rules connote simple scenarios, which have no necessary application to the complexities of actual disputes. Hence, no textual basis exists for determining whether the intricacies of the case at hand materially differ from the spare picture envisaged in the rule, or whether the differences between the case and the rule's core concept are immaterial.[5] In short, judges cannot simply "find" the governing law; rather, they must choose whether legal standards apply based on extra-textual factors.

Reconsider the speed limit. Does it apply to police chasing a fleeing suspect? An ambulance driver rushing an accident victim to the emergency room? A worried parent who is late to pick up a child from school? Under the literal terms of the law, the speed limit applies to each scenario equally, requiring a judge to fine the police, ambulance driver, and parent alike. But surely judicial decision-making is not so mechanical. Rather than blindly apply the rule as written, judges will decide whether these cases are analogous to the paradigmatic scenario of an ordinary driver, who carelessly exceeds the speed limit. The text of the law does not control this decision; it merely provides a blanket rule that seems over-inclusive. Accordingly, when applying the law in practice, judges will look beyond its literal terms and determine whether the speed limit *should* govern a specific dispute.

Building on these insights, legal realists in the 1920s and 1930s argued that judges inevitably rely on their policy preferences and sense of fairness when determining the scope of rules. Based on these arguments, they posited a "political jurisprudence," which, at its most extreme, turns formalism on its head. Specifically, whereas formalists envisage judges deducing a result from preexisting rules, legal realists assert that judges start with a desired result and then find rules that rationalize their decision. Therefore, realists see every legal decision as a policy decision. Moreover, any explicit reliance on rules, or "law talk," is verbal legerdemain aimed at preserving the appearance of neutrality.[6]

Legal realism has been enormously influential among political scientists who study the courts.[7] However, in recent years, the legal model has made a comeback under the banner of "post-positivism." The genetic marker of post-positivist theory lies in its conception of the law as an internal, as opposed to an external, constraint on judicial decision-making. In a trenchant essay, Howard Gillman explains as follows:

> "[P]ostpositivist" legalists make claims, not about the predictable behavior of judges, but about their state of mind—whether they are basing their decisions on honest judgments about the meaning of the law. What is post-positivist about this version is the assumption that a legal state of mind does not necessarily mean obedience to conspicuous rules; instead, it means a sense of obligation to make the best decision possible in light of one's general training and sense of professional obligation.[8]

From this perspective, analyzing patterns of consensual and discordant rule application during the override process is somewhat beside the point. The crucial issues do not involve patterns of judicial outcomes. In fact, post-positivism implies that counting judicial votes can be misleading, because there may be cases of discordant rule application that reflect good-faith disagreements over legal principles that weakly constrain judicial discretion. There also may be cases of consistent rule application that reflect freewheeling policy-making among like-minded judges. Thus, under post-positivism, we should focus not on judges' votes but on how judges experience the process of judging and how this process shapes their reasoning.

The "Behavioralist Model"

Behavioralists object to both positivist and post-positivist strands of the legal model. With respect to positivism, behavioralists have rigorously tested the assertion that legal rules strongly constrain judicial discretion, especially in connection with the Supreme Court. They have found, time and time again, that Justices' underlying ideological preferences—as opposed to the text of preexisting law—offer a parsimonious explanation of voting patterns in Supreme Court decisions. The leading advocates of the behavioralist model, Jeffrey Segal and Harold Spaeth, sum up decades of careful studies as follows: "Simply put, Rehnquist votes the way he does because he is extremely conservative; Marshall voted the way he did because he is extremely liberal."[9]

With respect to post-positivism, behavioralists object on methodological grounds. They argue that if inconsistent voting patterns may or may not be legally motivated, and if consistent voting patterns may or may not be legally motivated, then one cannot systematically test post-positivist claims concerning legal influence as an "internal constraint." Behavioralists add that, for obvious reasons, asking judges whether their decisions reflect their policy preferences, as opposed to the law, is not promising. As Segal and Spaeth argue, "Judicial nominees who can state under oath before the entire nation that they had never thought about *Roe v. Wade* can hardly be fruitful candidates for traditional survey measures."[10]

Under the behavioralist model, whether overrides can clarify the law or check the courts is an empirical question that depends on whether judges interpret overrides consistently with the law's language. To operationalize this issue, behavioralists would engage in the following steps: (1) predict judicial outcomes based on the *language* of the override; (2) assess whether post-override judicial interpretations are consistent with these predictions; and (3) evaluate the effects of competing determinants of judicial outcomes, especially the presiding judges' attitudes and policy preferences.

It should be added that overrides are unlikely to constrain judicial discretion under a strict behavioralist approach because it is unlikely that the bare text of any law mechanically constrains judicial decision-making; language is simply too pliable. Moreover, to the extent that we observe judicial consensus after Congress acts, behavioralists would predict that such consensus would reflect the presiding judges' common policy preferences, as opposed to the constraining affects of an override. In short, from a behavioralist perspective, we would expect to find that the passage of overrides is largely symbolic, changing the terms of written rules that are made to be broken—or at least manipulated—by politically selected American judges.

The Current Impasse

The debate between the post-positivists and behavioralists has reached an impasse. Post-positivists argue that the law matters as an internal constraint, which requires judges to apply their good-faith—but often contested—understanding of legal doctrine and principles. Behavioralists reply that no set of observable judicial outcomes can disprove post-positivists' claims that law serves as an internal constraint. As such, these claims cannot serve as the conceptual basis for a productive research agenda. Post-positivists rejoin that behavioralists test legal formalism, a form of the legal model that has long been abandoned. Gillman identifies the heart of the problem as follows:

> Behavioralists want to force legalists into offering testable hypotheses, so that beliefs about law's influence can be verified by a kind of scientific knowledge that behavioralists consider more authoritative; however, legalists believe that doing such tests has the effect of changing the concept of legal influence so that it no longer represents what they believe.[11]

The Institutionalist Model: An Alternative Approach

The institutionalist model—or what Edward Rubin calls the "microanalysis of institutions"—offers a third approach, which attempts to sidestep this conceptual morass over judicial motivations. Rather than make strong claims about judicial motivations, the institutionalist approach assumes that judicial motivations are complex, reflecting a combination of policy, legal, and strategic factors.[12] From this perspective, the key issue is not determining what drives judicial decision-making, but identifying under which conditions the law—as socially, politically, and strategically constructed—matters.

To elaborate, consistent with behavioralism, the argument recognizes that judges, like all lawmakers, seek to maximize their policy preferences given the competing preferences of other actors, such as other judges, the public, and other branches of government. It also concedes that the text of legal rules is often ambiguous and pliable when standing alone. Consistent with post-positivism, however, the institutionalist model stresses that judges differ from other policy makers because they operate within networks of norms and expectations about how the law should be read and applied.[13]

This combination of legal rules, norms, and expectations can constrain judicial outcomes on at least two levels. First, these norms and expectations can produce shared understandings about what the law means and when it should be applied.[14] In terms of the speed limit, the issue is not merely what the rule says but also its *ascribed* meaning, which is developed through interaction over its application. Thus, judges and police may come to understand that the speed limit protects public safety against ordinary carelessness. Given this understanding, they may agree that the rule should not apply to police officers or ambulance drivers in emergencies, but to drivers facing stressful but not necessarily dangerous situations, like the parent running behind schedule. Although this understanding cannot be derived directly from the text of the rule, it is part of the legal understanding that imbues the speed limit with clear and predictable meaning, and it renders its application routine in most cases.[15]

Second, some scholars argue that legal norms and expectations serve as strategic constraints on judicial policy-making. For example, in their account of Supreme Court decision-making, Lee Epstein and Jack Knight argue that the justices not only seek to maximize their preferences but also aim to preserve the Court's institutional legitimacy. Given this combination of goals, Epstein and Knight posit that justices will modify their positions "to take account of a *normative constraint*—such as *stare decisis*—to produce a decision as close as possible to their preferred outcome."[16] Why? If the justices radically departed from general norms and expectations of judicial decision-making, they would undermine the Court's institutional standing.[17]

In a somewhat similar vein, Malcolm Feeley and Edward Rubin argue that to the extent judges are motivated to make policy, they must persuade other judges to adopt their decisions. To do so, Feeley and Rubin contend, they must work within the rule of law, showing how their decisions build on existing precedent and rules.[18] Roger Traynor, a justice on California's Supreme Court from 1964 to 1970 and no stranger to judicial policy-making, echoed this theme when he argued that even creative judges must remain "close to his house of the law," proceeding "at the pace of the tortoise that steadily advances though it carries the past on its back."[19]

From the institutional model perspective, overrides are best understood as part of an ongoing colloquy over the meaning of statutes. In the context of this interactive process, the passage of an override can increase levels of judicial consensus (i.e., significantly contribute to turning hard cases, which produce litigation and disagreement among judges in the pre-override period into matters of routine rule application, which engender consensus or no litigation in the post-override period).

Several implications bear emphasis. First, under institutionalism, any causal claim about the effect of the text of override legislation—as a written command in the U.S. Code—is weak by necessity, because the communicative impact of overrides cannot be fully separated from the norms, expectations, and strategic considerations that have accrued during the pre-override period and during passage of the override itself. Second, any claims about judicial motivation are modest. Specifically, it is assumed that judicial motivations are complex, reflecting a combination of legal, political, and strategic factors. No claims are made about the relative significance of these factors. Rather, the only claims are that the passage of overrides significantly contributes to triggering judicial consensus, and that judicial consensus is not *wholly* a function of the presiding judges' preferences.

Once rule application is seen as an interactive process, whether social or strategic, it seems likely that the effectiveness of rules will vary from setting to setting. For example, some policy issues rest on a well-established repertoire of conventions and understandings. Under these circumstances, the passage of overrides will be likely to produce judicial consensus. By contrast, other policy areas are less settled, either because they are novel or because changes in markets, technology, or political values have called old agreements, assumptions, and understandings into question. Under these circumstances, overrides likely will be less effective because the underlying conventions and norms are unsettled or contested.

Similarly, some overrides may send more credible signals than others. For example, if the relevant lawmaking coalition spends the time and resources to hammer out highly specific overrides, judges—as strategic actors—may believe that the legislative coalition is greatly concerned about override issue and hence will be more likely to reverse judicial decisions that stray from carefully constructed legislative bargains. By contrast, if the composition of Congress has significantly changed since the passage of an override, strategic judges may feel less constrained to apply the override as originally drafted.

In sum, the competing models focus attention on different aspects of judging and judicial policy-making. Post-positivists focus our sights on judicial self-perception, raising questions about how judges see their role as decision makers and interpreters of legal principles. Behavioralists focus our attention on judges' votes, raising questions about the predictive value of legal rules in judicial decision-making. Institutionalists are less concerned with judicial motivations. They emphasize the context of rulemaking and judicial decision-making—whether that context is seen as legal, strategic, political, or some combination of these traits—and raise questions about the conditions under which socially, politically, and strategically constructed rules shape policy outcomes.

Assumptions

Given this book's emphasis on the dynamics of inter-branch policy-making, the institutionalist model seems most appropriate to the questions at hand. Accordingly, it is assumed that overrides are best understood as part of a broader interactive process and, as part of that process, can significantly increase judicial consensus.

I believe these assumptions are reasonable. As a general matter, given the long-standing nature of the legalists–behavioralists debate, it seems likely that both are partially right. Sometimes judges will faithfully apply the law, despite their personal preference;[20] sometimes they will ignore the letter of the override and mete out justice on their own terms;[21] and other times the law will be vague and judges will legislate interstitially, filling the gaps that inevitably appear when applying general rules to specific, nonroutine cases.[22] The institutionalist approach allows for each of these possibilities because it assumes rule application will vary across settings. Thus, it avoids the pitfalls of either extreme and expects neither too much nor too little from the law.

In addition, despite behavioralists' justified skepticism of judicial proclamations that law matters, judges do seem to take the law seriously. The most dramatic examples involve cases of "judicial can'ts": decisions in which judges apply the law as they find it, despite personal opposition.[23] In the context of overrides, "invitations to override" offer the most obvious examples. In these cases, judges apply the law as written, they recognize that their decision produces absurd policy results, and they explicitly ask Congress to take corrective action.[24] Consider the famous snail-darter case: *TVA v. Hill*.[25] In *TVA*, the Supreme Court applied the Endangered Species Act (ESA) as drafted, even though it required the halting of a $110 million dam project that was nearly complete and was started long before the passage of the ESA. In applying the law literally, the majority invoked the doctrine of "judicial can't" and urged Congress to reverse its decision. (Congress promptly obliged, passing two laws: one that dealt directly with *TVA* and another that created an administrative board, known as the "God Squad," that allows the suspension of the ESA's protections on an ad hoc basis.[26])

Similarly, if rules do not meaningfully constrain judicial discretion, as the most extreme versions of legal realism and behavioralist arguments seem to imply, we would expect high levels of judicial dissensus in contentious policy areas. Although the judicial behavior literature does find *relatively* higher levels of dissensus in contested policy areas, *absolute* levels of judicial consensus remain impressively high. Jon Gottschall, for example, has found that 83 percent of appellate court opinions are unanimous in controversial policy areas, such as civil liberties, race and sex discrimination, labor relations, and others.[27] In these cases, judges of various ideological stripes are not only *saying* the law requires an outcome but also *voting* together. Although some consensus surely reflects ideological—as opposed to doctrinal—agreement,[28] it seems likely that routine cases of rule application exist in which judges believe themselves constrained under the law (for doctrinal, political, or strategic reasons), regardless of ideological preference.

Finally, as noted, Congress has passed hundreds of overrides since the mid-1970s. So if overrides are largely symbolic and cannot send effective signals, why do sophisticated interest groups and governmental agencies spend so much time and energy lobbying Congress? Again, it seems the most common-sense approach assumes that the passage of overrides is part of an ongoing process that can send constraining signals, but allows that their effectiveness will vary across settings.[29]

Do Overrides Significantly Increase Levels of Judicial Consensus?

Assuming overrides *can* significantly affect patterns of judicial behavior does not mean they will, in fact, do so. Instead, the institutional model focuses attention on the following question: given the political and legal context of the passage of overrides, would we expect overrides to increase levels of judicial consensus significantly? The answer is far from clear. Drawing on the logic of hyperpluralist accounts of the statutory construction process, we can construct a plausible null hypothesis that predicts the passage of overrides will not significantly increase levels of judicial consensus. Under this view, political controversy that produced litigation and congressional dissatisfaction in the pre-override period should spill over to the post-override period. By contrast, the logic of pluralist and capture theory points toward an alternative hypothesis that predicts overrides will send strong and effective signals. Under the logic of these views, the passage of overrides should significantly increase levels of judicial consensus on override issues.

The Hyperpluralist Null Hypothesis

Hyperpluralism suggests that the passage of overrides will not significantly increase levels of judicial consensus. This thesis, in turn, rests on an argument about the legislative process and an argument about the judicial process, both of which were suggested in earlier chapters. First, according to hyperpluralism, members of Congress are likely to pass vague overrides that will do little to rein in the courts. Second, even if Congress manages to pass clear overrides, or agencies enact clear interpretive rules, politically selected and ideologically diverse American judges are unlikely to apply the law faithfully or consistently. The net result should be persistent legal uncertainty, stemming from unclear legal standards and inconsistent statutory interpretations.

The Hyperpluralist Legislative Premise: Overrides Will Be Vague. In their magisterial comparison of British and American law, Professors Patrick S. Atiyah and Robert Summers maintain that American statutes tend to be less clear than their British counterparts. The reason, they argue, lies in differences between each nation's statutory drafting processes. In Great Britain, legislation is drafted in the Office of Parliamentary Counsel, a small, centralized office staffed with highly skilled professionals who specialize in writing statutes.[30] The office's monopoly over the drafting process is complete, extending to amendments and whatever revisions are needed to reconcile preexisting laws to new ones. The result is no panacea. Atiyah and Summers readily concede that British laws are arcane and tortuous to the untrained eye. However, they claim that "inconsistencies and conflicting provisions are rarely . . . found between one statute and another, still less within the same statute, [because of] the ability of British governments to control the content of statutes which are passed by Parliament, and to ensure that they are drafted by lawyers of high professional competence."[31]

Congress also has a professional legislative drafting staff: the Legislative Counsel. The Legislative Counsel, however, operates within an entirely different institutional environment than does the Parliamentary Counsel. Although members of the Legislative Counsel may be as skilled as their British counterparts, they do not control the drafting process; they merely initiate it. As a result, their handiwork is subject to multiple rounds of ad hoc revisions by specialized committees and subcommittees, each of which possesses different areas of technical expertise and answers to different and often competing constituencies. In addition, unlike the Parliamentary Counsel, which takes orders from a ruling coalition, the Legislative Counsel takes orders from multiple committees and subcommittees. This means not only multiple taskmasters, who may give conflicting instructions, but also more work, which may result in less care given to each bill. Finally, the Legislative Counsel does not serve as a clearinghouse that ensures internal consistency of new laws or their consistency with existing statutes. Instead, American laws tend to grow piecemeal. Thus, "what started out as an adequately drafted bill [in the U.S.] may end up as crude patchwork."[32]

Why should overrides be different? They, too, must run the lawmaking gauntlet in Washington. Hence, overrides should be equally prone to ambiguity and incoherence. Moreover, overrides may be particularly vague, because override issues, by definition, generate litigation and multiple rounds of legislation. Such high levels of activity in courts and

Congress may suggest that competing interest groups are well mobilized on the issue. If so, representatives seeking to maximize their re-election chances are likely to favor vague laws that send tough issues back to the courts such as the Civil Rights Act of 1991. The reason is that passing general, "feel good" measures allows elected officials to claim credit for taking action; avoid difficult policy trade-offs, which may alienate voters or become campaign fodder for political rivals; and blame courts for problems that inevitably arise during implementation.[33]

The Hyperpluralist Judicial Premise: Even If Overrides Are Clear, Courts Will Ignore Them.   Even if members of Congress manage to pass clear overrides, or agencies promulgate clear interpretive regulations, courts may circumvent them. After all, as discussed in Chapter 2, the U.S. "coordinate" judicial system seems hardwired for flexible, and inconsistent, rule application. Specifically, in contrast to European hierarchical systems of justice, the American justice system decentralizes decision-making authority, which protects the discretion of trial court judges, who are closest to the facts of each case, and limits top-down control. Moreover, unlike European judges, who are selected for their legal skill and reputation, American judges are selected for their political experience and problem-solving skills. Given this difference in backgrounds, it is not surprising that comparative scholars find that American judges approach rule application less formally than their European counterparts.[34]

In addition, the override process may be particularly likely to produce inconsistent court decisions. By the time Congress has passed an override, contending interests have already spent considerable resources litigating and legislating the override issue. Given these sunken costs, it seems unlikely that the "losers" in Congress would suddenly drop the issue. Instead, we would expect these litigation-tested groups to return to court and try to exploit any ambiguities in the override laws. At the same time, we would expect the "winners" in Congress to resist such lawsuits vigorously, pointing to Congress's iterative attempts to clarify the law. One might expect such hotly contested lawsuits to produce disagreement over the interpretation of the law, as ideologically diverse American judges apply their discretion on a case-by-case basis to reach fair results. The bottom line is the null hyperpluralist hypothesis that the passage of overrides will not significantly increase levels of judicial consensus.

Pluralism and Capture Theory, and the Alternative Hypothesis

Different strands of pluralism and capture theory imply an alternative hypothesis, which posits that overrides will significantly increase judicial consensus. This argument directly challenges hyperpluralism's legislative and judicial premises that underlie the null hypothesis. Namely, although pluralism and capture imply very different patterns of interest group participation during the passage of overrides, both predict that members of Congress will pass clear rather than vague override statutes, and that judges will typically adhere to, not ignore, overrides.

The Alternative Legislative Premise: Overrides Will Be Targeted and Clear. Override statutes may be targeted and clear for several reasons, both of which stem from the iterative nature of the override process. From a pluralist perspective, statutory construction should involve a form of organizational learning or feedback.[35] This perspective stresses that members of Congress face a significant contracting problem: they cannot anticipate all potential applications of statutes, much less changes in technology, markets, and political values that may render statutes obsolete. As a result, Congress may pass general rules initially, which courts then flesh out through adjudication. As Congress's second stab at an issue, however, overrides are different because members of Congress are not writing on a clean slate. They can review the courts' attempts to apply the law and revise it accordingly. The product should include clearer and more specific rules that provide better formal guidance to judicial decision-making.

One need not adopt this (somewhat rosy) view of inter-branch relations to believe overrides will be targeted. Indeed, consistent with hyperpluralism, one might concede that members of Congress seek to maximize their chances of re-election. Accordingly, members of Congress tend to pass vague *original* statutes, which allows them to claim credit and to shift blame to the courts for any problems that arise during the implementation of their general edicts.

Once the original statute is in place, however, members of Congress may shift their strategic focus and adopt legislative strategies consistent with capture theory. Specifically, rather than pass general laws that allow credit-claiming with the public, members of Congress may pass specific overrides that provide key constituents legislative relief from unfavorable court decisions. By combining broad initial statutes with targeted overrides, members of Congress claim credit twice. They can tout the broad original statute to the general public, and then pass specific overrides to cement the loyalty of key constituents who have lost in court. Whether one adopts the pluralist account of inter-branch feedback, or the capture theorist's account of strategic credit-claiming, overrides should be highly specific.

The Alternative Judicial Premise: Courts Will Adhere to Overrides. Judges may take overrides seriously. After all, an override is Congress's second statute on an issue, which should clarify legal standards. As such, if one is inclined to focus on the legal context of judicial decision-making, it seems reasonable to assume that clarified rules should provide better formal guidance to judicial discretion. Hence, the passage of overrides should promote consistent rule application.

If one is inclined to emphasize the strategic context of judicial decision-making, overrides should send credible signals, which should rein in judicial policy-making. This argument stems from studies that envisage court-Congress relations as an iterated signaling game with asymmetric information.[36] Specifically, signaling games assume that judges are motivated to maximize their policy preferences, but lack perfect information about congressional preferences and the costs of passing future overrides. Under these circumstances, judges must guess whether a legislative majority will reverse their decisions, relying on a patchwork of signals, such as the text of statutes, legislative history materials (such as committee reports), and public post-enactment statements.

Gleaning information from congressional signals is usually problematic for several reasons. First, statutes often send static-filled messages to the courts: some statutes are vague, some are conflicting, and some are obsolete. Second, even if a statute accurately reflects the preferences of pivotal members of Congress when it passes, congressional membership and preferences change over time. Elections and retirements create turnover in Congress; fluctuations in public opinion or tough re-election campaigns can force incumbents to reconsider positions; and external factors, such as changes in markets, technology, or demographics, can shift constituencies. Finally, the credibility of congressional signals can be hard to assess. Indeed, judges may reasonably believe that members of Congress will routinely exaggerate the intensity of their preferences in an attempt to (1) encourage judicial compliance with legislative bargains, and (2) reduce the costs of monitoring court decisions.

Under these circumstances, legislative majorities need *credible* means to convey the intensity of their preferences to the judiciary. Overrides provide such signals because, unlike doctoring legislative history or making public statements, passing overrides is costly. After all, passing any statute is hard work, and in the case of overrides, members of Congress have run the policy-making obstacle course twice: once when passing the original statute and again when passing the override. Barring dramatic changes in the composition of Congress, such determined political effort should convince judges that a legislative majority cares about the override issue and is poised to reverse future errant decisions. Under this logic, because judicial activism would be strategically fruitless if it merely triggered congressional reversal, overrides offer a credible threat of reversal that should deter even ideologically motivated judges from ignoring their plain meaning. The net result is the alternative hypothesis that the passage of overrides will significantly increase levels of judicial consensus.

Table 3.1   Do Overrides Significantly Increase Levels of Judicial Consensus? Summary of Competing Views

Issue	Hyperpluralist	Alternative
Is Congress likely to pass clear overrides?	No	Yes
Assuming overrides are clear on their face, will courts apply them consistently?	No	Yes
Will the override process significantly increase levels of judicial consensus?	No (The null hypothesis)	Yes (The alternative hypothesis)

Summary

Does the passage of overrides significantly increase levels of judicial consensus? As seen in Table 3.1, there are competing views. Hyperpluralism suggests that the passage of overrides will not significantly increase levels of judicial consensus. Instead, Congress will tend to pass the buck and, even when the rules are clear, politically selected and ideologically diverse judges will interpret the law inconsistently. Pluralism and capture theory suggest the opposite—the passage of overrides will significantly increase levels of judicial consensus—albeit for different reasons. Pluralists typically envisage statutory construction as an open, ongoing policy dialogue that engenders inter-branch feedback and policy consensus over time. Thus, as Congress's second signal on an issue, overrides should send effective clarifying signals to the courts.

Capture theorists offer a more cynical account. In order to maximize their chances for reelection, strategic members of Congress will pass targeted overrides, which provide key constituents relief from unfavorable court decisions. In order to maximize their policy preferences and avoid reversals of their decisions, strategic judges will adhere to overrides because overrides credibly convey that a legislative majority is (1) monitoring their decisions and (2) capable of reversing errant judicial interpretations. The next chapter probes the validity of the null and alternative hypotheses.

Notes

1. For insightful, concise overviews on the nature of legal constraints and the role of law and courts in policy-making, see Robert A. Kagan, *Regulatory Justice: Implementing a Wage-Price Freeze* (New York: Russell Sage Foundation, 1978), 85–90; see also Martin Shapiro, "Courts of Law, Courts of Politics," in

Courts in the Political Process: Jack W. Peltason's Contributions to Political Science, ed. Austin Ranney (Berkeley, Calif.: IGS Press, 1996), 99–115; Edward Rubin, "The New Legal Process, the Synthesis of Discourse and the Microanalysis of Institutions," *Harvard Law Review* 109 (1996): 1393–411; Michael McCann, "How the Supreme Court Matters in American Politics: New Institutionalists Perspectives," in *The Supreme Court in American Politics,* ed. Howard Gillman and Cornell Clayton (Lawrence: University of Kansas Press, 1999), 63–97; Howard Gillman, "What's Law Got to Do with It? Judicial Behaviorialists Test the 'Legal Model' of Judicial Decision Making," *Law & Social Inquiry* 26, no. 2 (Spring 2001): 485–95.

2. For more on the establishment of law schools in American universities, see Robert Stevens, *Law School: Legal Education in America from the 1850s to the 1980s* (Chapel Hill: North Carolina Press, 1983).

3. For a concise distillation of Weber's typology of law and legal systems, see David M. Trubek, "Max Weber on the Rise of Capitalism," *Wisconsin Law Review* (1972): 725–31.

4. See H. L. A. Hart, *The Concept of Law* (Oxford: Oxford University Press, 1961), 120, 124–26, 132.

5. Kagan, *Regulatory Justice,* 87.

6. See Martin Shapiro, *Courts: A Comparative and Political Analysis* (Chicago: University of Chicago Press, 1981), 1–8.

7. For classic examples of political scientists who argue that judicial decisions can be predicted by nonlegal factors, see Joel Grossman, "Social Background and Judicial Decisions: Notes for a Theory," *Journal of Politics* 29 (1967): 29; Glendon Schubert, *The Judicial Mind: The Attitudes and Ideologies of Supreme Court Justices, 1946–1963* (Evanston, Ill.: Northwestern University Press, 1965); Glendon Schubert, *Quantitative Analysis of Judicial Behavior* (Glencoe, Ill.: The Free Press, 1954); Jeffrey A. Segal and Harold J. Spaeth, *The Supreme Court and the Attitudinal Model* (Cambridge: Cambridge University Press, 1993); Jeffrey A. Segal, *The Supreme Court and the Attitudinal Model Revisited* (Cambridge: Cambridge University Press, 2002); Harold Spaeth, *Supreme Court Policy Making: Explanation and Prediction* (San Francisco: W. H. Freeman, 1979); Sidney Ulmer, "The Analysis of Behavior Patterns in the Supreme Court of the United States," *Journal of Politics* 22 (1960): 429; Harold Lasswell, *Power and Personality* (New York: W. W. Norton, 1958).

8. "What's Law Got to Do with It?" 486; see also Steven J. Burton, *Judging in Good Faith* (Cambridge: Cambridge University Press, 1992), xi–xii, 44; Lawrence Baum, "Case Selection and Decision Making in the U.S. Supreme Court," *Law & Society Review* 27 (1993): 445; Ronald Dworkin, *Taking Rights Seriously* (Cambridge, Mass.: Harvard University Press, 1977), 15–17.

9. *Supreme Court and the Attitudinal Model,* 65; see also Harold J. Spaeth and Jeffrey A. Segal, *Majority Rule of Majority Will: Adherence to Precedent on the U.S. Supreme Court* (Cambridge: Cambridge University Press, 1999).

10. Quoted in Gillman, "What's Law Got to Do with It?" 476.

11. Gillman, "What's Law Got to Do with It?" 484. There has been some encouraging movement. For example, in *Majority Rule or Minority Will* (Cambridge: Cambridge University Press, 2001), the leading advocates of the behavioralist model, Jeffrey Segal and Harold Spaeth, attempt to grapple with a central aspect of post-positivists' accounts of the legal model: the role of precedent in Supreme Court decision-making. Unfortunately, despite heroic data-collection efforts, their operationalization of adherence to precedent is highly problematic; thus, their book, which vindicates behavioralism, is unlikely to convince post-positivists. See Gillman, "What's Law Got to Do with It?" 482–83.

12. See generally Rubin, "New Legal Process," 1424–33 (providing an overview of "microanalysis of institutions"); see also Richard Posner, *The Problems of Jurisprudence* (Cambridge, Mass.: Harvard University Press, 1990), 73, 101–5; Lee Epstein and Jack Knight, *The Choices Justices Make* (Washington, D.C.: CQ Press, 1998), 45; Mark J. Richards and Herbert M. Kritzer, "Jurisprudential Regimes in Supreme Court Decision-Making," *American Political Science Review* 96, no. 2 (2002): 305. It must be recognized that the term *new institutionalism* connotes a wide range of approaches, some of which may be inconsistent with what I call the "institutionalist model." Again, my goal is not to summarize specific authors. I seek to characterize different styles of argument about the nature of legal constraint in order to clarify the analysis' assumptions and how this approach relates to existing schools of thought.

13. As Emile Durkheim wrote over a century ago, "Everything in the contract is not contractual" (*The Division of Labor in Society* [1893; reprint, New York: The Free Press, 1964]).

14. Kagan, *Regulatory Justice*, 89; see also Malcolm M. Feeley and Edward L. Rubin, *Judicial Policy-Making and the Modern State: How the Courts Reformed America's Prisons* (Cambridge: Cambridge University Press, 1998), 241–48.

15. Kagan, *Regulatory Justice*, 90–91. Others take the concept of socially constructed laws further, arguing that legal norms are "constitutive" of the judging process. See generally Rogers M. Smith, "Political Jurisprudence, the 'New Institutionalism,' and the Future of Public Law," *American Political Science Review* 82 (1988): 89. Taken to its extreme, these scholars suggest that legal norms cannot meaningfully be separated as a constraint on judicial decision-making. Although this book's approach is not wholly inconsistent with this argument—I believe that legal norms should be seen as "part" of the law—I only incorporate it to the extent that legal norms, as strategic considerations or social expectations, serve to enrich the common understanding of how rules should be read and hence give them predictable and binding meaning in most cases.

16. Epstein and Knight, *Choices Justices Make*, 45 (emphasis added).

17. Ibid.; see also Shapiro, *Courts: A Comparative and Political Analysis*, 1–8.

18. Feeley and Rubin, *Judicial Policy-Making and the Modern State*, 241–48.

19. Roger J. Traynor, "The Limits of Judicial Creativity," *Iowa Law Review* 63 (1977): 6. See also Gunther Teubner, "Introduction to Autopoietic Law," in *Autopoietic Law: A New Approach to Law and Society*, ed. Gunther Teubner (Berlin: de Gruyter, 1987). For a brief overview of variations on the argument that law is a form of discourse that constrains judicial decision-making, see Shapiro, "Courts of Law, Courts of Politics," 109–13.

20. See generally Robert Cover, *Justice Accused: Antislavery and the Judicial Process* (New Haven, Conn.: Yale University Press, 1975), 119–23.

21. See, for example, H. Laurence Ross and James P. Foley, "Judicial Disobedience of the Mandate to Imprison Drunk Drivers," *Law & Society Review* 21 (1987): 315.

22. See Benjamin N. Cardozo, *The Nature of the Judicial Process* (1978, reprint; New Haven, Conn.: Yale University Press, 1921), 103 (discussing the need for judges to legislate within the "interstitial limits" of the law).

23. See Cover, *Justice Accused*, 119–23.

24. Lori Hausegger and Lawrence Baum, "Inviting Congressional Action: A Study of Supreme Court Motivations in Statutory Interpretation," *American Journal of Political Science* 43, no. 1 (1999): 162.

25. 437 U.S. 153 (1978).

26. See Energy and Water Development Appropriation Act of 1979, Pub. L. No. 96-69, 93 Stat. 437, 449 (1979) (specifically reversing *TVA*); Endangered Species Act Amendments of 1978 Pub. L. No. 95-632, 92 Stat. 3751 (creating the "God Squad").

27. Jon Gottschall, "Reagan's Appointments to the U.S. Court of Appeals: The Continuation of a Judicial Revolution," *Judicature* 70 (July 1986): 51, table 1; see also Harry T. Edwards, "Collegiality and Decision Making on the D.C. Circuit," *Virginia Law Review* 84 (1998): 1335; but see Richard Revesz, "Environmental Regulation, Ideology, and the D.C. Circuit," *Virginia Law Review* 83 (1997): 1717.

28. See Donald Songer, "Consensual and Nonconsensual Decisions in Unanimous Decisions of the United States Courts of Appeals," *American Journal of Political Science* 26, no. 2 (1982): 225; Harold J. Spaeth, "Consensus in Unanimous Decisions of the U.S. Supreme Court," *Judicature* 72 (1989): 274; Lee Epstein, Jeffery Segal, Harold Spaeth, and Thomas Walker, *The Supreme Court Compendium: Data, Decisions, and Developments* (Washington, D.C.: CQ Press, 1993), 424 (all discussing the role of ideology in unanimous court decisions).

29. For more on how the culture of rule application can offer a meaningful constraint on judicial policy-making, see Feeley and Rubin, *Judicial Policy-Making and the Modern State*, 241–48.

30. Patrick S. Atiyah and Robert Summers, *Form and Substance in Anglo-American Law: A Comparative Study of Legal Reasoning, Legal Theory, and Legal Institutions* (Oxford: Clarendon Press, 1987), 315–23.

31. Ibid., 317.

32. Ibid., 319.

33. See generally Douglas R. Arnold, *The Logic of Congressional Action* (New Haven, Conn.: Yale University Press, 1990), 101; Morris Fiorina, *Congress, Keystone of the Washington Establishment,* 2d ed. (New Haven, Conn.: Yale University Press, 1989), 48. See also Terry Moe, "The Politics of Bureaucratic Structure," in *Can the Government Govern?*, ed. John Chubb and Paul Patterson (Washington, D.C.: Brookings Institution, 1989), 277–79.

34. See generally Robert Summers and Michele Taruffo, "Interpretation and Comparative Analysis," in *Interpreting Statutes: A Comparative Study,* ed. D. Neil MacCormick and Robert Summers (Brookfield, Vt.: Dartmouth University Press, 1991), 472–73.

35. Guido Calabresi, *A Common Law for the Age of Statutes* (Cambridge, Mass.: Harvard University Press, 1982), 1–7 (arguing that statutory construction by the courts can update laws and induce legislative action).

36. As noted in the last chapter, the best of these signaling models takes into account Congress's uncertainty about the future costs of passing overrides and the courts' uncertainty about the intensity of Congress's preferences. See, for example, Edward Schwartz, Pablo T. Spiller, and Santiago Urbiztondo, "A Positive Theory of Legislative Intent," *Law & Contemporary Problems* 57 (1991): 72. Other relevant game theoretic studies include Matthew McCubbins, Roger Noll, and Barry Weingast, "Structure and Process, Politics and Policy: Administrative Arrangements and the Political Control of Agencies," *Virginia Law Review* 75 (1989) 431; William Eskridge Jr., "Overriding Supreme Court Statutory Interpretation Decisions," *The Yale Law Journal* 101 (1991): 372; Rafael Gely and Pablo T. Spiller, "A Rational Choice Model of Supreme Court Statutory Interpretation Decisions with Applications to the *State Farm* and *Grove City* Cases," *Journal of Law, Economics, and Organization* 6 (1990): 263; see also John Ferejohn and Charles Shipan, "Congressional Influence on Bureaucracy," *Journal of Law, Economics, and Organization* 6 (1990): 1. For articles that test these models, compare Pablo T. Spiller and Rafael Gely, "Congressional Control or Judicial Independence: The Determinants of U.S. Supreme Court Labor-Relations Decisions, 1949–1988," *RAND Journal of Economics* 23, no. 4 (1992): 463; with Jeffrey A. Segal, "Separation-of-Powers Games in the Positive Theory of Congress and the Courts," *American Political Science Review* 91, no. 1 (March 1997): 28.

4 Data, Methods, and Findings

Does the passage of overrides significantly increase levels of judicial consensus? As discussed in Chapter 3, there are competing hypotheses. This chapter makes the analysis more concrete. It describes the data, sets forth a strategy for probing the validity of these hypotheses, and discusses the findings. The data suggest that overrides do significantly increase levels of judicial consensus, casting doubt on hyperpluralism's simple null hypothesis that overrides do not matter. However, substantial levels of judicial dissensus persist even after Congress acts, as indicated by post-override judicial dissents, reversals, and circuit splits on the override issue. This finding implies that the effectiveness of overrides varies and that the passage of overrides defies any single, or simple, characterization. Part II grapples with the underlying complexity of the override process, exploring the patterns of court-Congress relations in the sample.

Data

Sample

I collected original data on 100 randomly identified override processes.[1] The sample was constructed in four stages. I first took a random sample of 100 overrides from a list of about 270 overrides passed from 1974 through 1990. This list is a compilation of data from a variety of secondary sources, mainly William Eskridge's published data on overrides passed from 1967 through 1990. (For a summary of overrides analyzed, see the Appendix.) To compile his list, Eskridge and his research assistants combed through the *United States Code Congressional and Administrative*

News (U.S.C.C.A.N.), which collects committee reports and other legislative history materials for most public laws enacted by Congress. They noted each time a report stated that a bill "overruled," "modified," "clarified," or in some cases "responded to" a statutory interpretation decision. Eskridge supplemented this list with a review of transcripts from 1979 to 1988 from the Judiciary Committees, the most active judicial oversight committees.

Although his is widely accepted as the best single published list of overrides, Eskridge concedes that his "method has some gaps. Not all public laws generate committee reports, not all committee reports are reproduced in U.S.C.C.A.N. (which also edits the reports), and not all overrides of judicial decisions are reported in committee reports."[2] To fill some of these gaps, I cross-referenced Eskridge's list with other override studies and studies of court-Congress interaction over federal statutes.[3]

To check the comprehensiveness of this list and assess its potential biases, I independently compiled a list of overrides for the 101st Congress, using the LEXIS-NEXIS Congressional Universe database that collects all reports. Specifically, a research assistant and I searched for any report that used the terms *modify, clarify, reverse, overrule,* or *override* (using appropriate variations and root expanders), or any report that used the term *court* or any variation of federal citations (e.g., *F.2d* or *F.Supp.*). We found no statute that was not already in the sampling frame. We then repeated these searches using the LEXIS-NEXIS Congressional Universe database for the Congressional Record of the 101st Congress, and also found no omissions from the list. (Note that this database begins with the 101st Congress, so that a similar search was not possible for overrides passed prior to this Congress.)

Having randomly selected 100 overrides from this list, I then identified the corresponding original statutes, namely, the preceding statutory provision of each override, based on an independent review of the overridden decision and the override's legislative history. Using this list of 100 override provisions and 100 original statutory provisions, I performed a broad computer search for every federal court decision using the Westlaw and LEXIS databases, including courts of special jurisdiction (such as tax and bankruptcy courts), which cited the relevant statutes up to January 2001. In addition, I used Westlaw, LEXIS, and LegalTrac to find articles that cited the original statute, override, or overridden decisions.

Using these materials, I coded each period of statutory interpretation as involving a period of "judicial consensus" or "judicial dissensus" using specific criteria (to be discussed). In addition, I analyzed whether the pattern of rule application was partisan, as indicated by the rulings of Democratic and Republican judicial appointees, as well as whether judicial dissensus was relatively contemporaneous or reflected shifts over time. In addition to these legal analyses, I observed a host of other attributes of each override process, including (1) whether Congress delegated significant aspects of the override issue (as it defined the issue), (2) the time between the passage of the original statute and override, (3) the time between the overridden decision and the passage of the override, (4) the reporting committee(s) on the override bill, (5) whether there was divided government at the time the override passed, and (6) the public salience of the bill (as indicated by a content analysis of *The New York Times Index*). As noted in Chapter 1, these data can be visualized as 100 timelines, each of which begins at the passage of the original statutes and continues to January 2001.

Case Selection

The decision to focus on overrides passed from 1974 through 1990 reflects a combination of substantive and practical considerations. Substantively, the best available data suggest that 1974 marks a significant historical shift in congressional oversight of the courts. Prior to 1974, Congress passed an average of fourteen overrides per session. In 1974, after the expansion of congressional staffs and the growth of inter-branch mistrust following Watergate, that number nearly tripled.[4] Focusing on override processes that center on post-1974 overrides allows me to "control" for this historical shift.

As a practical matter, one cannot assess patterns of rule application in the post-override period unless the courts are given adequate time to act. To estimate a reliable period for patterns of rule application to emerge, I analyzed patterns of post-override judicial behavior following the 20 oldest overrides in the sample, which were enacted in the mid-1970s. Of those 20 cases, 3 overrides produced no litigation. Of the remaining 17 cases, the cases divided into 2 patterns of rule application. In 8 cases, a stable pattern of rule application emerged within 7 years of the override. In the final 9 cases, a pattern emerged between 7 and 10 years. Thus, it seemed prudent to allow about a decade from the passage of the most recent override in the sample.

Issues of Selection Bias

Because I take a random sample of overrides, there is no reason to suspect that the sampling method correlates with either the dependent or independent variables. Two caveats bear emphasis, however. First, sampling strategies are tied to issues of generalizability. Because I focus on judicial behavior before and after the passage of overrides, the sample does not allow me to test the effectiveness of formal constraints on the courts in general, because overrides may not be typical of all statutes and I have not systematically addressed what triggers overrides. The sample does, however, allow consideration of the questions at hand, such as: Given an override, do levels of judicial consensus shift? What patterns of court-Congress relations underlie the passage of overrides?

A possible counterargument is that members of Congress may act only when they expect judicial consensus to emerge.[5] But there is no evidence that Congress overrides "easy" cases only. To the contrary, Congress almost always addresses override issues that have divided the courts, and often passes overrides in contested policy areas, such as civil rights, environmental law, immigration, and others. Thus, far from shying away from divisive issues, the data suggest that the overriding Congresses typically addresses them.

Second, selection bias can be introduced through the choice of sampling frame, the actual list of cases from which the sample is drawn. I believe the sampling frame is the most comprehensive available, but it is not perfect. Data never are. Indeed, a complete list of overrides is probably impossible to compile because Congress sometimes overrules decisions without mentioning them by name.

In a world without time or resource constraints, I would overcome this problem by reading every case, the entire legislative record, and interviewing all members of Congress and their staff. But this is clearly impracticable. The next best line of defense is considering how potential bias in the sampling frame would qualify the findings. Using this line of defense, I believe the most likely gap in the sampling frame is substantively minor: overrides that are not prominently mentioned in the legislative history *and* have not been the subject of scholarly analysis. If this gap introduces bias, it would limit the findings to explicit congressional reversals or cases salient enough to gain scholarly attention.

Testing Strategy

The alternative hypothesis predicts that levels of judicial consensus will significantly increase following the passage of overrides. This hypothesis, in turn, involves two claims: the *factual claim* that overrides significantly increase levels of judicial consensus, and the *counterfactual claim* that if Congress had not acted, levels of judicial consensus would not have significantly increased. I use four sets of comparisons to examine these claims: (1) comparison of judicial consensus levels before and after the passage of overrides; (2) comparison of judicial consensus levels following "prescriptive" versus "partial" overrides and pre-override judicial dissensus; (3) comparison of judicial consensus levels on the delegated and nondelegated portions of the override issue following the passage of partial overrides; and (4) comparison of the effect of overrides that are passed at different points in the interpretive process. Each comparison is discussed separately in the following sections.

Comparison 1: Levels of Judicial Consensus Before and After the Passage of Overrides

The first comparison involves a simple before-and-after analysis, comparing the proportion of judicial consensus cases following the passage of overrides versus the proportion of judicial consensus cases following the pre-override, or "original," statutes. If the proportion of judicial consensus cases is significantly greater after overrides, preliminary evidence exists that overrides matter. By contrast, if the proportion of judicial consensus cases is not significantly greater following the passage of overrides, we cannot reject the simple null hypothesis that overrides do not matter.

Comparison 2: Levels of Judicial Consensus Following Prescriptive Versus Partial Overrides

This before-and-after test has strong intuitive appeal. However, it fails to address the counterfactual claim that levels of judicial consensus would not have increased absent congressional action. To probe this counterfactual claim, which is admittedly difficult, the next comparison analyzes patterns of judicial decisions following prescriptive versus partial overrides after pre-override judicial dissensus.[6] As noted earlier, prescriptive overrides include bills that, on their face, attempt to resolve the override issue (as defined by the overriding Congress). Partial overrides include bills that do not seek to resolve the override issue (as defined by the overriding Congress). Instead, a partial override expressly delegates significant aspects of the override issue to the courts. If the proportion of judicial consensus cases was significantly greater following prescriptive overrides, further evidence would exist to support the alternative hypothesis that overrides matter. If not, we cannot reject the simple null hypothesis.

Analogizing to the language of experimental design may help clarify the explanatory logic of this comparison. One might think of pre-override judicial dissensus as the "pre-test condition," the passage of substantive follow-up signals on the override issue as the "treatment," and the levels of post-override judicial consensus as the "outcome" to be observed. In cases of prescriptive overrides, Congress gives the treatment: it passes an override that, on its face, sends a substantive signal to the courts on the divisive override issue. In cases of partial overrides, Congress does not give the full treatment; it explicitly forbears from sending a comprehensive signal to courts on the divisive override issue. As such, cases of partial overrides offer a theoretically interesting "control group," which provides some leverage over the counterfactual scenario of what would have happened if Congress had not acted.

To operationalize this comparison, I first identified cases of significant pre-override judicial dissensus, meaning cases of inter-circuit splits or multiple dissents and reversals under the original statutes. I then identified cases of prescriptive versus partial overrides based on a detailed content analysis of the overridden court cases, the language of the override bill, and its legislative history. As noted, in cases of prescriptive overrides, Congress passes a bill that, on its face, attempts to resolve the override issue as defined by the overriding Congress. In cases of partial overrides, the bill or accompanying legislative history expressly directs courts to develop some significant aspect of the override issue on a case-by-case basis; remains explicitly neutral on an aspect of the override issue that divided the courts in the pre-override period; or employs an inherently vague "reasonableness" or "fairness" standard.

The coding of partial overrides is probably best demonstrated by example. Consider the Insider Trading and Securities Fraud Enforcement Act of 1988 (the Securities Fraud Enforcement Act). Prior to the Securities Fraud Enforcement Act, controversy arose as to whether shareholders who traded contemporaneously, but unwittingly, with insider trading were entitled to damages.[7] The circuits split on the issue. An early Second Circuit decision—*Shapiro v. Merrill Lynch, Pierce, Fenner & Smith*—held that so-called contemporaneous traders could recover damages from insider traders, provided insiders withheld material information.[8] In *Fridrich v. Bradford*, the Sixth Circuit flatly rejected *Shapiro*. It held that "[i]nvestors must be prepared to accept the risk of trading in an open market without complete or always accurate information."[9] In other words, caveat emptor.

After the Sixth Circuit handed down the *Fridrich* decision, the Second Circuit further muddied the waters. In *Wilson v. Comtech Telecommunications Corp.*, the Second Circuit seemed to take a step away from *Shapiro*. It recognized insider liability to contemporaneous traders, but held that a trade one month after the insider trade was not contemporaneous, even though the plaintiff traded *before* the securities fraud was disclosed.[10] In *Moss v. Morgan Stanley, Inc.*, the Second Circuit seemed to contradict itself, and rejected insider liability to contemporaneous traders. Consistent with the Sixth Circuit's approach, *Moss* held that plaintiffs who traded on the market without knowledge of the insider trading could not demonstrate that the fraud caused their harms.[11] Nevertheless, *Shapiro* remained on the books, resulting in a potential circuit split and conflicting standards within the Second Circuit, which is the Court of Appeals for Wall Street.

In 1988, Congress stepped in and passed the Securities Fraud Enforcement Act. The Act reversed *Fridrich* and *Moss*, providing that insider traders could be liable to contemporaneous traders.[12] Congress explained that the override would provide "express private rights of action for those who trade contemporaneously with, and on the other side of, a transaction from the insider trader . . . and is intended, in part, to overturn court cases which have precluded recovery by plaintiffs who were victims of [insider trading]."[13] In addition, the overriding Congress explicitly refused to define the meaning of contemporaneous trades, indicating that it wanted to provide "courts leeway to develop" the law.[14]

Given the language of the override and legislative history, I reasoned that the override issue was the liability of insider traders to contemporaneous traders. In response to this issue, Congress passed a classic partial override: it ordered courts to abandon cases that denied insider liability to contemporaneous traders, such as *Fridrich* and *Moss*, but invited judges to develop the specific meaning of contemporaneous trading. Thus, the nondelegated aspect of the override issue was the rejection of the *Fridrich* and *Moss* cases, which denied contemporaneous traders a cause of action against insider traders, and the delegated aspect of the override issue involved the development of a specific test for contemporaneous trades.

Comparison 3: Levels of Judicial Consensus on the Delegated and Nondelegated Aspects of the Override Issue Following Partial Overrides

To further probe what would have happened if Congress had not acted in the cases, the third comparison examines levels of judicial consensus on delegated and nondelegated issues following partial overrides and pre-override judicial dissensus.[15] If significantly greater levels of judicial consensus emerge under the nondelegated, or prescribed, aspects of the override issue (i.e., the portion of the override issue that Congress attempts to resolve), further evidence would exist to support the alternative hypothesis that overrides matter. If not, we cannot reject the simple null hypothesis.

Again, a brief analogy using the language of experimental design may help clarify the explanatory logic of this comparison. As noted earlier, we can think of pre-override judicial dissensus as the pre-test condition and the passage of overrides as the treatment. In cases of partial overrides, Congress seeks to resolve some aspects of the override issue but expressly delegates other aspects of the override issue to the courts. Thus, with respect to the nondelegated aspects of the override issue, Congress applies the treatment (and sends a substantive signal to the courts). With respect to the delegated aspects of the override issue, Congress does not send a signal; it sends the issue back to the courts. Accordingly, the delegated portion of the override issue provides another "control group" for Congress not acting at all.[16]

Comparison 4: Levels of Judicial Consensus Following Overrides Passed at Different Points in the Override Process

The final set of comparisons seeks to address a slightly different issue, namely, whether change in levels of judicial consensus stems from processes that unfold over time and that are distinct from the passage of overrides. Returning to the language of experimental design should help clarify the issue. In cases of a medical condition, it is possible that the disease will run its course without any treatment. If so, the treatment would be incidental to the cure. In the case of overrides, it is possible that judicial consensus would increase without the passage of overrides due to some historical or maturation process, such as learning within the policy community or the common law process. If so, the passage of overrides would be incidental to increases in levels of judicial consensus.

How can we address this concern? In the case of a medical treatment, we would gain confidence in the treatment's efficacy if it had a similar effect when applied soon after symptoms appear and when applied to chronic symptoms. Extending this logic to the override process, we would gain confidence that overrides matter if the passage of overrides had similar effects when overrides are passed soon after judicial dissensus emerges (and soon after the original statute is enacted) and in cases of long-standing judicial dissensus (and long after the original statute is enacted).

Accordingly, I compared the effects of overrides that are passed within 0–2, 2–4, 4–8, and 8 or more years after judicial dissensus first emerges under the original statute as well as the effect of overrides passed within 0–4, 4–8, 8–16, and 16 or more years of the original statute. If the effect of overrides is similar across these periods, it seems unlikely that the passage of overrides is incidental to any increases in judicial consensus. By contrast, if their effect is not stable at different points in the interpretive process, it seems more likely that the passage of overrides is incidental and that increases in judicial consensus reflect underlying historical or maturation processes.

Measuring the Dependent Variable

To implement this testing strategy, levels of judicial consensus under the relevant statutes must be measured.[17] As seen in Table 4.1, nearly all of the cases fell into one of four empirical categories: (1) inter-circuit judicial dissensus, (2) significant intra-circuit judicial dissensus, (3) consistent rule application, and (4) no reported post-override decision. Each category raised distinct coding issues, which are discussed in the following sections.

Table 4.1   Summary of Judicial Consensus Coding

Coding of Statute	Primary Coding Rationale	Original Statute	Override
"Judicial dissensus under the statute"	Inter-circuit judicial dissensus	48	31
	Significant intra-circuit judicial dissensus	40	17
	Other*	1	1
"Judicial consensus consistent with the statute"	Consistent rule application	11	35
	No reported post-override decisions	N/A	16
	Totals	100	100

*In the pre-override period, one case involved conflicting statutes, which the court recognized allowed multiple interpretations. In the post-override period, one case involved consistent rule application, but the pre-override winners in court won in the post-override period, and Congress passed a follow-up override that indicates courts had misconstrued the override. As a result, neither case seemed to involve judicial consensus consistent with underlying statute.

Inter-Circuit Judicial Dissensus

Inter-circuit judicial dissensus occurs when courts in two or more circuits explicitly disagree on the meaning of a statute (as opposed to distinguishing the cases on their facts). Of 200 statutes examined, 79 involved inter-circuit judicial dissensus. In 77 of 79 cases, the split was among U.S. Court of Appeals decisions in different circuits. In the remaining two cases, the splits were among multiple lower courts in at least three circuits (as opposed to cases of an isolated lower court decision that contradicts a multi-circuit majority interpretation). In all 79 cases of inter-circuit splits in the sample, the underlying statute was coded as judicial dissensus. Overall, the category of inter-circuit splits has strong facial validity as a measure of the key outcome; it is hard to argue an underlying statute has engendered judicial consensus if judges from different circuits explicitly disagree on its meaning.

Intra-Circuit Judicial Dissensus

Intra-circuit judicial dissensus exists when there are dissents or appellate court reversals of lower court decisions on statutory grounds. Thus, judges in the same case, with the same facts, explicitly disagree on the proper interpretation of the law governing the override issue. Of 200 cases in the sample, 57 involved some intra-circuit dissensus. In coding these cases, the key issue was whether the intra-circuit dissensus was pervasive or isolated. Accordingly, I examined whether the available decisions—in the official reporters and Westlaw and LEXIS databases—reflected clear patterns of dissents and reversals under the relevant statutes.

Of the 57 cases, 19 involved multiple dissents or reversals within the circuits as well as a divided Supreme Court decision on the override issue. In an additional 13 cases, there were multiple dissents and reversals on the override issue (but no Supreme Court cases). In these 32 cases, the period of rule application was coded as "significant intra-circuit dissensus." The reasoning was similar to cases of inter-circuit splits: it is hard to argue that a statute has engendered judicial consensus consistent with the language and legislative history of the override if judges repeatedly disagree on the statute's meaning.

The remaining 26 cases of intra-circuit judicial dissensus involved a single dissent or reversal. In one case, involving an original statute, there was a single appellate court reversal of a lower court decision, whose reading of the original statute contradicted a consistent, bipartisan, and multi-circuit majority interpretation. This case was treated as isolated judicial dissensus. Accordingly, the period of statutory interpretation was coded as judicial consensus.

In 25 cases (involving 19 original statutes and 6 overrides), intra-circuit dissensus emerged in the only reported litigation under the statute (in either the official reporters or the Westlaw and LEXIS databases). These cases were tentatively coded as judicial dissensus under the law because the only available decisions indicate explicit judicial disagreement on the interpretation of the statute. For purposes of all analyses (both in this and later chapters), however, these cases were coded both ways, because not all cases are published and, hence, one cannot make a definitive judgment as to whether the dissensus is pervasive or isolated. (Results were substantively similar.)

It should be added that 55 cases of inter-circuit splits also included intra-circuit splits. The finding of both intra- and inter-circuit splits in so many override processes not only gives assurance with respect to the coding of these individual cases but also lends "convergent validity" to the measures: different measures of judicial dissensus tended to crop up together, which is what we would expect if they measure the same concept.

Consistent Rule Application

Forty-seven cases involved consistent rule application. In these cases, the crucial issue is whether consistent rule application reflects judicial consensus, which is consistent with the language and legislative history of the statute, or ideological consensus—or what some call "ideological herding"—among the presiding judges in the reported cases. After all, if consistent rule application only reflects the common ideological preferences of the rule judges, one cannot assert that the override, as socially and politically constructed, triggered judicial consensus. In describing the coding of these cases, it is useful to discuss consistent rule application under original and override statutes separately.

Consistent Rule Application Under Original Statutes. Under the original statutes, there were 11 cases of consistent rule application (including the case of isolated intra-circuit dissensus discussed earlier). To assess whether these cases likely involved judicial consensus under the statute or ideological consensus among the presiding judges, the following three factors were examined: whether (1) the judicial consensus was bipartisan, meaning that Democratic and Republican appointees agreed on the statute's meaning; (2) the overriding Congress indicated the original statute was vague, antiquated, or otherwise flawed (as opposed to asserting the courts had consistently misconstrued the statute); and (3) courts invited an override. I reasoned that judicial consensus was more likely to reflect agreement on the meaning of the law, as opposed to ideological consensus, if Democratic and Republican appointees agreed on the meaning of the statute; the overriding Congress indicated that the original statute was flawed (as opposed to noting that courts had consistently misconstrued the statute); and/or courts invited an override (suggesting that they disagreed with the policy outcome required under their reading of the law).

In 7 of 11 cases, Democratic and Republican appointees consistently applied the original statute. In 8 cases, including all cases of bipartisan judicial consensus, the overriding Congress indicated that the original statute had grown outdated as a policy matter (as opposed to the courts misconstruing the original law). Each of these cases was coded as cases of judicial consensus.

The Electronic Communications Act of 1986 was typical. The 1986 act replaced the Omnibus Crime Control and Safe Streets Act of 1968, which regulated government wiretaps and electronic surveillance. Consistent with the legislative history of the original statute, courts uniformly ruled that the 1968 act did not apply to "pen registers," mechanical devices that record numbers dialed on a telephone but do not record the underlying conversation or whether the call is completed.[18] The 1986 override reversed these cases, requiring the government to petition courts before installing pen registers. In explaining the purpose of the new law, Congress did not state the courts had consistently misconstrued the 1968 statute. Rather, it indicated the old law was "hopelessly out of date" and "has not kept pace with the development of communications and computer technology. Nor has it kept pace with changes in the structure of the telecommunications industry."[19]

Hence, in these cases, there was no indication that judicial consensus was only the result of underlying ideological consensus among judges. Instead, it seemed most likely that judges applied the law in good faith, even though the law had grown antiquated. Accordingly, these cases were coded as involving a period of judicial consensus under the original statute.

In 2 of the 3 remaining cases of pre-override and consistent rule application, courts invited Congress to override its literal interpretation of the tax code. In these cases, courts adhered to the literal terms of the law, even though they believed it produced absurd results. As such, it seemed appropriate to code these cases as involving judicial consensus under the statute. Indeed, courts may have interpreted these statutes too faithfully, forcing Congress to close an unintended loophole in the tax code.

In the final case of consistent pre-override rule application, there was only one lower court decision interpreting the override in the official reporters, Westlaw and LEXIS databases. Hence, in a narrow sense, the original statute was interpreted consistently. Moreover, if there was a contrary decision, it seems likely that it would have been reported. Consequently, this case was tentatively coded as involving judicial consensus; however, given the dearth of authority under the statute, it was coded both ways for the purpose of all analyses. (Again, results were nearly identical.)

Consistent Rule Application Under Overrides.   There were 36 cases of consistent rule application under overrides. To assess whether consistent post-override rule application should be seen as judicial consensus under the statute, or a result of ideological consensus among the presiding judges, the following three factors were examined: whether (1) the judicial consensus was bipartisan; (2) Congress sent subsequent signals indicating that courts had misconstrued the override; and (3) the winner in pre-override litigation lost in the post-override period. I reasoned that judicial consensus was more likely to reflect consensus on the meaning of the law, as opposed to only ideological consensus, if judicial appointees from both parties applied the override consistently; Congress did not send follow-up signals; and the winners in court switched following the override.

In 28 of 36 cases, all three conditions were met: judicial consensus was bipartisan; Congress did not send follow-up signals on the override issue; and the winners in the overridden decision lost on the override issue during the post-override period. These cases were coded as involving judicial consensus.

In 7 cases of consistent post-override rule application, two conditions were met. The winners in the overridden decision lost in court following the passage of the override, and there was no evidence of post-override congressional signals indicating that the courts' interpretation was incorrect. It should be added that, in these cases, there was no indication that the override issue was likely to engender partisan judicial interpretations. To the contrary, there was non-partisan, pre-override judicial dissensus in each case. Consequently, for these cases, the period of statutory interpretations was coded as involving judicial consensus consistent with the override.

Two cases technically involved judicial consensus, but these were coded as "other" and placed under the heading of judicial dissensus. In the pre-override period, one case involved a conflict between the tax code and ERISA provisions governing the conditions under which employees can recoup contributions to pension funds. This case was coded as involving judicial dissensus under the original statute because the court stated that the meaning of the underlying statutory framework was unclear and subject to multiple interpretations. In the post-override period, a case technically involved judicial consensus because it was the only case that interpreted the override. However, the post-override decision did not change the result on the override issue (the winner in the pre-override litigation also won in the post-override period), and Congress passed a subsequent override rejecting the courts' interpretation as misconstruing the first override. As a result, it seemed inappropriate to code this case as involving judicial consensus under the override.

No Post-Override Litigation

Sixteen cases involved no reported decisions under the override in the official reporters, Westlaw, or LEXIS databases. These cases were coded as involving judicial consensus. One might argue that the absence of reported cases is consistent with a variety of interpretations. Perhaps insufficient time has passed for courts to construe the override; perhaps potential litigants lack resources to bring lawsuits; perhaps the stakes are too low to warrant the time and expense of litigation; or perhaps, as assumed, litigation or published decisions are moot following the override.

As a practical matter, the final alternative seems most likely in the sample. As noted earlier, the sampling period allows ample time for courts to consider cases under the override; thus, insufficient time is unlikely to account for an absence of decisions in official reporters or the Westlaw or LEXIS databases in the cases. In addition, parties have already taken the time and expense to litigate the underlying issues in the pre-override case. It seems unlikely they would drop the issue without trying their luck in the courts, absent the conviction that litigation would be a waste of time and money.

An example should help clarify the coding logic. Prior to 1990, federal courts divided over calculating penalties under the Clean Air and Water Acts. Controversy hinged on determining fines when regulators estimated daily violations based on emissions over a period of time. The majority of courts held that polluters should be fined for each day that average daily emissions violated relevant standards.[20] A number of other courts, by contrast, held that multi-day average violations constitute a single violation. These courts reasoned that if the government seeks penalties for each day, it should prove rather than estimate daily violations.[21] The difference between these approaches is considerable. Under one interpretation, violation of monthly standards on average results in as many as 31 mandatory $10,000 fines. Under the alternative, the same violation results in a single fine of $10,000.[22]

In 1990, Congress overhauled the governing penalty provision. With respect to multi-day average violations, language was added to make "clear that each day during the averaging period is a separate violation."[23] After the override, the issue disappeared from view, even though Congress more than doubled the maximum daily fines to $25,000 and empowered the courts to order the forfeiture of any economic benefit or savings resulting from failure to comply.[24] Are industrial polluters likely to forego credible challenges to a law that increases their exposure to liability and reduces the evidentiary burden on regulators? Not likely. Polluters have a strong incentive to challenge the override as long as a plausible argument can be made. As a result, this case and others like it were coded as involving judicial consensus.

Reliability

In order to make credible inferences from the distribution patterns of judicial interpretations in the sample, the coding procedures must be reliable, meaning the coding must reflect actual variation in the cases as opposed to idiosyncrasies of the analyst. To assess reliability, a third party independently coded the cases in a 30-percent random sample of the cases. The degree of significance of inter-coder agreement was measured using Kappa. As seen in Table 4.2, the analysis shows that had the cases been coded

Table 4.2   Inter-Coder Agreement

Coding	Coder 1	Coder 2
Judicial dissensus	43	43
Judicial consensus	17	17
Totals	60	60

$N = 60$
Agreement: 100%
Expected agreement: 53%
Kappa = 1.0
Z = 7.75
p < .001

randomly (but with the probabilities equal to the overall proportion of cases), we would have expected agreement in about 53 percent of the cases. In fact, there was agreement in 100 percent of the cases, which is significantly above that which would be expected by chance (p < .001).

Findings and Discussion

Do Overrides Matter?

The data suggest that the passage of overrides does significantly increase levels of judicial consensus, but substantial judicial dissensus nevertheless persists. As seen in Figure 4.1, the patterns of rule application before and after the passage of overrides in the sample were striking. Specifically, a period of judicial consensus followed about 10 percent of the original statutes in the sample. Thus, in the vast majority of cases when Congress chooses to pass an override, there is some form of judicial dissensus on the override issue. Following the passage of the overrides, the pattern of judicial behavior shifts: judicial consensus followed about 50 percent of overrides in the sample. Thus, the ratio of judicial consensus to judicial dissensus cases went from about 1 to 9 in the pre-override period to about 1 to 1 in the post-override period. Not surprisingly, as seen in Table 4.3, this sharp difference in proportions is statistically significant (p > .001), using a one-tailed test. (It should be stressed that this finding held even when all the tentatively coded cases were recoded.) This finding offers some evidence in support of the alternative hypothesis that overrides significantly increase levels of judicial consensus.

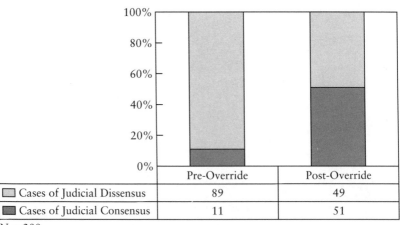

	Pre-Override	Post-Override
▢ Cases of Judicial Dissensus	89	49
▪ Cases of Judicial Consensus	11	51

N = 200

FIGURE 4.1   Levels of Judicial Consensus Pre- and Post-Override

Table 4.3   Summary of Difference in Proportions Test: Levels of Judicial Consensus Pre- and Post-Override

Period of Interpretation	Proportion of Cases with Judicial Consensus	Standard Error	$p > |z|$
Post-override period (x)	.51	.05	. . .
Pre-override period (y)	.11	.03	. . .
Difference (x) − (y)	.40	.06	.001*

*Rounded up

N = 100 for each period

Null hypothesis: proportion (x) − proportion (y) = 0

Alternative hypothesis: proportion (x) − proportion (y) > 0

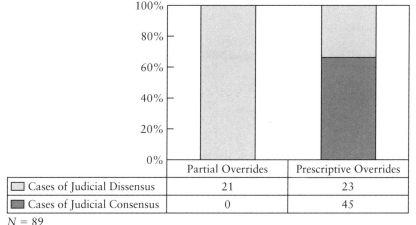

	Partial Overrides	Prescriptive Overrides
☐ Cases of Judicial Dissensus	21	23
▉ Cases of Judicial Consensus	0	45

N = 89

FIGURE 4.2   Levels of Judicial Consensus Following Partial Versus Prescriptive Overrides

Comparing post-override patterns of rule application following prescriptive and partial overrides and a period of judicial dissensus offers additional evidence in support of the alternative hypothesis. As seen in Figure 4.2, when Congress passed prescriptive overrides that sought to resolve the override issue following judicial dissensus, judicial consensus emerged in 45 of 68 cases (66 percent). When Congress passed partial overrides on divisive issues, not a single case of judicial consensus—0 of 21—emerged. As seen in Table 4.4, that difference is highly statistically significant (p > .001) using a one-tailed test. (Again, this finding holds when the tentatively coded cases are recoded.)

Table 4.4   Summary of Difference in Proportions Test: Levels of Judicial Consensus
Following Partial Versus Prescriptive Overrides

Period of Interpretation	Proportion of Cases with Judicial Consensus	Standard Error	$p > |z|$
Post-prescriptive overrides (x)	.66	.06	. . .
Post-partial overrides (y)	0	. . .	. . .
Difference (x) − (y)	.66	.06	.001*

*Rounded up

N = 89

N for prescriptive overrides = 68

N for partial overrides = 21

Null hypothesis: proportion (x) − proportion (y) = 0

Alternative hypothesis: proportion (x) − proportion (y) > 0

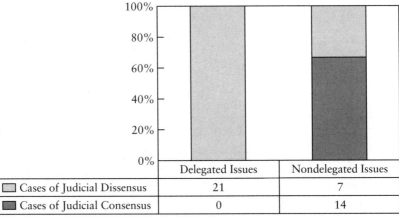

	Delegated Issues	Nondelegated Issues
☐ Cases of Judicial Dissensus	21	7
■ Cases of Judicial Consensus	0	14

N = 21

FIGURE 4.3   Levels of Judicial Consensus on Delegated and Nondelegated Issues
in Cases of Partial Overrides

Comparing post-override patterns of rule application following partial
overrides further buttresses the alternative hypothesis. As seen in
Figure 4.3, on the aspect of the override issue that Congress did not delegate to the courts—that is, on the aspect of the override that Congress tried
to resolve—judicial consensus emerged in 14 of 21 cases (67 percent). On

Table 4.5 Summary of Difference in Proportions Test: Levels of Judicial Consensus on Delegated and Nondelegated Issues in Cases of Partial Overrides

Period of Interpretation	Proportion of Cases with Judicial Consensus	Standard Error	$p > |z|$
Post-nondelegation (x)	.67	.10	...
Post-delegation (y)	0	...	...
Difference (x) − (y)	.67	.15	.001*

*Rounded up

N = 21

N for nondelegated issues = 21

N for delegated issues = 21

Null hypothesis: proportion (x) − proportion (y) = 0

Alternative hypothesis: proportion (x) − proportion (y) > 0

the portion of the override issue that Congress did delegate, not a single case of judicial consensus emerged (0 of 21). As seen in Table 4.5, that difference is statistically significant (p > .001) using a one-tailed test. (Again, this finding holds when the tentatively coded cases are recoded.)

Examining the effects of overrides that are passed at different points in the interpretive process also suggests that overrides matter. Indeed, the data indicate that the effect of overrides is remarkably stable regardless of when pre-override judicial dissensus emerges or when the original statute is passed. For example, as seen in Table 4.6, the passage of overrides triggers judicial consensus in about 50 percent of the cases, regardless of whether Congress acts with 0–2, 2–4, 4–8, or 8 or more years after judicial dissensus emerges under the original statute. Similarly, as seen in Table 4.7, overrides have a similar effect on levels of judicial consensus regardless of whether the original state was passed 0–4, 4–8, 8–16, or 16 or more years prior to the override. Given the stability of overrides' effect, it seems unlikely that the passage of overrides is incidental to the increased levels of judicial consensus.

Several additional points should be highlighted. First, as discussed earlier, judicial consensus in the sample is not likely to reflect ideological consensus among the presiding judges. Indeed, post-override judicial consensus was overwhelmingly bipartisan: 28 of 36 cases of consistent post-override rule application involved agreement among Republican and Democratic appointees.[25] Moreover, the substantive results do not significantly change if all cases of partisan consistent rule application are recoded.

Second, the overrides in the sample were selected randomly, *not* for their low levels of pre-override judicial consensus. Hence, it is unlikely

Table 4.6 The Effect of Overrides Over Time: Cases of Recent Versus Long-Standing Judicial Dissensus

Post-Override Consensus?	Time From Emergence of Pre-Override Judicial Dissensus to Passage of Override				Totals
	0–2 Years	2–4 Years	4–8 Years	8+ Years	
Yes	20	6	6	12	44
(row %)	(45%)	(14%)	(14%)	(27%)	(100%)
(col. %)	(51%)	(40%)	(46%)	(55%)	(49%)
No	19	9	7	10	45
(row %)	(42%)	(20%)	(16%)	(22%)	(100%)
(col. %)	(49%)	(60%)	(54%)	(45%)	(51%)
Totals	39	15	13	22	89
(row %)	(44%)	(17%)	(15%)	(25%)	(100%)
(col. %)	(100%)	(100%)	(100%)	(100%)	(100%)

N = 89
Pearson chi-2(3) = .8733
Pr. = .83
Note: Errors due to rounding.

Table 4.7 The Effect of Overrides Over Time: Cases of Recent Versus Long-Standing Original Statutes

Post-Override Consensus?	Time From Passage of the Original Statute to Passage of Override				Totals
	0–4 Years	4–8 Years	8–16 Years	16+ Years	
Yes	5	14	11	19	49
(row %)	(10%)	(29%)	(22%)	(39%)	(100%)
(col. %)	(50%)	(64%)	(52%)	(40%)	(49%)
No	5	8	10	28	51
(row %)	(10%)	(16%)	(20%)	(55%)	(100%)
(col. %)	(50%)	(36%)	(48%)	(60%)	(51%)
Totals	10	22	21	47	100
(row %)	(10%)	(22%)	(21%)	(47%)	(100%)
(col. %)	(100%)	(100%)	(100%)	(100%)	(100%)

N = 100
Pearson chi-2(3) = 3.3687
Pr. = .34
Note: Errors due to rounding.

that any increase in levels of judicial consensus in the sample reflects "regression to the mean," which poses its greatest threat to internal validity when cases are selected based on an extreme pre-test score.[26]

Third, it seems unlikely that levels of judicial dissensus would rise to pre-override levels if judges were given more time to maneuver around the law. Compare patterns of statutory interpretation of the most recent overrides in the sample, those passed during the 101st Congress (1990–1991), versus patterns of statutory interpretation of the oldest overrides in the sample, those passed during the 94th Congress (1974–1975). In both sets of cases, the percentage of overrides that triggered post-override judicial dissensus was about 40 percent.

Taken together, these findings suggest that the passage of overrides—as part of an iterative process—significantly increases levels of judicial consensus, turning hard cases into routine ones. This finding is particularly notable because the data support a central tenet of the hyperpluralist null hypothesis: override issues are divisive. Specifically, judges explicitly disagreed on the meaning of the original statute in about 9 of 10 cases. According to the logic of hyperpluralism, such issues should engender persistent judicial dissensus because in enacting the override, members of Congress will pass the buck. Or, in applying the override statute, politically selected American judges will read the law along partisan lines. Contrary to this expectation, however, Congress was able to resolve judicial dissensus among politically selected American judges in a significant proportion of cases.

At the same time, the data do not tell a simple pluralist or capture story, which assumes overrides will almost always rein in the courts. Instead, judicial dissensus followed the passage of an override in nearly half the cases, which suggests that a substantial proportion of cases comport with general hyperpluralist expectations of persistent legal uncertainty.[27] In short, although the data cast doubt on the simple hyperpluralist null hypothesis, there is nothing simple about the underlying patterns of court-Congress relations in the sample.

Summary

Does the passage of overrides significantly increase levels of judicial consensus on override issues? Contrary to the hyperpluralist null hypothesis, the data provide strong *prima facie* evidence that the passage of overrides significantly increases overall levels of judicial consensus, even though (1) override issues are highly divisive, as indicated by frequent circuit splits, dissents, and reversals under the original statutes; (2) members of Congress face a number of obstacles to passing specific overrides through the fragmented policy-making process in Washington; and (3) the coordinate system of justice in the United States gives judges substantial leeway to adapt the rules to the individual merits of specific cases.

At the same time, overrides failed to produce judicial consensus in about half of the cases. This variation hints at the rich diversity of court-Congress relations in the sample and raises issues concerning the relative frequency of pluralist, capture, and hyperpluralist patterns of court-Congress relations underlying the override process. To assess these issues, we must take a closer look at the cases and examine patterns of interest group participation as well as the nature of judicial consensus and dissensus in the sample. Part II takes on that task, creating a new typology of pluralist, capture, and hyperpluralist override scenarios and applying this typology to the sample. The results offer fresh insights into the role of override passage in the current age of statutes as well as the dynamics of court-Congress relations in connection with the passage of overrides.

Notes

1. All data are available upon request from the author.

2. William Eskridge Jr., "Overriding Supreme Court Statutory Interpretation Decisions," *The Yale Law Journal* 101 (1991): 337.

3. See, for example, R. Shep Melnick, *Between the Lines: Interpreting Welfare Rights* (Washington, D.C.: Brookings Institution, 1994); Richard Paschal, "The Continuing Colloquy: Congress and the Finality of the Supreme Court," *Journal of Law & Politics* VIII (1991): 143; Michael E. Solomine and James L. Walker, "The Next Word: Congressional Response to Supreme Court Statutory Decisions," *Temple Law Review* 65 (1992): 425.

4. Eskridge, "Overriding Supreme Court Statutory Interpretation Decisions," 338, table 1.

5. I thank Eric Schickler from my dissertation committee for this argument.

6. Using more formal notation, this comparison can be denoted as follows: (Proportion of Judicial Consensus Cases|Pre-Override Judicial Dissensus and Prescriptive Overrides) versus (Proportion of Judicial Consensus Cases|Pre-Override Judicial Dissensus and Partial Overrides).

7. See generally Stephanie F. Barkholz, "Insider Trading, the Contemporaneous Trader, and the Corporate Acquirer: Entitlement to Profits Disgorged by the SEC," *Emory Law Review* 40 (1991): 537.

8. *Shapiro v. Merrill Lynch, Pierce, Fenner & Smith*, 495 F.2d 228, 241 (2d Cir. 1974).

9. 542 F.2d 307, 318 (6th Cir. 1976), certiorari denied 429 U.S. 1053 (1977).

10. 648 F.2d 88, 94 (2d Cir. 1981).

11. 719 F.2d 5, 12 (2d Cir. 1983), certiorari denied 465 U.S. 1025 (1984).

12. 15 U.S.C. sec. 78t-1.

13. See United States Code Congressional and Administrative News (U.S.C.C.A.N) (1988): 6075–76.

14. Ibid., 6064.

15. Using more formal notion, this comparison can be denoted as follows: (Proportion of Judicial Consensus Cases on the Delegated Aspects of the Override Issue|Partial Overrides and Pre-Override Judicial Dissensus) versus (Proportion of Judicial Consensus Cases on the Nondelegated Aspects of the Override Issue|Partial Overrides and Pre-Override Judicial Dissensus).

16. Another possibility is to look at cases in which Congress initially tries and fails to pass an override and, in later Congresses, passes an override. Unfortunately, however, too few of such cases were in the sample.

17. As discussed in the text, I coded levels of judicial consensus dichotomously. One might argue that there is a continuum between judicial consensus and dissensus, and as a result, coding should not be dichotomous. The response is three-fold. First, in the sample, the vast majority of cases of dissensus involved high levels of inter- or intra-circuit dissensus or clear patterns of consistent rule application. Accordingly, even if a continuum exists between judicial consensus and dissensus as a conceptual matter, the dichotomous dependent variable adequately describes my observations as an empirical matter. Second, coding continuously would not affect the analysis of the null and alternative hypotheses. For example, if one coded all cases of inter-circuit judicial dissensus as "low consensus," all cases of intra-circuit judicial dissensus as "medium consensus," and all cases of consistent rule application and no post-override litigation as "high consensus," the findings would not change. Specifically, the number of high consensus cases would significantly increase following the passage of the overrides, and there would be a reduction in both cases of high and medium judicial dissensus. Finally, in deciding to use a dichotomous variable, I interviewed a dozen lawyers, some of whom are litigators and others of whom are corporate attorneys, and asked them when they believed the law was unsettled for purposes of planning. All agreed that the threshold for treating the law as unsettled or uncertain was low. Specifically, once significant intra-circuit judicial dissensus emerges, as I have defined it, they believed that the law becomes unsettled. Admittedly, the lawyers interviewed were not selected at random and represent a small sample; however, the interviews, in my judgment, buttress the decision to treat judicial consensus versus dissensus dichotomously.

18. See, for example, *Application of United States in re Pen Register Order,* 538 F.2d 956, 958–9 (2d Cir. 1976) (affirming district court holding that the 1968 wiretapping statute does not apply to pen registers), affirmed under the name *U.S. v. New York Telephone,* 434 U.S. 166 (1977); *U.S. v. Illinois Bell Telephone Co.,* 531 F.2d 809, 811 (7th Cir. 1976) (affirming district court and parties agreeing that pre-override statute did not apply to pen registers); *U.S. v. Southwest Bell Telephone Co.,* 546 F.2d 243, 247 (8th Cir. 1976) (affirming district court with a justice dissenting on whether the courts have the authority to force cooperation in installing pen registers); *Michigan Bell Telephone Co. v. U.S.,* 565 F.2d 385, 388 (6th Cir. 1976) (affirming district court with a justice dissenting on whether the courts have the authority to force cooperation in

installing pen registers); *U.S. v. Falcone,* 505 F.2d 478, 482 (3d Cir. 1974) (affirming district court with dissent on other grounds), certiorari denied 420 U.S. 955 (1975); *Hodge v. Mountain States Telephone Co.,* 555 F.2d 254, 257 (9th Cir. 1977) (affirming district court with dissent on other grounds); *U.S. v. Clegg,* 509 F.2d 605, 610, n. 6 (5th Cir. 1975) (affirming district court).

19. U.S.C.C.A.N. (1986): 3556.

20. See, for example, *Atlantic States Legal Foundation v. Tyson Foods, Inc.,* 897 F.2d 1128, 1139–40 (11th Cir. 1990); *Public Interest Research Group of NJ v. Powell Duffryn Terminals, Inc.,* 913 F.2d 64, 78 (3d Cir. 1990); see generally *Law of Environmental Protection,* vol. 1, ed. Sheldon Novick, Donald Stever, and Margaret Mellon (Deerfield, Ill.: Clark Boardman Callaghan, 1987) §8.01 [8][a] (collecting additional authority).

21. See, for example, *EPA v. Hill Petroleum Co.,* 17 Envtl. L. Rep. 20457, 20460 (W.D. La. 1986); *SPIRG of N.J. Inc. v. Monsanto Co.,* 18 Envtl. L. Rep. 20999 (D. N.J. 1988).

22. The relevant provision, section 211(d), of the Clean Air Act provided that "[a]ny person who violates . . . the regulations prescribed under subsection (c) of this section . . . shall forfeit and pay to the United States a civil penalty of $10,000" codified at (42 U.S.C. sec. 7545[d]).

23. U.S.C.C.A.N. (1990): 3512.

24. 42 U.S.C. sec. 7545(d)(1); see also U.S.C.C.A.N. (1990) at 3511 (Senate Report).

25. It should be added that in 18 of 28 cases of bipartisan post-override judicial consensus, diverse Democratic and Republican appointees agreed on the meaning of the law as well. Thus, in many cases, agreement was between not only Democratic and Republican appointees but also Kennedy, Johnson, and Clinton appointees as well as Nixon, Ford, and Reagan appointees, which underscores the ideological diversity among judges that applied the override consistently.

26. Donald Campbell and Julian Stanley explain the distinction as follows: "If a group *selected for independent reasons* turns out to have an extreme mean, there is less a priori expectation that the group mean will regress on a second testing, for the random or extraneous sources of variance have been allowed to affect the initial scores in both directions. But for a group selected *because* of its extremity on a fallible variable, this is not the case. Its extremity is artificial and it will regress toward the mean of the population from which it was selected" (*Experimental and Quasi-Experimental Design* [Boston: Houghton Mifflin, 1963], 11–12; emphasis in original).

27. In 44 percent of the cases, judicial dissensus in the pre-override period persisted in the post-override period. In 5 percent of the cases, judicial dissensus emerged after a period of legal consensus under the original statute.

Part II   What Patterns of Court-Congress Relations
Underlie the Override Process?

5   A Typology of Override Scenarios

Part I addressed the threshold question raised by the pluralist, capture, and hyperpluralist views: does the passage of overrides significantly increase levels of judicial consensus on the override issue? Comparing patterns of rule application before and after Congress acts, the data imply that overrides significantly increase judicial consensus on override issues, even though these issues generated high levels of judicial dissensus in the pre-override period. At the same time, overrides are hardly definitive. Substantial judicial dissensus persisted in the post-override period in about half the cases. Thus, overrides seem to matter, but their effect varies.

These findings represent an important first step in assessing the pluralist, capture, and hyperpluralist views, but it is only a first step. Many important issues remain unexplored. For example, does judicial consensus follow open congressional deliberation, as implied by pluralism, or one-sided congressional deliberation, as suggested by capture theory? If congressional deliberation is one-sided, do courts check Congress by ruling for groups that did not participate in the legislative process, consistent with pluralism, or do courts uniformly rule for groups that dominated the legislative process, consistent with capture theory? Moreover, when Congress passes partial overrides, does its decision to delegate reflect a broad policy consensus, consistent with pluralism, or congressional passing the buck, consistent with hyperpluralism? Finally, if Congress tries but fails to resolve the override issue following open deliberation, consistent with hyperpluralism, does this failure reflect unclear override legislation or judicial resistance to congressional oversight?

These questions raise complex issues that require careful examination of the legislative record, court cases, and expert commentary during the override process. Part II navigates this complexity in stages. This chapter opens the analysis by setting forth an original typology of override scenarios based on the logic of pluralism, capture theory, and hyperpluralism. In introducing this typology, it describes the general logic of the competing views of court-Congress relations, identifies the implied override scenarios under each view, and provides illustrative examples. The purposes are to present the typology in a narrative fashion, which locates each override scenario in a broader theory of inter-branch relations, and to highlight the potential diversity of pluralist, capture, and hyperpluralist override scenarios.

Chapter 6 lays out the typology more systematically. It develops a framework for coding each scenario, which underscores the analytic dimensions of the typology. Once this framework is in place, chapter 6 addresses key issues of measurement, reports the distribution of override scenarios in the sample, and discusses the implications for understanding the passage of overrides. Chapter 7 then generates hypotheses about the conditions that tend to produce the predominant patterns of court-Congress relations in the sample.

The Competing Images of the Override Process

As seen in Figure 5.1, the typology consists of nine core override scenarios: the pluralist scenarios of effective deliberative revision, consensual delegation, judicially thwarted one-sided revision, and judicially thwarted one-sided partial revision; capture theory's effective one-sided revision and effective one-sided partial revision; and hyperpluralist's delegation by default, weak congressional signals, and partisan judicial resistance.

Before turning to specifics, a few caveats are in order. First, these scenarios are only *implied* in the literature. Accordingly, the following discussion is not a summary of specific authors, but a distillation of underlying assumptions and styles of argument about the nature of court-Congress relations and the role of overrides in American politics. Second, the goals are modest. In the following analysis, I do not provide a prescriptive theory of what government should do (and when each branch should act). I am content to provide an original synthesis of the literature's implicit approaches, and break new ground by offering a generalized description of recurring patterns of court-Congress interaction in a relatively large number of cases, which in turn can be used to generate hypotheses about the politics of contemporary court-Congress interaction related to the passage of overrides.

Third, these categories carry normative connotations. In the literature, pluralist modes of court-Congress interaction are deemed "healthy"; non-pluralist override processes are not. Such connotations are unavoidable, because pluralism, capture theory, and hyperpluralism conflate empirical

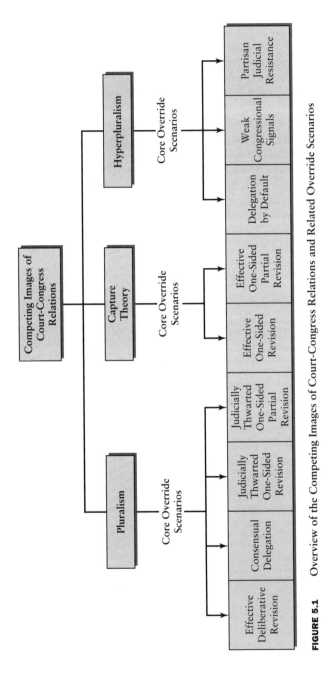

FIGURE 5.1 Overview of the Competing Images of Court-Congress Relations and Related Override Scenarios

and normative considerations. However, even if one rejects the normative assessments in the proposed distillation of the literature, the typology of override scenarios and their relative frequency in the sample should still be of general interest to scholars of inter-branch political dynamics and statutory construction.

A brief example should illustrate the latter point. As will be developed, pluralism encompasses judicially thwarted one-sided revision: cases in which courts rule for groups that won under the original statute but did not participate in congressional deliberations on the override bill. From a pluralist perspective, such judicial behavior is laudable, because it checks the effects of one-sided—or procedurally unfair—legislative processes. From a legal or "textualist" perspective, such behavior constitutes rank judicial activism, which violates a judge's core obligation to apply the law faithfully as written.[1] Regardless of normative perspective, findings on whether congressional deliberation is one-sided and the extent to which courts use statutory interpretation to blunt one-sided congressional deliberation are valuable. They provide insight into interest group activity related to congressional oversight of the courts as well as the relationship between the procedural fairness of legislative processes and how judges use their power of statutory construction.

The Pluralist Perspective

With these caveats in mind, we can turn to the competing images of court-Congress relations, beginning with pluralism. Pluralist theory of American policy-making traces its roots to the writings of James Madison, especially Federalist Papers 10 and 51. According to this view, the primary threat to republican government is the "mischief of faction": the natural tendency of groups—whether majority or minority—to pursue narrow self-interests, which are inimical to others or the aggregate interests of the community.[2]

Given this definition of the problem, the Framers' challenge was to design political institutions that would limit the specter of minority and majority tyranny without extinguishing the spirit of popular sovereignty or restricting individual liberty unduly. With respect to the threat of minority tyranny, the Framers' solution was straightforward. They provided regular elections so that popular majorities would have ample opportunities to remove corrupt or biased representatives.

The threat of majority tyranny poses a thornier problem, however, because a majority faction, by definition, cannot be voted out of office. As a result, the Framers had to look beyond elections to contain the risk of majority tyranny. Specifically, they employed a series of complementary institutional strategies designed to reduce the likelihood that any single faction will control the policy-making process.

Most obviously, the Framers fragmented policy-making power. They divided legislative power between the Senate and House of Representatives, which they viewed as the most susceptible to majority faction, and adopted federalism, separation of powers, and an elaborate system of checks and balances. This dispersal of power ensures that policy-making power is shared: Congress is given the primary power to draft laws, subject to the president's veto and judicial review; the executive branch is given the primary power to implement laws, subject to congressional oversight and judicial review; and the courts have the primary power to interpret laws, subject to a variety of legislative and executive checks, including the passage of overrides.[3] Consequently, if a tyrannical majority seizes control over one branch of government, it cannot unilaterally impose its will on the other branches. Instead, the faction must persuade other branches to endorse its preferences.

Fragmenting lawmaking power offers only an imperfect safeguard against majority tyranny, because dividing power by itself does not prevent a faction from monopolizing *all* branches of government. Accordingly, the Framers buttressed fragmented authority in two ways. First, they designed each branch of government to respond to different constituencies. Thus, members of the House of Representatives are elected by voters in local congressional districts; members of the Senate originally were elected by state representatives (and now are elected by voters in statewide elections); the president is selected by a majority of electoral college votes following a nationwide election; and federal judges are insulated from electoral pressures as political appointees with lifetime tenure and salary protection. By making the branches diversely representative, the Framers built political tension into the American policy-making process, which decreases the likelihood that any single constituency will control all branches of government simultaneously. Second, the Framers staggered the terms of the Senate, House, and president, and provided that the Senate would be a continuing body, in that only one-third of its members run for re-election at a time. This system of staggered terms requires majority coalitions to persist over multiple election cycles, which decreases the likelihood that a temporary surge in popular sentiment will sweep a tyrannical majority into the elected branches of government.

According to pluralist theory, this complex system of checks and balances serves both negative and positive functions. The negative function has already been discussed: checks and balances limit any single branch of government or faction from unilaterally implementing self-serving laws. The positive function is that fragmented and open policy-making structures should promote ongoing policy discourse among separate institutions sharing power. Such policy discourse, in turn, should promote inter-branch feedback, revision of vague or outmoded laws, and, over time, policy consensus and legal certainty.[4]

Three points bear emphasis. One, pluralism does not guarantee protection of all minority interests all of the time, or that all interests will fully and equally participate in policy-making. Instead, pluralism envisages a policy-making process that affords meaningful procedural opportunities for participation. It also assumes that reasonably diverse groups will naturally coalesce to take advantage of these opportunities, a point that modern capture theory strongly contests on the grounds that the costs of participating in multiple policy-making forums are not equally distributed. Two, pluralism's ideal is open deliberation and inter-branch policy consensus, not open deliberation and inter-branch stalemate; such gridlock constitutes hyperpluralism, not pluralism.[5] Three, pluralism predicts that open, inter-branch policy-making will generate policy consensus among lawmakers. It does not hold that such policy-making will terminate all interest group conflict on the override issue. Indeed, in Federalist Paper 10, Madison explicitly argues that factionalism is sown in the seeds of human nature and any attempt to eliminate conflict among factions in a large republic would entail unacceptable restrictions of individual liberty. Thus, from the perspective of pluralism, the question is not whether open congressional deliberation produces overrides that end all litigation, but whether open congressional deliberation promotes overrides that trigger judicial consensus and, hence, enhance legal certainty.

Pluralism and the Override Process

The logic of pluralism suggests four override scenarios: effective deliberative revision, consensual delegation, judicially thwarted one-sided revision, and judicially thwarted one-sided partial revision. Effective deliberative revision reflects the positive, consensus-building function of fragmented political authority. It involves the following attributes: open congressional deliberations on the override bill, which feature competing viewpoints; the passage of prescriptive overrides, which seek to resolve the override issue as Congress defines it; and post-override judicial consensus, which is consistent with the override bill's language and legislative history.[6] Figure 5.2 depicts this scenario.

Of course, not all issues lend themselves to comprehensive legislation. Sometimes experts agree that Congress should resolve some—but not all—aspects of the override issue, because the override issue is imperfectly understood or it involves a fact-intensive inquiry that defies bright-line legal rules. Under these circumstances, pluralism would not require members of Congress to overreach. Instead, pluralism envisages consensual delegation: cases in which, consistent with a broad consensus, Congress passes a partial override that allows courts flexibility to develop significant aspects of the override issue on a case-by-case basis. Following the passage

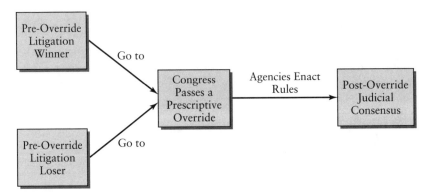

FIGURE 5.2   The Pluralist Scenario of Effective Deliberative Revision

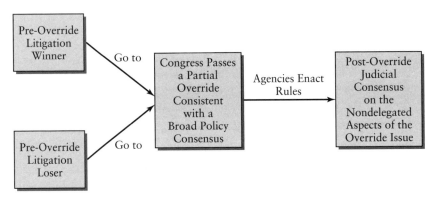

FIGURE 5.3   The Pluralist Scenario of Consensual Delegation

of the partial override, judicial consensus emerges on the nondelegated aspects of the override issue, but not necessarily on the delegated aspects of the override issue. Figure 5.3 sets forth this scenario.

Judicially thwarted one-sided revision and judicially thwarted one-sided partial revision embody the negative, institution-checking function of fragmented political authority envisaged by pluralism. The difference lies in the scope of the override bill. In judicially thwarted one-sided revision, congressional deliberations are one-sided and the overriding Congress passes a *prescriptive* override, which seeks to resolve the override issue. After the override, at least some courts rule for the group that won under the overridden decision but failed to participate in congressional deliberations. Figure 5.4 illustrates this scenario.

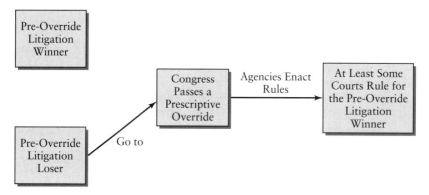

FIGURE 5.4   The Pluralist Scenario of Judicially Thwarted One-Sided Revision

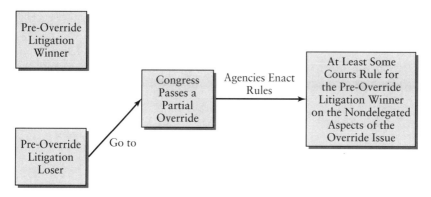

FIGURE 5.5   The Pluralist Scenario of Judicially Thwarted One-Sided
Partial Revision

In judicially thwarted one-sided partial revision, congressional deliberations are one-sided and the overriding Congress passes a *partial* override, which seeks to resolve some—but not all—aspects of the override issue. After Congress acts, at least some courts rule for the group that won under the original statute on the nondelegated aspects of the override issue, but failed to participate in congressional deliberations. Figure 5.5 depicts this scenario.

One might object that the passage of partial overrides after one-sided congressional deliberations is unlikely. After all, if a group dominates congressional deliberation, it would presumably seek a prescriptive override that aims to resolve all aspects of the override issue in its favor—as opposed to a partial override, which would send significant aspects of the override issue back to the courts that have already proven unsympathetic. At worst, if the prescriptive override produced unanticipated consequences, the group could return to Congress and seek another override. Moreover, without opposition from other groups, Congress would have little reason to object.

These points are well taken. Nevertheless, the passage of partial overrides following one-sided deliberations is not wholly implausible. We can imagine situations in which members of well-organized groups seek a partial override because they object to only some aspects of the courts' interpretations of the original statute. Alternatively, members of powerful groups may generally agree that Congress should pass a prescriptive override, but disagree over the specifics of comprehensive legislation. Under those circumstances, they may adopt a piecemeal approach, which passes a partial override and leaves the final resolution of the override issue to a later date. Far more important, in creating a typology of override scenarios, it is better to define the landscape broadly than to prejudge the distribution of cases. Indeed, the emergence of "null sets" can be theoretically interesting. Thus, the possibilities of judicially thwarted one-sided partial revision and effective one-sided partial revision, even if somewhat unlikely, will be considered.

Effective Deliberative Revision Illustrated

Effective deliberative revision represents the classic, pluralist consensus-building scenario. Consistent with pluralism, congressional deliberations are open, meaning they reflect competing viewpoints. Moreover, Congress does not shy away from tackling override issues. It passes prescriptive overrides that attempt to settle the override issue. These overrides are "effective" in that Congress successfully achieves its stated goal of clarifying the override issue, as indicated by post-override judicial consensus that is consistent with the override's language and legislative history.

In practice, effective deliberative revision takes several forms. Sometimes effective deliberative revision addresses conflicting statutes. Recall the Information Act, discussed in Chapter 1.[7] In that case, litigation revealed tension between the Privacy Act and FOIA, which were passed to enhance public access to governmental records. This tension confused the courts. One line of cases interpreted the laws broadly to maximize public disclosure. Another read them narrowly, limiting public access to governmental files.

Stalemated in court, interest groups on both sides of the issue—including the CIA, ACLU, and American Bar Association—turned to Congress, which passed an override that harmonized the statutes and sought to eliminate any confusion. Congress succeeded. In the post-override period, judicial consensus emerged on the override issue. Indeed, a circuit court noted that the clarity of the override was "stunning." It should be added that capture was unlikely. All sides testified before Congress on the override bill, and the overriding Congress championed a citizen's right of access over the objections of powerful governmental interests.

In other cases, effective deliberative revision addresses unintended consequences of statutes. This pattern is common in tax law, in which litigation uncovers loopholes in the tax code, which produce double deductions or other anomalous policy outcomes. Court-Congress interaction over *Textron, Inc. v. U.S.* is typical.[8] The case concerned rules governing a parent company's use of tax benefits related to an unprofitable subsidiary. Specifically, Textron, a Fortune 500 company, owned a subsidiary company that operated a fleet of cruise ships from the West Coast to the Hawaiian Islands. The business was a bust, losing millions of dollars. In 1959, Textron claimed a $6-million deduction on the grounds that its subsidiary's stock had become worthless. A year later, Textron bought a substantial interest in Bell Aircraft, which builds helicopters, and merged this new business into its failed cruise ship subsidiary. Textron then used the operating losses from its cruise ship operations to protect the profits of its successful helicopter business.

The Internal Revenue Service (IRS) audited Textron and disallowed its 1959 deductions for worthless stock. It maintained that the subsidiary's stock was not worthless, because the subsidiary had significant operating losses that proved valuable for Textron's helicopter business. The district court rejected the IRS's argument, holding that Textron had complied with the literal terms of the tax code. The IRS appealed.

In a divided decision, the First Circuit of the U.S. Court of Appeals affirmed the district court's decision. The First Circuit conceded that a literal reading of the tax code would produce a double deduction for Textron. However, they reasoned that Congress or the IRS—not the courts—should close any loophole in the law. It explained as follows: "Textron has turned its Hawaiian sow's ear into a silk purse—and filled it at Treasury's expense. But it is a matter that should be cured by statute or regulation, not by a far reaching retroactive court decision."[9] As a policy matter, the majority stressed that legal certainty under the tax code trumped any other concerns, and it declined to "inject [a] massive and unsettling dose of 'equity' into the tax laws without a clear invitation from the Service and a careful exploration of the issue by both sides."[10]

Eventually, the IRS appealed to Congress for an override. During its deliberations on the override issue, Congress heard from the IRS and various members of Textron, including its chairman and president, and the president and marketing manager of its Bell Helicopter operations, who explained Textron's internal accounting procedures. After hearing from all sides, Congress reversed *Textron*.[11] Following the override, courts have treated the issue as settled.[12] In short, Congress made the law; courts applied the original statute as written and invited Congress to revisit the issue; and, consistent with the court's invitation, Congress effectively eliminated the unintended consequences of the original statutory framework.

Effective deliberative revision also updates antiquated laws. Court-Congress interaction surrounding the Immigration Act of 1990 offers a case in point. The act's override provision grew out of long-standing controversy over the treatment of gay immigrants. Specifically, under the 1952 Immigration Act, aliens "afflicted by psychopathic personality" were excluded from the United States.[13] In the early 1960s, controversy arose as to whether this provision—as applied to homosexuals—was unconstitutionally vague.[14]

In 1964, Congress sought to erase any doubt. It amended the statutory definition of *psychopathic personality* to include "sexual deviation." In 1967, in *Boutilier v. INS*, the Supreme Court ruled that psychopathic personality language, as amended, barred homosexuals from entering the United States, and that such a bar was constitutional.[15]

Until 1979, the Immigration and Naturalization Service (INS) referred suspected homosexuals to Public Health Services (PHS), which examined the applicant and provided a medical certificate regarding sexual preference. In 1979, however, PHS stopped issuing these certificates on the grounds that homosexuality is not a mental disorder and that being gay is not medically diagnosable. The Justice Department advised the INS to continue excluding gay aliens, irrespective of the PHS change in policy.

This controversy within the executive branch soon spilled into the courts. The legal issue was whether the INS needed a medical certificate to exclude gay aliens, because the psychopathic personality provision constituted medical grounds for exclusion. In a divided decision, the Fifth Circuit held that a medical certificate was not required;[16] the Ninth Circuit held the opposite.[17]

In 1990, after hearing from a wide range of groups, Congress finally overrode *Boutilier*. The Judicial Committee explained that the law was both unclear and obsolete:

> The law . . . needs to be updated in its treatment of sexual orientation. The term "sexual deviation" . . . was included with the other mental health exclusion grounds expressly for the purpose of excluding homosexuals. Not only is this provision out of step with current notions of privacy and personal dignity, it is also inconsistent with contemporary psychiatric theories. . . . Nonetheless the law remains on the books, and court interpretations have been inconsistent and confusing. . . . Therefore, in order to make clear that the United States does not view personal decisions about sexual orientation as a danger to other people in our society, the bill repeals the "sexual deviation" exclusion ground.[18]

After the override, the issue disappears from view.[19] Again, there is no reason to suspect capture. To the contrary, representatives from all sides testified before Congress, and the bill granted a victory to gay noncitizens, who hardly represent a traditional powerhouse on Capitol Hill. In sum, whether reconciling statutory conflicts, addressing unintended statutory consequences, or updating statutory anachronisms, effective deliberative revision embodies the pluralist ideal of inter-branch feedback in which open congressional deliberations produce comprehensive overrides that trigger judicial consensus and hence greater legal certainty.

Consensual Delegation Illustrated

In consensual delegation, Congress does not seek to settle every aspect of the override issue. Instead, following open deliberation and consistent with a broad expert consensus, Congress passes a partial override that delegates significant aspects of the override issue to the courts, at least for the time being. Consistent with this partial override, judges uniformly rule on the nondelegated aspects of the override issue, but they typically struggle to develop a consistent standard for the delegated aspects of the override issue.

Court-Congress relations surrounding the Trademark Clarification Act of 1984 illustrate this scenario. The Trademark Clarification Act addressed a thorny trademark law issue: when do terms such as *aspirin, thermos,* or *cellophane* become generic and hence lose their trademark protection?[20] Traditionally, Congress allowed courts to develop the definition of *genericness* on a case-by-case basis, which resulted in alternative tests for assessing public perception of the relevant term.[21]

In the late 1970s and early 1980s, the Ninth Circuit, in litigation known as the *Anti-Monopoly* case, offered an entirely novel test for genericness, which departed from the existing public perception tests. Specifically, in *Anti-Monopoly,* a company developed a board game titled "Anti-Monopoly: The Bust the Trusts Game" and sought a judicial declaration that *Monopoly* had become a generic term. In response, General Mills, the maker of the popular board game *Monopoly,* sued for trademark infringement. Rather than examine public perception of the term *Monopoly,* the Ninth Circuit examined whether purchasers were motivated to buy the product *solely* because of its name.[22] If not, the term would be deemed generic.

The Ninth Circuit's "purchaser motivation" test was highly controversial. After hearing testimony from small and large businesses as well as legal experts, Congress passed the Trademark Clarification Act of 1984. This act was a classic partial override: it reversed the Ninth Circuit's purchaser motivation test, but refrained from providing a statutory definition of *genericness.* Instead, Congress left further refinement of the genericness doctrine to the courts. The Judiciary Committee explained as follows:

> [T]he bill is not intended to effect important substantive changes in the mainstream of trademark law. Thus its purpose remains primarily that of clarifying and rendering more precise in the statute what the law is today and should be in the years to come, undisturbed and undiverted by the troubling and potentially dangerous elements of the [*Anti-Monopoly*] case.[23]

Congress succeeded in its goals. On one hand, it effectively reversed *Anti-Monopoly*. Following the override, courts have uniformly abandoned the purchaser motivation test, and the post-override court decisions have remained within the approved framework of public perception.[24] On the other hand, Congress did not resolve the override issue of when a common term becomes generic. Indeed, considerable judicial dissensus persists over the precise test of public perception.[25] But Congress did not intend to resolve this intricate issue; rather, it passed a partial override that intentionally, and prudently, allowed courts the discretion to determine genericness on a case-by-case basis.

It is tempting to counter that the Trademark Clarification Act involves capture theory's effective one-sided revision, which is discussed in the next section. After all, General Mills, a large corporation, used the override process to reverse an unfavorable court decision. In fact, Representative Kastenmeier expressed fear that the Judiciary Committee would become a "quasi-appellate forum" for litigation losses in trademark cases.[26]

But capture theory is an unlikely explanation of the Trademark Clarification Act for several reasons. First, as a procedural matter, modern capture theory envisages one-sided congressional deliberations. But, in this case, a range of legal experts, small business interests, and industry groups testified before Congress. Second, as a policy matter, General Mills was not the only critic of the Ninth Circuit approach. Legal experts, Democrats, and Republicans sharply attacked the purchaser motivation test as unworkable.[27] Although General Mills may have captured all of these groups, it seems more likely that the *Anti-Monopoly* decision was widely perceived as flawed and warranted reversal.

Third, if large firms, such as General Mills, had captured the process, we would have expected Congress to pass a prescriptive override, which affords greater protection to well-established brand names than does the Trademark Clarification Act. In fact, they tried. Specifically, the House passed a bill that provided a single public perception test. It also eliminated the use of so-called indirect evidence of genericness, such as dictionary definitions and usage in newspapers and magazines, which is widely considered to favor those challenging trademarks.[28] That bill, however, died in the Senate. In its place, Congress passed a partial override that gives courts considerable flexibility in determining the relevant evidence and legal standard for genericness.

It is also tempting to place a hyperpluralist spin on the Trademark Clarification Act. At some level, members of Congress came, they saw, and they fudged. As a result, judicial dissensus persists over the precise definition of *genericness*. Indeed, some legal experts have criticized the overriding Congress for not passing more comprehensive legislation.[29]

Several factors cut against this argument. First, many key members, such as Senator Orrin Hatch, who sponsored the override, endorsed the basic judicial approach prior to the *Anti-Monopoly* case.[30] Under these circumstances, Congress was trying to restore the law to its previous condition, even if the preexisting law was less than crystal clear. In hyperpluralism's delegation by default, by contrast, the overriding Congress concedes that the judicial status quo is unacceptable. Nevertheless, it cannot reach accord on a prescriptive override and passes a stopgap measure, which by its own admission will not adequately address the override issue.

Second, in the Trademark Clarification Act case, experts agreed that the override issue—namely, whether a brand name has become generic—involves a fact-intensive inquiry into the common usage and understanding of language, which cannot be reduced to a simple statutory formula. Accordingly, even experts who favored more comprehensive legislation than the Trademark Clarification Act did not call for a prescriptive override. They recognized that courts needed flexibility in determining genericness and argued that the House's bill went too far in limiting the courts' discretion.[31]

In short, the weight of evidence suggests that Congress did not pass the buck when passing the Trademark Clarification Act. Instead, Congress engaged in consensual delegation: consistent with an expert consensus, it reversed *Anti-Monopoly* while leaving further legal refinements to the courts. Moreover, Congress achieved its stated goals. Following the override, the controversial Ninth Circuit approach was abandoned, and courts continued to adapt the law within the lines of the general approach favored by Congress.

Judicially Thwarted One-Sided Revision Illustrated

As noted earlier, pluralism asserts that fragmented political authority has a negative institution-checking function as well as a positive consensus-building function. Hence, pluralism does not assume that the passage of all overrides will be procedurally open. It holds that, in the absence of broad participation in congressional deliberation, disgruntled groups that did not participate in the legislative process will take their case—literally—to the courts, which will serve as a check on one-sided legislative processes.

As will be discussed in the next chapter, there were very few cases of one-sided congressional deliberation in the sample and no cases of judicially thwarted one-sided partial revision. The Crime Control Act of 1990, however, illustrates judicially thwarted one-sided revision. This override addressed judicial dissensus over the treatment of criminal fines, penalties, and restitution orders under the Bankruptcy Code. The issue was whether these obligations were "debts" for bankruptcy purposes and hence "dischargeable," meaning whether the Bankruptcy Code would absolve the debtors from payment following their bankruptcy cases. Some courts held that such obligations were dischargeable debts;[32] others held that they were not.[33]

In *Pennsylvania Public Welfare Department v. Davenport*,[34] the Supreme Court granted certiorari to resolve the split. The case involved a married couple who pleaded guilty to welfare fraud and were ordered to pay monthly restitution to the state. The Davenports eventually filed for bankruptcy under Chapter 13, which suspends debt collection by creditors, allows consumer debtors to pay a percentage of their debts according to a plan, and discharges their pre-bankruptcy debts once the plan is complete. During the bankruptcy proceedings, the couple sought an injunction against any collection actions by the state and a declaration that their monthly restitution obligations were dischargeable. The Court ruled for the Davenports, holding that criminal restitution payments are dischargeable in a Chapter 13 case.

States and law enforcement officials appealed to Congress and obtained an override of *Davenport*. Congress did not hear testimony from any group representing consumer debtors, the poor, or criminal rights groups. In passing the override, Congress crafted language that dealt explicitly with the discharge of criminal restitution orders in Chapter 13 cases, but did not explicitly deal with the discharge of all obligations arising from criminal proceedings, such as criminal fines and penalties. Instead, the Committee Report stated that the override had codified an earlier Supreme Court decision, *Kelly v. Robinson*,[35] which expressed "serious doubts whether Congress intended to make criminal penalties 'debts' [for purposes of bankruptcy proceedings]."[36]

Following the override, several courts held that the overriding Congress did not clearly indicate its intent with respect to criminal penalties other than restitution orders. In so holding, these courts emphasized the need to give bankruptcy debtors the benefit of any statutory ambiguity and protect their right to a "fresh start."[37] In short, the courts engaged in judicially thwarted one-sided revision: they used their power of statutory construction to protect the rights of groups, such as bankruptcy consumer debtors and convicted criminals, who are unlikely to—and, in fact, did not—make their case in Congress.

The Capture Perspective

Capture theory challenges pluralism's assumption that inter-branch policy-making in a system of fragmented power will promote broad political participation. Instead, capture theory posits that "elites," variously defined, will dominate American policy-making. This view is nothing new. In the 1950s, for instance, C. Wright Mills warned that the "higher circles" of corporations, federal bureaucracies, and the military had formed an inter-locking directorate, which controls decision-making on fundamental issues.[38] Under this view, members of Congress represent a "middle level" power, whose actions on secondary issues serve to obscure the power structure that operates beyond the public's view.[39]

Early versions of capture theory, such as Mills's argument, suffered a central weakness. They failed to articulate clear mechanisms by which elites monopolized the sprawling American policy-making process, which features multiple veto points and diversely representative lawmakers.[40] In the 1970s, a number of scholars stepped into the breach. Using the language of economics, they posited a general theory of interest group formation, political participation, and agenda-setting, which challenged pluralism at its roots.[41] This argument, sometimes called "public choice theory," has been enormously influential among those who study over-rides, especially legal scholars.[42]

What is public choice theory? Public choice theory reads like a rational choice "whodunit": well-organized, wealth-maximizing groups have captured the lawmaking process because they have the motive, opportunity, and means to do so. The motive and means are relatively straightforward. The motive for capture is the passage of favorable statutes and regulations. The most obvious examples include direct subsidies to regulated industries or restrictions on competition, such as licensing laws that allow regulated industries to charge above-market prices or "rents."[43] More subtle examples are changes in legal procedures, such as lowering a party's burden of proof in lawsuits, which facilitate pursuing and defending legal claims. The means of capture are political resources, such as campaign contributions, information, organizational support, or bureaucratic assistance, which well-organized groups can use to reward compliant representatives in future elections and sympathetic administrators in future budget battles.

Understanding the opportunity for capture—from a rational choice perspective—is more complex, because public choice scholars must assume voters and elected officials are as rational as the groups that seek to capture the lawmaking process. Specifically, modern capture theorists assume that voters seek to maximize their wealth and that elected officials seek to maximize their chances of re-election. Hence, voters would never elect officials who disproportionately favor narrow interests at their expense in direct and informed elections; likewise, elected officials would never openly thwart popular majorities, who could turn them out of office.

The problems, according to public choice theory, are that elections are rarely if ever direct or informed and that the policy-making process is rarely transparent to the public. Congressional elections are indirect because citizens vote for candidates who fight over a number of policies and overlapping constituencies. Hence, unlike single-issue referenda, congressional elections rarely send a clear message to elected officials, because there are many issues, only one vote per office, and no means to register the intensity of individual policy preferences. Elections seem to send particularly fuzzy signals in an era of divided government, when citizens often vote for members of Congress and presidents from different parties who expressly disagree on policy.

Elections are uninformed because, unlike markets that feature voluntary agreements among parties who are motivated to educate themselves, elections involve large segments of the community, regardless of each citizen's interest, knowledge, or intensity of preferences on the relevant issues.[44] Indeed, citizens often vote for reasons unrelated to the candidate's policy positions, such as party loyalty, disaffection with past candidates, the candidate's personality or "image," or habit.

Similar reasons explain why policy-making is usually obscure to voters. Bills rarely address single issues. Instead, they address a host of issues, which are often unrelated, especially in massive omnibus and appropriation bills. Hence, votes on specific bills rarely send clear signals to the public about their representatives' legislative activities. In addition, the policy-making process involves endless rounds of bureaucratic, committee, and judicial processes, which are often opaque to ordinary voters.

Under public choice theory, two implications follow from indirect and uniformed elections and the difficulty of monitoring policy-making. First, because elections provide attenuated lines of communication between voters and their representatives, elected officials tend to respond only to strong preferences, which are articulated through more direct and costly means than the ballot box, such as lobbying. Second, because most voters lack the information and motivation to monitor their representative's actions, elected officials enjoy some organizational "slack," which allows them to reap the advantages of serving well-organized—and well-heeled—constituents without fear of losing office.[45]

Given this opportunity, the question remains why some groups mobilize effectively while others do not. The answer, according to public choice theory, lies in the combination of two factors: (1) the "free rider" or "collective action" problem and (2) the costs associated with participating in multiple and diversely representative lawmaking forums.[46] Specifically, the free rider problem holds that, all things being equal, individual group members face a dilemma: they must share the fruits of their labors with the group at large. Thus, individual group members have an incentive to piggyback on the efforts of others—that is, do nothing and let others incur the costs of taking action that benefits the group. Put differently, individual incentive to act is blunted when rewards must be shared.

The free rider problem, moreover, should not affect groups equally. As a theoretical matter, smaller groups are more likely to overcome the costs of free riding, because group benefits are less widely dispersed and the costs of a few free riders are more easily absorbed. By contrast, the free rider problem is often daunting for large groups, because individuals must widely share benefits, which makes it less likely that the individual costs of acting on the group's behalf will exceed the individual benefits of taking such action. Consequently, it is argued that small groups, especially those with large stakes in policy outcomes, enjoy systematic political advantages over large, diffuse groups, particularly when members of large groups are one-shotters who have no other reason to organize because they tend to focus on the outcomes of particular disputes as opposed to the rules of the game.

The free rider problem is not the only obstacle facing diffuse interest and one-shotters; the other lies in the costs of participating in a system of fragmented power. Specifically, in a system of fragmented political power, it is not enough to mobilize for action in any single forum. Groups must gird themselves for battle in multiple forums that approach policy-making differently and are designed to respond to different political constituencies. In such a system, modern capture theory predicts that well-organized interest groups will outlast and outmaneuver diffuse interests and one-shotters. With respect to Congress, the argument is that well-organized groups have long-standing relationships with members of Congress, federal agencies, and other groups. This paves the way for favorable laws and regulations. Diffuse interests and one-shotters, by contrast, are unlikely to have the needed experience or allies to push their agendas on Capitol Hill.

A similar argument can be made with respect to the courts. Specifically, well-organized groups are often repeat players in the judicial system: groups that litigate often and face a large number of similar claims.[47] As such, they are able to litigate with an eye toward shaping legal precedents in their favor. Why? Unlike one-shotters, who face discrete claims and lack litigation experience, repeat players can pick and choose their battles in court. Accordingly, repeat players can settle unfavorable claims and vigorously pursue claims that place their view of the law in the best light and before the most sympathetic judges. Careful selection of cases, in turn, enables repeat players to shape legal precedents in their favor. Of course, if litigation takes an unexpected turn against repeat players, they can always appeal to Congress for a favorable override and continue the process until the rules are advantageous.

Capture and the Override Process

From the perspective of modern capture theory, overrides should not differ from other legislation. Indeed, the costs of playing the override game may be especially high because a group must have the resources, allies, and determination to endure multiple rounds of legislation and litigation. Consistent with this reasoning, some argue that Congress typically serves as a politically skewed court of appeals that favors industry groups, especially in the area of environmental regulation.[48] Others charge that governmental agencies have captured the override process, using overrides to reverse judicial decisions that favor politically marginalized groups, such as noncitizens, who are unlikely to have legislative clout.[49]

The net result should be either effective one-sided revision or effective one-sided partial revision: cases in which well-organized groups unilaterally appeal to Congress to reverse unfavorable court decisions, and then use litigation to cement their legislative advances. The difference in these scenarios lies in the scope of the override. In effective one-sided revision, the overriding Congress passes a prescriptive override following one-sided deliberations and seeks to resolve the override issue. After the override, courts uniformly apply the override in favor of the winner in Congress. Figure 5.6 depicts this scenario.

In effective one-sided partial revision, congressional deliberations are one-sided and the overriding Congress passes a partial override that seeks to resolve some but not all aspects of the override issue. After Congress acts, courts uniformly apply the nondelegated aspects of the override in favor of the winner in Congress and, hence, locks in its gains. Figure 5.7 depicts this scenario.

Effective One-Sided Revision Illustrated

As will be discussed in the next chapter, cases of capture were rare in my sample, even when the definition was relaxed, and there were no cases of effective one-sided partial revision. Indeed, the only cases of one-sided congressional deliberation seem to involve relatively autonomous agencies, such as the Justice Department. The Fine Improvements Act discussed in

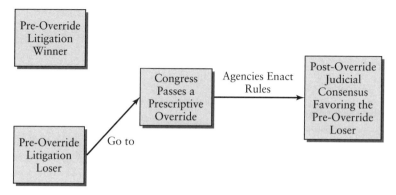

FIGURE 5.6   The Capture Scenario of Effective One-Sided Revision

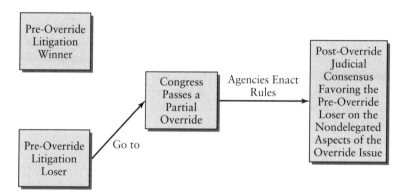

FIGURE 5.7   The Capture Scenario of Effective One-Sided Partial Revision

Chapter 1 was typical.[50] In that case, government prosecutors were able to appeal unfavorable interpretations of federal criminal law to Congress without opposition. Congress, without hearing competing views, passed a prescriptive override that codified the government's position.

The False Claims Act of 1986 provides another example. In that case, Congress overrode a Sixth Circuit decision that required the government to establish allegations of fraud under the False Claims Act by "clear, unequivocal and convincing evidence."[51] The government sought an override that would lower its burden of proof in suing for fraud. After hearing from law enforcement and governmental interests only, the overriding Congress wrote these groups' preference into law.[52] After the override, the U.S. Court of Appeals unequivocally adopted this lower standard of proof for the government.[53] Thus, in both cases, well-organized groups achieved effective one-sided revision: they unilaterally appealed unfavorable court decisions to Congress, which rewrote the law in their favor and then these groups persuaded judges to lock in their legislative gains.

The Hyperpluralist Perspective

Hyperpluralists would agree with pluralists that fragmented government promotes diverse, active political participation; however, they reject the pluralist assumption that inter-branch policy-making engenders judicial consensus consistent with the override signal. Instead, hyperpluralists argue that fragmented political authority is a formula for policy stalemate and legal uncertainty. The reasoning was detailed in Chapter 3 in connection with the null hypothesis and will not be fully restated here. Suffice it to say that hyperpluralists argue that elected officials, when faced with divisive issues, have political incentives to pass vague laws that allow claiming credit for taking some action while avoiding specific policy stands that could alienate key constituents or haunt them in future elections. Moreover, even if members of Congress are motivated to tackle tough issues, it is difficult to maneuver specific statutes through the fragmented lawmaking process in Washington. Finally, even if a clear law is passed, or agencies manage to promulgate clear regulations interpreting the law, politically selected American judges, in a coordinate system of justice, are likely to eschew the letter of the law and decide cases according to their policy preferences, which often conflict given American judges' ideological diversity.[54]

Hyperpluralism and the Override Process

The logic of hyperpluralism connotes three override scenarios, each of which entails open congressional deliberations and persistent legal uncertainty. One is delegation by default: cases in which members of Congress intentionally delegate significant aspects of the override issue to the courts, even though experts recommend that Congress resolve the override issue. Figure 5.8 depicts this scenario.

Under the remaining scenarios—partisan judicial resistance and weak congressional signals—congressional deliberation is open, Congress passes a prescriptive override, and judicial dissensus emerges in the post-override period. The difference between these scenarios lies in the nature of post-override judicial dissensus. In partisan judicial resistance, partisan judicial dissensus arises in the post-override period, which indicates that the courts have evaded congressional oversight on the override issue. In weak congressional signals, non-partisan judicial dissensus emerges in the post-override period, which suggests that Congress has sent confusing signals to the courts. Figures 5.9 and 5.10 lay out each of these scenarios.

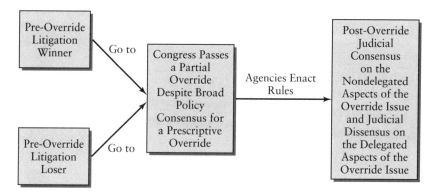

FIGURE 5.8   The Hyperpluralist Scenario of Delegation by Default

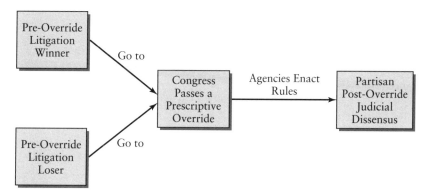

FIGURE 5.9   The Hyperpluralist Scenario of Partisan Judicial Resistance

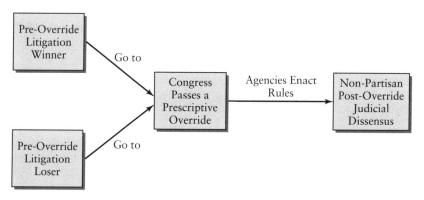

FIGURE 5.10   The Hyperpluralist Scenario of Weak Congressional Signals

Delegation by Default Illustrated. In delegation by default, experts urge Congress to pass a prescriptive override, but Congress fails to do so. Consider the Judicial Improvements and Access to Justice Act (the Judicial Improvements Act), which concerned a cluster of procedural issues involving lawsuits against the government. Specifically, prior to the override, courts had hopelessly split on the meaning of the Tucker Act, which waives sovereign immunity for a host of monetary claims against the federal government; assigns jurisdiction for such claims greater than $10,000—so-called large Tucker Act claims—to the U.S. Court of Appeals for the Federal Circuit; and gives the U.S. Claims Courts and regular federal courts concurrent jurisdiction for claims under $10,000, or "small Tucker Act claims."[55]

At the time of the override, almost everyone agreed that Congress needed to clarify the law and end wasteful litigation over where to litigate Tucker Act claims.[56] Nevertheless, members of Congress could not reach agreement on the underlying jurisdictional issues, which included the following: (1) where to bring mixed Tucker Act and non–Tucker Act claims; (2) the interplay between the Tucker Act and the Administrative Procedure Act, both of which provide procedures for bringing claims against the government; (3) the treatment of large Tucker Act claims improperly brought before the district courts; and (4) whether parties must first litigate Tucker Act claims in the lower courts and address jurisdictional issues on appeal, or simply may take an interlocutory appeal to settle jurisdictional issues prior to trial. In the absence of an agreement, Congress passed a narrow partial override, which allowed interlocutory appeals of jurisdictional disputes under the Tucker Act but did not address the underlying jurisdictional controversies that plagued the courts.[57] Thus, the overriding Congress provided a limited procedural fix that left the vexing substantive issues unresolved.

The legislative record indicates that the overriding Congress recognized that the Judicial Improvements Act itself needed improvement. For example, the Judiciary Committee admitted the override would not resolve the underlying substantive issues, especially the relationship between the Administrative Procedure Act and the Tucker Act, and that those issues would "be the subject of continuing controversy in the courts."[58] It further conceded that Congress would have to review these issues "in the near future."[59] In short, by its own admission, the overriding Congress largely punted to the courts.[60]

Not surprisingly, judicial dissensus on the jurisdictional issues persisted after the override.[61] To reiterate, unlike the Trademark Clarification Act, experts did not urge Congress to give judges discretion on these issues. Instead, experts implored Congress to resolve the underlying jurisdictional controversies once and for all to eliminate unproductive litigation over procedural matters. Thus, instead of consensual delegation, members of Congress engaged in delegation by default: it passed a partial override, despite a broad expert consensus for a prescriptive override.[62]

Partisan Judicial Resistance Illustrated.   In partisan judicial resistance, congressional deliberation is open and the overriding Congress passes a prescriptive override. Unlike effective deliberative revision, however, the override fails to trigger judicial consensus. Instead, judges interpret the override along partisan lines.

Court-Congress interaction over the meaning of the Age Discrimination in Employment Act (ADEA) illustrates partisan judicial resistance. The override issue stemmed from section 4(f)(2) of the ADEA, which is convoluted even by the standards of American statutes. It provides: "it shall not be unlawful for an employer . . . to observe the terms of a bona fide employee benefit plan such as a retirement, pension, or insurance plan, which is not a subterfuge to evade the purposes of this [act], except that no such employee benefit shall excuse the failure to hire any individual."[63]

Courts struggled to apply this jumble of double negatives to mandatory retirement plans that were adopted prior to the ADEA's passage in 1967. On one hand, the Fifth Circuit focused on the "subterfuge" language. It reasoned that the ADEA did not apply to good-faith mandatory retirement plans unless the plans represented a "subterfuge" to avoid its provisions. Given this reasoning, the ADEA clearly does not apply to pre-enactment mandatory retirement plans. After all, how could practices adopted prior to the passage of the ADEA be a subterfuge for avoiding its ban on age discrimination? Accordingly, under the Fifth Circuit interpretation, the ADEA provided a safe harbor for all good-faith plans enacted before 1967.

The Fourth Circuit rejected this interpretation. It focused on the "employee benefit" language, ruling that the subterfuge language was limited to employee benefits and hence did not apply to mandatory retirement provisions.[64] Under this reading, the ADEA did not provide a safe harbor for mandatory retirement plans adopted prior to 1967. After all, the court suggested, why create an automatic exception for employment practices that plainly violate the spirit of the ADEA's protection of older workers?

In *United Air Lines, Inc. v. McMann,* the Supreme Court granted certiorari to resolve the split.[65] In a 7 to 2 decision, which divided along ideological lines, the conservative majority sided with the Fifth Circuit and employers, holding that mandatory retirement plans established significantly prior to 1967 did not violate the ADEA. In support of its view, the majority stressed the "subterfuge" language and stated that the Court's "function is narrowly confined to discerning the meaning of the statutory language; we do not pass on the wisdom of fixed mandatory retirements at a particular age."[66]

The leading liberals on the Burger Court—Justices Brennan and Marshall—found that the ADEA was not so cut and dried. They argued that the statute permitted conflicting interpretations. Consistent with the majority's approach, one could emphasize the "subterfuge" language and exempt all pre-1967 mandatory retirement plans from the ADEA. Consistent with the Fourth Circuit's view, however, one could focus on the "employee benefit" language and require mandatory retirement plans to pass muster under the ADEA. In favoring the Fourth Circuit approach, the dissent leaned heavily on statements in the legislative history, and on a policy argument that the majority's construction produced the following anomaly:

> [Under the majority's interpretation of the ADEA,] the individual [facing mandatory retirement] has a simple route to regain his job: He need only reapply for the vacancy created by his retirement. As a new applicant, the individual plainly cannot be denied the job because of his age. And as someone with experience in performing the tasks of the "vacant" job he once held, the individual likely will be better qualified than any other applicant. Thus the individual retired one day would have to be hired the next. We should be loath to attribute to Congress an intention to produce such a bizarre result.[67]

McMann did not end the controversy. Instead, the competing interests converged on Congress. After hearing from a broad array of groups, including business representatives, the Chamber of Commerce, the American Association of Retired Persons, labor interests, and the medical community, Congress responded to *McMann*.[68] As James Brudney argues, the legislative history provides a number of strong indications that Congress intended to override the holding and reasoning of *McMann*, and hence eliminate a safe harbor for pre-ADEA plans.[69] First, the conference report clearly states that plans should not be judged based on their establishment date. Second, many key proponents of the bill explicitly reaffirmed that the override would reverse the Supreme Court's reading of the "subterfuge" language and eliminate an exemption for pre-1967 plans. Third, the overall gist of the amendments was to *strengthen* protection of older workers.

Despite these relatively clear signals, controversy emerged over whether Congress had, in fact, wholly overridden *McMann*. Specifically, in *Betts v. Hamilton County Board of Mental Retardation*,[70] the Sixth Circuit split on this issue. The majority of circuit court judges, as well as the district court judge, held that Congress expressly repudiated *McMann's* creation of a safe harbor for pre-1967 plans. Thus, it required employers to show that their pre-1967 benefit plans were nondiscriminatory under the ADEA.[71] The dissenting view rejected this approach, arguing that the overriding Congress did not remove the "subterfuge" language from the ADEA. Under this interpretation, Congress reversed the outcome of *McMann* with respect to mandatory retirement provisions, but did not affect *McMann's* creation of a safe harbor for employee benefit plans pre-dating the ADEA.[72]

The Supreme Court granted certiorari to review *Betts*.[73] Again, the Court divided along ideological lines in a 7 to 2 decision. Not surprisingly, the conservative majority adopted the narrow interpretation of the override. It concluded: "we see no reason to depart from our holding in *McMann* that the term 'subterfuge' is to be given its ordinary meaning, and that as a result an employee benefit plan adopted prior to the enactment of the ADEA cannot be a subterfuge."[74] Justice Marshall, joined again by Justice Brennan, was nonplussed by the majority's refusal to examine the legislative history of the override. In a sharply worded dissent, Marshall lamented that "the majority today puts aside conventional tools of statutory construction and, relying instead on artifice and invention, arrives at a draconian interpretation of the ADEA which Congress assuredly did not contemplate, let alone share, in 1968, in 1978, or now."[75] In sum, the ADEA involved the erratic and syncopated beat of partisan judicial resistance, in which courts read the law along partisan lines notwithstanding Congress's efforts to set the record straight.

A coda to *Betts* further illustrates the texture of court-Congress relations in the politically charged arena of employment discrimination law and civil rights in the sample. Specifically, within weeks of the *Betts* decision, Congress passed a second override that aimed to reverse *McMann* once and for all. The new bill, the Older Workers Benefit Protection Act of 1990, removed the term *subterfuge* from the ADEA and expressly stated that employee benefit plans must comply with the ADEA, regardless of when they were established.[76]

The aftermath of the second override is notable on two counts. First, following the 1990 override, courts generally have abandoned *McMann* and *Betts* with respect to the ADEA.[77] Thus, Congress was able to overcome partisan judicial splits on the override issue eventually. To do so, however, Congress had to spend considerable legislative resources to revisit the override issue and close any possible loophole in the statute.

Second, despite multiple rounds of overrides, courts still are finding ways to revive *McMann* and *Betts* in the area of employment discrimination. Specifically, the Americans with Disabilities Act (ADA), which was passed in 1991, contains a provision stating that insurance classification and underwriting "shall not be used as a subterfuge to evade" the ADA.[78] In *Modderno v. King*,[79] the D.C. Circuit relied on both *McMann* and *Betts* interpretations of the term *subterfuge* when construing the ADA. The court argued as follows: "when Congress chose the term 'subterfuge' for the insurance safe-harbor of the ADA, it was on full alert as to what the

Court understood the word to mean and possessed (obviously) a full grasp of the linguistic devices available to avoid that meaning."[80] The D.C. Circuit was so certain of its interpretation of *subterfuge*, it ruled that the Labor Department's interpretation of the term, which explicitly rejects *Betts,* plainly violated the statute.[81]

A glance at the legislative history of the ADA, however, seems to contradict the D.C. Circuit's assertions. The House Report states that the ADA "subterfuge" language "may not be used to evade the [act's] protections . . . *regardless of the date an insurance plan or employee benefit was adopted.*"[82] On the floor of Congress, Senator Kennedy added that Congress's use of the term *subterfuge* in the ADA "should not be interpreted in the manner in which the Supreme Court interpreted the term in [*Betts.*]"[83] Representative Owens explained: "It is not our intent that the restrictive reading of *Betts,* with which we do not agree, should be carried over to the ADA."[84]

In short, despite repeated signals from Congress, judges are still finding ways to sidestep congressional signals on this ideologically divisive issue. Such patterns of judicial behavior, in turn, cast a shadow of legal uncertainty over the American workplace and place a heavy burden on Congress, which must pass repetitive laws, not because the old laws were skewed or flawed, but because courts resist following them.

Weak Congressional Signals Illustrated.   Similar to partisan judicial resistance, weak congressional signals involve open congressional deliberation and the passage of prescriptive overrides that fail to clarify the law. Contrary to partisan judicial resistance, however, the fault appears to lie with Congress and not the courts. The National Defense Authorization Act of 1987 is illustrative. The override issue involved government contracting practices. Specifically, in the 1960s, Congress passed the Truth in Negotiations Act (TINA) to improve governmental contracting. Under TINA, the government can reduce contract prices if the contractor overestimates its costs; however, courts have allowed contractors to offset such reductions by any underestimates of costs.

In 1986, the Federal Circuit of the U.S. Court of Appeals handed down *U.S. v. Rogerson,*[85] which seemed to expand a contractor's right of offset significantly. Specifically, it suggested a contractor could offset both intentional and unintentional cost underestimates. Within a year, after hearing from a range of interests, Congress sought to override *Rogerson.* The new law provides that contractors cannot offset cost underestimates unless such estimates are unintentional and pertain to "factual," as opposed to "judgmental," data. Perhaps not surprisingly, the distinction between factual and judgmental data has proven unwieldy. Indeed, a year after the override, members of Congress admitted the override has "created more confusion than clarity."[86]

Table 5.1   Summary of Pluralist, Capture, and Hyperpluralist Override Scenarios

Image	Scenario	Brief Definition
Pluralist	Effective deliberative revision	Following open deliberation, Congress passes a prescriptive override that precipitates judicial consensus on the override issue.
	Consensual delegation	Following open deliberation, and consistent with a broad expert consensus, Congress passes a partial override that precipitates judicial consensus on the nondelegated aspects of the override issue.
	Judicially thwarted one-sided revision	Following one-sided congressional deliberations and the passage of a prescriptive override, at least some courts rule for interests that won in the overridden judicial decision but did not participate in congressional deliberation on the override bill.
	Judicially thwarted one-sided partial revision	Following one-sided congressional deliberation and the passage of a partial override, at least some courts rule for interests that won in the overridden judicial decision on the nondelegated portion of the override issue but did not participate in congressional deliberation on the override bill.
Capture	Effective one-sided revision	Following one-sided congressional deliberation and the passage of a prescriptive override, courts uniformly rule for the winner in Congress.
	Effective one-sided partial revision	Following one-sided congressional deliberation and the passage of a partial override, courts uniformly rule for the winner in Congress on the nondelegated portion of the override issue.
	Delegation by default	Following open congressional deliberation, Congress passes a partial override, despite a broad expert consensus that Congress should have passed a prescriptive override.
Hyperpluralist	Partisan judicial resistance	Following open congressional deliberation, Congress passes a prescriptive override, which precipitates partisan judicial dissensus on the override issue.
	Weak congressional signals	Following open congressional deliberation, Congress passes a prescriptive override, which precipitates non-partisan judicial dissensus on the override issue.

Unfortunately, Congress could not muster the votes for a second override, and this confusing distinction remained on the books. Thus, instead of effectively clarifying the law based on lessons learned from litigation, members of Congress—by their own admission—passed a weak congressional signal: a prescriptive override that managed to cloud, not illuminate, the underlying issue.

Summary

What patterns of court-Congress relations underlie the override process? To begin addressing this question, this chapter described nine types of override scenarios, which flow from the logic of pluralism, capture theory, and hyperpluralism, and, for the first time, provide a systematic means to describe the potential variation in override scenarios. Table 5.1 summarizes each scenario. With these types in mind, chapter 6 operationalizes these scenarios and analyzes their distribution in the sample.

Notes

1. For a leading example of the "textualist" argument, see Anthony Scalia, *A Matter of Interpretation: Federal Courts and the Law: An Essay* (Princeton, N.J.: Princeton University Press, 1997).

2. James Madison, Federalist Paper No. 10, in *The Federalist Papers* (1788, reprint; New York: Penguin Books, 1987), 122–28.

3. For more about checks on judicial power, see Chapter 2 at pages 31–34 and accompanying notes.

4. See Terri Jennings Peretti, *In Defense of a Political Court* (Princeton, N.J.: Princeton University Press, 1999), 209–17; Cass R. Sunstein, *A Partial Constitutional* (Cambridge, Mass.: Harvard University Press, 1993), 133–45; Robert A. Dahl, *A Preface to Democratic Theory* (Chicago: University of Chicago Press, 1956), 132–34. See also Madison, Federalist Papers Nos. 10 and 51, 122–28, 318–22.

5. Sunstein, *Partial Constitution*, 137.

6. Based on this definition, "judicial invitations to override" that lead to open participation in congressional deliberation and the passage of an override that triggers judicial consensus is a subset of effective deliberative revision.

7. See Chapter 1 at pages 9–10 and accompanying notes.

8. 561 F.2d 1023 (1st Cir. 1977).

9. 561 F.2d at 1026.

10. Ibid., 1026–27.

11. Public Law 100–203, sec. 10225; United States Code Congressional and Administrative News (U.S.C.C.A.N.) (1987): 2313–711. It should be noted that *Textron* was anomalous in one respect: it took ten years to pass the override. In

the other tax cases in the sample, Congress typically acted within four years of the contested court decision.

12. See, for example, *In re Prudential Lines, Inc.*, 107 B.R. 832, 841, n. 18 (Bankr. S.D.N.Y. 1989).

13. 8 U.S.C. sec. 1182(a)(4) (1952).

14. Compare *Fluenti v. Rosenberg*, 302 F.2d 652, 658 (9th Cir. 1962) ("afflicted by psychopathic personality" is unconstitutionally vague) and *Lavoie v. INS*, 360 F.2d 27, 28 (9th Cir. 1966) (same) with *Boutilier v. INS*, 363 F.2d 488 (2d Cir. 1966) (admission of homosexuality was sufficient to exclude applicant).

15. 387 U.S. 118, 119 (1967).

16. *Matter of Longstaff*, 716 F.2d 1439, 1450 (5th Cir. 1983).

17. *Hill v. INS*, 714 F.2d 1470 (9th Cir. 1983).

18. U.S.C.C.A.N. (1990): 6736.

19. A broad computer search of the Westlaw and LEXIS databases revealed no cases from the override's enactment date to January 2001 that explicitly turned on the override issue. However, courts did indicate that the override issue was resolved in *dicta*. For example, in *Yepes-Prado v. INS*, 10 F.3d 1363 (9th Cir. 1993), the Ninth Circuit addressed the deportation of a lawful resident who had been convicted for possession of 14.25 grams of heroin. Although the case did not turn on the alien's sexual orientation, the court analyzed the 1990 amendments as part of explaining standards for deporting immigrants for illegal or objectionable conduct. Consistent with the argument that the overriding Congress resolved the issue, the Ninth Circuit stated that statutory revisions to immigration laws "evidence Congress' intent that private sexual conduct among consenting adults should no longer be considered a legitimate basis for making immigration decisions" (10 F.3d at 1369). It should be noted that a district court, in *dicta*, indicated an immigrant's homosexuality is still a factor in cases of deportation for crimes of moral turpitude (see *Toutounjian v. INS*, 959 F.Supp. 598, 603 [W.D.N.Y. 1997]). But the reasoning in *Toutounjian* is suspect; the court did not even mention the 1990 override or cite any post-override decisions. More important, this case falls far outside the override issue as Congress defined it. *Toutounjian* involves deportation for criminal activity, whereas the override issue involved deportation for homosexuality as a medical condition.

20. See generally Wayne S. Osoba, "The Legislative Response to *Anti-Monopoly*: A Missed Opportunity to Clarify the Genericness Doctrine," *University of Illinois Law Review* (1985): 197–211 (providing an overview of trademark law and the genericness doctrine).

21. Some courts adopt Learned Hand's standard: "the single question . . . is merely one of fact: What do the buyers understand by the word for whose use the parties are contending?" (*Bayer Drug Co. v. United Drug Co.*, 272 F. 505, 509 [S.D.N.Y. 1921]). Others have adopted the Supreme Court's *dicta* in *Kellogg Co. v. National Biscuit Co.*, which provides that the manufacturer "must show that the primary significance of the term in the minds of the

consuming public is not the product but the producer" (305 U.S. 111, 118 [1938]). Other courts ask whether the trademark refers to a "genus" of products or a group of products that consumers can reasonably interchange; see *Surgicenters of America, Inc. v. Medical Dental Surgeries Co.*, 601 F.2d 1011, 1014 (9th Cir. 1979); *Abercormbie & Fitch Co. v. Hunting World, Inc.*, 537 F.2d 4, 9 (2d Cir. 1976). See generally Osoba, "Legislative Response to *Anti-Monopoly*," 201–2 (describing these and other standards).

22. *Anti-Monopoly, Inc. v. General Mills Fun Group, Inc.*, 611 F.2d 296, 306 (9th Cir. 1979) (remanding for consideration of the purchasers' motivations in buying the product); *Anti-Monopoly, Inc. v. General Mills Fun Group, Inc.*, 684 F.2d 1316, 1326 (9th Cir. 1982) (reversing the district court decision after remand and holding the district court's rejection of the purchaser motivation survey was clearly erroneous), certiorari denied 459 U.S. 1227 (1983).

23. U.S.C.C.A.N. (1984): 5724 (quoting Senator Hatch's floor remarks introducing the bill).

24. See, for example, *H. Marvin Ginn v. International Association of Fore Chiefs*, 782 F.2d 987, 990 (Fed. Cir. 1986) (stating that the 1984 act clarified that "genericness" should turn on the buyers' perceptions and applying the "genus" test); *Magic Wand Inc. v. RBD, Inc.*, 940 F.2d 638, 640–1 (Fed. Cir. 1991) (stating that Congress rejected the *Anti-Monopoly* standard and employing Judge Hand's test).

25. See generally Osoba, "Legislative Response to *Anti-Monopoly*," 211. One court has explained that although it is accepted that "genericness" hinges on the perception of the purchasing public, "[t]here is no uniform test or formula to be applied in determining whether a term has become a common or generic name [in the public's perception]"; see *In re Montrachet S.A.*, 878 F.2d 375, 376 (Fed. Cir. 1989) (comparing *In re Bel Paese Sale Co.*, 1 U.S.P.Q. 1233, 1235 (TTAB 1986) (holding that magazine and newspaper articles are insufficient to render *Dolcelatte* a generic term for cheese); *In re Cooperativa Produttori Latte E Fontina Valle D'Acosta*, 230 U.S.P.Q. 131, 133 (holding that newspaper articles and dictionary definitions are enough to render *Fontina* a generic term for cheese). Moreover, lower and appellate courts often disagree on how to apply the same purchaser perception test to the same facts, even though the appellate courts use a deferential standard of review on questions of fact. See, for example, *H. Marvin Ginn Corporation*, 782 F.2d at 991 (reversing the lower court in its findings of genericness); *In re Montrachet S.A.*, 878 F.2d at 377 (same).

26. 129 *Congressional Record* E5700 (daily ed., 18 Nov. 1983).

27. See Osoba, "Legislative Response to *Anti-Monopoly*," 208–9, and accompanying notes.

28. See H.R. 4460, 98th Cong., 1st sess., sec. 2 (1983). Another issue concerns the burden of proof in genericness cases. Prior to the overrides, courts had split of the burden of proof in showing genericness. If well-established firms had captured the override process, they surely would have reversed cases that placed

the burden of proof on them, such as *Keller Products v. Rubber Linings Corp.,* 213 F.2d 382, 386 (7th Cir. 1954); *In re Meyer & Wendthe, Inc.,* 267 F.2d 945, 949 (C.C.Pa. 1959).

29. See generally Osoba, "Legislative Response to *Anti-Monopoly,*" 211–12.

30. See 129 *Congressional Record* S14379 (daily ed. 21 Oct. 1983); see also Senate Report No. 627, 98th Cong., 2d sess. (1984), 8. Senator Hatch was not alone. Representative Kastenmeier also stated that the override did not create a new test but codified existing ones. See 130 Congressional Record H10532 (daily ed., 1 Oct. 1984).

31. See Osoba, "Legislative Response to *Anti-Monopoly,*" 214.

32. See, for example, *In re Erickson,* 104 B.R. 364, 369–70 (Bankr.D.Colo. 1989); *In re Cullens,* 77 B.R. 825 (D.Colo. 1987).

33. See, for example, *In re Norman,* 95 B.R. 771, 772 (Bankr.D.Colo. 1989); *In re Ferris,* 93 B.R. 729, 731 (Bankr.D.Colo. 1988); see also *In re Hardenberg,* 42 F.3d 986, 990–91 (6th Cir. 1994) (collecting pre-override authority on both sides of the issue).

34. 495 U.S. 552 (1990).

35. 479 U.S. 36 (1986).

36. 479 U.S. at 50.

37. See, for example, *In re Hardenberg,* 42 F.3d at 991–3.

38. See, for example, C. Wright Mills, *The Power Elite* (Oxford: Oxford University Press, 1956): 8–9.

39. Ibid., 229, 244–5.

40. For classic pluralist critiques of stratificationist theory, see Robert Dahl, *Who Governs? Democracy and Power in an American City* (New Haven, Conn.: Yale University Press, 1961); Nelson Polsby, *Community Power and Political Theory* (New Haven, Conn.: Yale University Press, 1980); see also David Truman, *The Governmental Process* 2d ed. (New York: Alfred A. Knopf, 1971) (providing a standard pluralist account of the policy-making process).

41. See Marcus Olsen, *The Logic of Collective Action* (Cambridge, Mass.: Harvard University Press, 1971); George Stigler, "The Theory of Economic Regulation," *Bell Journal of Economic and Management Science* 2, no. 1 (1971): 3; Richard McKelvey, "Intransitivities in Multidimensional Voting Models and Some Implications for Agenda Control," *Journal of Economic Theory* 12 (1976): 472; see also Anthony Downs, *An Economic Theory of Democracy* (New York: Harper Collins, 1957); Kenneth Arrow, *Social Choice and Individual Values* (New Haven, Conn.: Yale University Press, 1963). For insightful overviews of these arguments, see Daniel A. Farber, "Democracy and Disgust: Reflection on Public Choice," *Chicago-Kent Law Review* 65 (1989): 161; Jerry Mashaw, "The Economics of Politics and the Understanding of Public Law," *Chicago-Kent Law Review* 65 (1989): 123.

42. See, for example, Frank Easterbrook, "Foreword: The Court and the Economic System," *Harvard Law Review* 98 (1984): 15–18 (arguing that

statutes that purport to be in the public interest are usually the product of special interest group lobbying); Frank Easterbrook, "Statutes' Domains," *University of Chicago Law Review* 50 (1983): 547–48 (arguing that statutes are likely to be the product of arbitrary agenda-setting). It should be emphasized that the term *public choice theory* represents a bit of a catchall. Any given public choice theorist would surely add a number of caveats and exceptions. As stressed in the text, however, my goal is not to summarize individual authors. Instead, I seek to characterize a style of argument about how organizational dynamics combined with fragmented political authority systematically advantage certain groups.

43. Stigler, "Theory of Economic Regulation," 5. According to Stigler, firms will prefer limits on competition because direct subsidies will only draw competitors into the market and the subsidies will have to be shared (ibid., 5). It should also be noted that Stigler recognizes that the benefits of regulation have limits—namely, regulation shifts control within an industry from large firms with market share to smaller firms with political clout, it is costly, and regulation subjects industry to forces that often do not have access to the board room but do have access to political forums (ibid., 6–7). These factors, however, are predictable and can be factored into the calculus to acquire regulation (ibid., 7). For an overview of "rent-seeking" or DUPs ("directly unproductive, profit-seeking" activities), see Robert D. Tollison, "Rent Seeking: A Survey," *Kyklos* 35, no. 4 (1982): 575–98; Jagdish N. Bagwati, "Directly Unproductive, Profit-Seeking (DUP) Activities," *Journal of Political Economy* 90, no. 5 (1984): 988–1000; Warren J. Samuels and Nicholas Mercuro, "A Critique of Rent-Seeking Theory," in *Neoclassical Political Economy: The Analysis of Rent-Seeking and DUP Activities*, ed. David C. Collander (Cambridge, Mass.: Ballinger Publishing, 1984), 55–70.

44. Stigler, "Theory of Economic Regulation," 12.

45. For an excellent overview of the problematic nature of the concept of political mandates, see Nelson Polsby and Aaron Wildavsky, *Presidential Elections: Strategies and Structures of American Politics* (Chatham, N.J.: Chatham House Publishers, 2000), 262–65.

46. Stigler, "Theory of Economic Regulation," 13. For a fuller discussion of the free rider or collection action problem, see Olsen, *The Logic of Collective Action*, part I, 5–52. For a balanced assessment of Olsen's analysis, see Jack L. Walker Jr. et al., *Mobilizing Interest Groups in America: Patrons, Professions and Social Movements* (Ann Arbor: University of Michigan Press, 1991), 45–51; see also Donald Green and Ian Shapiro, *Pathologies of Rational Choice: A Critique of Applications in Political Science* (New Haven, Conn.: Yale University Press, 1994).

47. Marc Galanter, "Why the 'Haves' Come Out Ahead: Speculations on the Limits of Legal Change," *Law & Society Review* 9 (1974): 95. For more on Galanter's argument, see the articles collected in *Law & Society Review* 33, no. 4 (1999).

48. See, for example, Michael Axline, "Forest Health and the Politics of Expediency," *Environmental Law* 26 (1996): 613 (criticizing the Salvage Logging Rider); Victor M. Sher and Carol Sue Hunting, "Eroding the Landscape, Eroding the Laws: Congressional Exemptions from Judicial Review of Environmental Laws," *Harvard Environmental Law Review* 15 (1991): 435 (discussing a string of congressional overrides of judicial environmental law decisions). For a contrary view of the Salvage Logging Rider, see Senator Slade Gorton and Julie Kays, "Legislative History of the Timber and Salvage Amendments Enacted in the 104th Congress: A Small Victory for Timber Communities in the Pacific Northwest," *Environmental Law* 26 (1996): 641.

49. Cf Kevin R. Johnson, "*Los Olvidados:* Images of the Immigrant, Political Power of Noncitizens, and Immigration Law and Enforcement," *BYU Law Review* (1993): 1139.

50. See Chapter 1 at pages 10–12 and accompanying notes.

51. See *U.S. v. Ueber* 299 F.2d 310, 314 (6th Cir. 1962).

52. 31 U.S.C. sec. 3731(c). In the Senate Report, Congress explained: "[N]otwithstanding the fact that the act permits a treble recovery, [claims] would be governed by the traditional civil burden of proof. The Committee notes in support of this proposition that the U.S. Supreme Court has upheld such a burden in cases of securities fraud and antitrust provisions" (U.S.C.C.A.N. [1986]: 5296).

53. See, for example, *Commercial Contractors, Inc. v. U.S.*, 154 F.3d 1357, 1362 (Fed. Cir. 1998); *Hagwood v. Sonoma County Water Agency*, 81 F.3d 1465, 1472 (9th Cir. 1996) (collecting Ninth Circuit authority); *Brooks v. U.S.*, 64 F.3d 251, 255 (7th Cir. 1995).

54. For more on the hyperpluralist view, see Chapter 3 at 66–68 and accompanying notes.

55. See generally Gregory Sisk, "Tucker Act Appeals to the Federal Circuit," *Federal Bar News & Journal* 36, no. 1 (January 1989): 41–5 (providing an overview of statutory framework and pre-override law); Gregory Sisk, "Two Proposals to Clarify the Tucker Act Jurisdiction of the Claims Court," *Federal Bar News & Journal* 37, no. 1 (January 1990): 47–9 (same).

56. See, for example, Sisk, "Two Proposals," 49; see also Justice Scalia's dissent in *Bowen v. Massachusetts*, 487 U.S. 879, 930 (1988), stating that "[n]othing is more wasteful than litigation about where to litigate particularly when they are all courts within the same legal system applying the same law."

57. One might argue that strategically motivated judges may see delegation by default and consensual delegation as functionally equivalent. After all, both cases result in partial overrides, which invite some judicial policy-making. I agree, but that is not the point. The point is that delegation by default and consensual delegation represent different types of *congressional* behavior from the perspective of pluralism and hyperpluralism.

58. U.S.C.C.A.N. (1988): 6014.

59. Ibid.

60. Based on the legislative record, it is difficult to assess precisely why Congress could not reach agreement on a prescriptive override. It may have simply been a matter of time, because the bill came up at the end of the session. However, this would not explain why Congress did not revisit the issue in later sessions. It may be that Congress, as a strategic matter, wanted to hand off tough issues to the courts, but this seems unlikely given the broad consensus favoring comprehensive congressional action. The more likely possibility, it seems to me, is that members of Congress agreed they should resolve the override issue, but could not agree on the specifics. However, Congress's ultimate reason—or combination of reasons—is beside the point. From the perspective of hyperpluralism, the point is that Congress passed the buck, despite an expert consensus that Congress should have tried to resolve the override issue.

61. See, for example, *Mitchell v. U.S.* 930 F.2d 893, 895 (Fed. Cir. 1991) (vacating district court on jurisdictional grounds and stating that the override "expedites resolution of complex Tucker Act disputes" and that concurrent jurisdiction of district and claims courts "raised thorny jurisdictional issues").

62. For more on why Congress may defer to the courts, see Mark Graber, "The Nonmajoritarian Difficulty: Legislative Deference to the Judiciary," *Studies in American Political Development* 7 (1993): 35. For an interesting transaction cost analysis of congressional delegation to agencies, see David Epstein and Sharyn O'Halloran, *Delegating Powers: A Transaction Cost Politics Approach to Making Policy Under Separate Powers* (Cambridge: Cambridge University Press, 1999).

63. 29 U.S.C. sec. 623(f)(2) (1967).

64. Compare *Brennan v. Taft Broadcasting Co.*, 500 F.2d 212 (5th Cir. 1974) with *United Airlines v. McMann*, 542 F.2d 217 (4th Cir. 1976).

65. 434 U.S. 192 (1977).

66. 434 U.S. at 203.

67. Ibid., 217.

68. Specifically, Congress added the following language to section 4(f)(2) of the ADEA: "and no such seniority system or employee benefit plan shall require or permit the involuntary retirement of any individual . . . because of the age of such individual" codified at 11 U.S.C. sec. 623(f)(2) (1978).

69. James J. Brudney, "Congressional Commentary on Judicial Interpretations of Statutes: Idle Chatter or Telling Response," *Michigan Law Review* 93, no. 1 (1994): 97–99.

70. 848 F.2d 692 (6th Cir. 1988).

71. 848 F.2d at 694.

72. Ibid., 700.

73. *Public Employees Retirement System of Ohio v. Betts*, 492 U.S. 158 (1988).

74. 492 U.S. at 168.

75. Ibid., 194.

76. Public Law No. 101-443, sec. 101 (1990).

77. See, for example, *Auerbach v. Board of Education,* 136 F.3d 104, 111 (1998).

78. 42 U.S.C. sec. 12201(c) (1991).

79. 82 F.3d 1059 (1996).

80. 82 F.3d at 1065.

81. Ibid.

82. U.S.C.C.A.N. (1990): 303, 419 (emphasis added).

83. 136 *Congressional Record* S9697 (daily ed., 13 July 1990).

84. Ibid., H4623; see also Representative Waxman's comments, H4626. For an argument supporting my reading of the legislative history, see Brudney, "Congressional Commentary on Judicial Interpretations of Statutes," 99–100 fn 395; for a different view, see David Copus and Glen Nager, "Benefit Plan Limitations After the Americans with Disabilities Act," *Employment Relations Law Journal* (1993): 77.

85. 785 F.2d 296, 297 (Fed. Cir. 1986).

86. H.R. Conf. Rep. No. 100-446, 100th Cong., 2d sess. (1987) quoted in Colleen A. Preston, "Truth in Negotiations Act: Is a New Definition of 'Cost or Pricing Data' Necessary?" *Federal Bar News & Journal* 34, no. 10 (1987): 451.

6 Operationalization of Typology, Findings, and Discussion

Chapter 5 introduced a typology of nine potential override scenarios: pluralism's effective deliberative revision, consensual delegation, judicially thwarted one-sided revision, and judicially thwarted one-sided partial revision; capture theory's effective one-sided revision and effective one-sided partial revision; and hyperpluralism's delegation by default, partisan judicial resistance, and weak congressional signals. The goals were to place each override scenario within the context of a broader theory of interbranch relations and illustrate the potentially rich diversity of court-Congress relations in connection with the passage of overrides.

This chapter develops a systematic framework for coding these scenarios and analyzes the passage of overrides along three main dimensions: (1) the openness of congressional deliberation, (2) the comprehensiveness of override signals, and (3) the nature of judicial responses to congressional override activity. To explain the framework, this chapter moves from the general to the specific. It begins by presenting a typology of congressional override activity. It then locates the alternative pluralist, capture, and hyperpluralist override scenarios within each mode of congressional override activity. With this overview in place, it fills in the details, explaining the measurement of key concepts. Finally, it summarizes and discusses the results.

The data show that the passage of overrides encompasses a wide range of pluralist, capture, and hyperpluralist scenarios. Within this diversity of override scenarios, several patterns emerged. First, the majority of cases involve some form of pluralism. Indeed, the most common override scenario by far was the pluralist ideal of effective deliberative revision, in which congressional deliberation is open, Congress passes a prescriptive override, and the override triggers judicial consensus. Second, contrary to capture theory, the override process is almost always open and does not systematically favor repeat players. Indeed, in almost three-quarters of the cases, the overriding Congress *reversed* court decisions that favored repeat players.

Third, contrary to hyperpluralism, Congress did not typically pass the buck in the sample, even though competing interest groups converged on Congress and the override issues were highly divisive. Specifically, in about three-quarters of the cases, open deliberation produced prescriptive overrides that sought to resolve the override issue. Moreover, when Congress passed partial overrides, which delegated significant aspects of the override issue to the courts, members of Congress did not engage in delegation by default, as in the case of the Judicial Improvements Act. Instead, similar to the Trademark Clarification Act, Congress engaged in consensual delegation, in which experts widely supported Congress's decision to give courts some flexibility on the override issue.

At the same time, it would be a mistake to dismiss the hyperpluralist view, because a substantial minority of cases involved some form of hyperpluralism, especially weak congressional signals and partisan judicial resistance: cases in which congressional deliberation is open, Congress passes a prescriptive override, but the override fails to resolve the override issue, as indicated by post-override judicial dissensus. Instead, the data show that the passage of overrides is open, but open deliberation produces a variety of pluralist and hyperpluralist override scenarios. The next chapter examines that variation and generates hypotheses about the dynamics of pluralism versus hyperpluralism in the sample.

Four Ideal Types of Congressional Override Activity

Table 6.1 sets forth the typology of congressional override activity. The horizontal dimension reflects the openness of congressional deliberations on the override bill, as primarily indicated by a content analysis of witness lists and congressional testimony. This dimension creates a continuum from *open* congressional deliberations, cases in which Congress acts after hearing from diverse interests on the override issue, to *one-sided* congressional deliberations, cases in which Congress acts after hearing only from interests that lost in the overridden court decision. The vertical dimension refers to the comprehensiveness of the override signal, meaning the extent to which the override bill attempts to resolve the override issue (as defined by the overriding Congress). This dimension creates a continuum from *prescriptive* overrides, overrides that seek to resolve the override issue comprehensively, to *partial* overrides, overrides that explicitly delegate significant aspects of the override issue to the courts.

Table 6.1 Typology of Congressional Override Activity

Comprehensiveness of the Override Bill	*Openness of Congressional Deliberation on the Override Bill*	
	Open Deliberation ⟵⟶	*One-Sided Deliberation*
Prescriptive Overrides	Attempted deliberative revision	Attempted one-sided revision
↕		
Partial Overrides	Attempted deliberative partial revision	Attempted one-sided partial revision

Pushing these continua to their extremes produces four "ideal types" of congressional override activity:

- **attempted deliberative revision**, cases in which Congress passes prescriptive overrides following open deliberation;
- **attempted one-sided revision**, cases in which Congress passes prescriptive overrides following one-sided deliberation;
- **attempted one-sided partial revision**, cases in which Congress passes partial overrides following one-sided deliberation; and
- **attempted deliberative partial revision**, cases in which Congress passes partial overrides following open deliberation.

Types of Congressional Override Activity and Pluralist, Capture, and Hyperpluralist Override Scenarios

As seen in Table 6.2, each type of congressional override activity encompasses a range of override scenarios. To understand this framework, it is useful to examine each mode of congressional override activity separately. Once the relationship between the types of congressional override activity and specific override scenarios is laid out, specific issues of measurement can be addressed.

Attempted Deliberative Revision: A Closer Look. Attempted deliberative revision, cases in which Congress passes prescriptive overrides after open deliberation, involves one of three override scenarios: pluralism's effective deliberative revision, hyperpluralism's partisan judicial resistance, or weak congressional signals. The threshold question in coding these scenarios is whether the override triggers judicial consensus, as indicated primarily by uniform, non-partisan judicial consensus that comports with

Table 6.2   Locating the Pluralist, Capture, and Hyperpluralist Override Scenarios in the Landscape of Congressional Override Activity

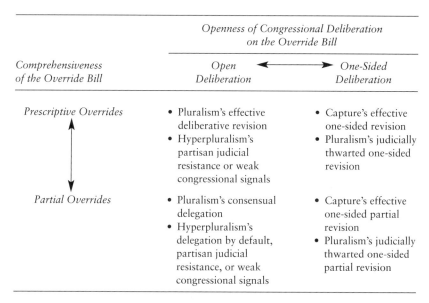

Comprehensiveness of the Override Bill	*Openness of Congressional Deliberation on the Override Bill*	
	Open Deliberation ←——————→	*One-Sided Deliberation*
Prescriptive Overrides ↑	• Pluralism's effective deliberative revision • Hyperpluralism's partisan judicial resistance or weak congressional signals	• Capture's effective one-sided revision • Pluralism's judicially thwarted one-sided revision
↓ *Partial Overrides*	• Pluralism's consensual delegation • Hyperpluralism's delegation by default, partisan judicial resistance, or weak congressional signals	• Capture's effective one-sided partial revision • Pluralism's judicially thwarted one-sided partial revision

the language and legislative history of the override bill. If attempted deliberative revision triggers judicial consensus, the override process involves pluralism's effective deliberative revision.[1]

If attempted deliberative revision triggers judicial dissensus, the override process involves hyperpluralism's partisan judicial resistance or weak congressional signals. Identifying these scenarios turns on whether the post-override judicial dissensus is partisan, as primarily indicated by the existence of splits among judges appointed by Democratic versus Republican presidents. If courts split along *partisan* lines following the passage of the override, it was assumed that judicial dissensus reflected resistance to congressional oversight by politically selected federal judges, and the case was coded as partisan judicial resistance. If post-override judicial dissensus was *non-partisan,* it was assumed that the dissensus reflected judicial refinement of unclear congressional signals, and the case was categorized as weak congressional signals. Table 6.3 summarizes attempted deliberative revision and its related override scenarios.

Attempted One-Sided Revision: A Closer Look.   Attempted one-sided revision, cases in which Congress passes prescriptive overrides after one-sided deliberations, involves capture theory's effective one-sided revision or pluralism's judicially thwarted one-sided revision. The key issue in

Table 6.3   Attempted Deliberative Revision: A Closer Look

		Common Congressional Attributes		Distinguishing Attributes		
Type of Override Scenario	Name of Override Scenario	Open Congressional Deliberation	Prescriptive Override	Post-Override Judicial Consensus	Post-Override Partisan Judicial Dissensus	Post-Override Non-Partisan Judicial Dissensus
Pluralist	Effective deliberative revision	X	X	X		
Hyper-pluralist	Partisan judicial resistance	X	X		X	
	Weak congressional signals	X	X			X

Key coding questions:
• Did the override effectively trigger judicial consensus?
• If not, is post-override judicial dissensus partisan?

coding these scenarios is whether the override triggers judicial consensus in favor of the winner in Congress. If so, the override process involves effective one-sided revision because interest groups unilaterally appealed to the overriding Congress and then cemented their legislative gains with post-override court victories. If judicial dissensus emerges following the override, the override process involves judicially thwarted one-sided revision: cases in which at least some judges blunt the effects of one-sided congressional deliberations by ruling for groups that won in the overridden decision but failed to participate in the passage of the override bill. Table 6.4 summarizes attempted one-sided revision and its related override scenarios.

It is important to stress that when congressional deliberation is one-sided, the partisanship of post-override judicial behavior is irrelevant from the perspective of capture theory and pluralism.[2] Under the logic of capture theory, the issue is whether groups that dominated congressional deliberation win in court as well, regardless of the partisan nature of judicial decision-making. Under pluralism, when congressional deliberation is one-sided, the issue is whether courts check Congress by ruling for groups

Table 6.4 Attempted One-Sided Revision: A Closer Look

Type of Override Scenario	Name of Override Scenario	Common Congressional Attributes		Distinguishing Attributes	
		One-Sided Congressional Deliberation	Prescriptive Override	Post-Override Judicial Consensus	Post-Override Judicial Dissensus
Capture	Effective one-sided revision	X	X	X	
Pluralist	Judicially thwarted one-sided revision	X	X		X

Key coding question:
- Did the override effectively trigger judicial consensus in favor of the winner in Congress?

that did not have a voice in the legislative process, regardless of whether courts rule along partisan lines. Indeed, pluralists would argue a benefit of politically selected judges is that such judges are more likely to act independently and consider the fairness of the statute before applying it. Of course, judicial independence has a potential downside from the perspective of pluralism as well: politically selected, independent judges may be more likely to cross the line into hyperpluralism and resist congressional signals following open deliberation. The threat of hyperpluralism does not exist when congressional deliberations are one-sided, however, because hyperpluralism, by definition, involves competing interest groups throughout the policy-making process.

Attempted One-Sided Partial Revision: A Closer Look. Attempted one-sided partial revision, cases in which Congress passes partial overrides following one-sided congressional deliberation, entails capture theory's effective one-sided partial revision or pluralism's judicially thwarted one-sided partial revision. The issue in coding these scenarios is whether the override process triggers judicial consensus on the *nondelegated* aspects of the override issue in favor of the winner in Congress. If so, the override process involves capture theory's effective one-sided partial revision because, in uniformly ruling for the winner in Congress, courts lock in the results of one-sided congressional deliberation.

Table 6.5 Attempted One-Sided Partial Revision: A Closer Look

				Distinguishing Attributes	
		Common Congressional Attributes		Post-Override Judicial Consensus on the	Post-Override Judicial Dissensus on the
Type of Override Scenario	Name of Override Scenario	One-Sided Congressional Deliberation	Partial Override	Override Issue's Nondelegated Aspects	Override Issue's Nondelegated Aspects
Capture	Effective one-sided partial revision	X	X	X	
Pluralist	Judicially thwarted one-sided partial revision	X	X		X

Key coding question:
- Did the override effectively trigger judicial consensus on the nondelegated aspects of the override issue in favor of the winner in Congress?

If the partial override fails to trigger judicial consensus on the nondelegated aspects of the override issue, the override process involves pluralism's judicially thwarted one-sided partial revision. The argument is that judicial dissensus on the nondelegated aspects of the override issue checks one-sided deliberation, in that courts give voice to interests that failed to participate in Congress on the override issue. Table 6.5 summarizes attempted one-sided partial revision and its related override scenarios.

Attempted Deliberative Partial Revision: A Closer Look. Attempted deliberative partial revision, cases in which Congress passes partial overrides following open congressional deliberations, represents the most complex mode of congressional override activity. It encompasses four override scenarios: pluralism's consensual delegation and hyperpluralism's delegation by default, partisan judicial resistance, and weak congressional signals.

Coding these scenarios involves several steps. If the partial override fails to trigger judicial consensus on the *nondelegated* aspects of the override, then the override process involves hyperpluralism's partisan judicial resistance or weak congressional signals. Why? Consistent with hyperpluralism, the overriding Congress sends a signal on significant aspects of an override issue and its signal fails to clarify the law. The issue then becomes whether the judicial dissensus on the nondelegated aspects of the override is partisan. If so, the case involves partisan judicial resistance. If not, the case involves weak congressional signals.

If the partial override effectively triggers judicial consensus on the nondelegated aspects of the override, then the issue is whether the overriding Congress's decision to delegate is consistent with pluralism's consensual delegation or hyperpluralism's delegation by default. Distinguishing these scenarios turns on a content analysis of the legislative record and expert commentary at the time of the override's passage. If experts widely endorsed the passage of a partial override, the case involved consensual delegation. If experts urged Congress to pass a prescriptive override but Congress enacts a partial override, the case was coded as delegation by default. Table 6.6 summarizes attempted deliberative partial revision and its related override scenarios.

Measuring the Key Concepts

Coding congressional override activity under this typology requires an assessment of whether congressional deliberations on the override bill are open or one-sided, and whether Congress passes a prescriptive or partial override. Coding override scenarios within each mode of congressional override activity requires an assessment of (1) whether the override triggers judicial consensus on the nondelegated aspects of the override issue; (2) whether post-override judicial dissensus is partisan; and (3) whether the passage of partial overrides following open congressional deliberation is consensual or by default. Measurement of each concept is discussed in the following sections.

Determining the Openness of Congressional Deliberations.   Coding congressional override activity turns, in part, on whether congressional deliberation on the override bill is open or one-sided. The analysis involved several steps. First, a research assistant and I performed a content analysis of the witness lists and congressional testimony on the override bill to determine whether competing interests testified in Congress on the override issue. Congressional deliberation was deemed open if one of the following conditions was satisfied: (1) the competing litigants in the overridden court decision, or closely related interest groups, testified on the override bill; (2) public interest groups testified in Congress against the override; (3) industry representatives testified on both sides of the issue; or (4) governmental interests testified against the override. If only the loser in the overridden decision—or their allies—testified, congressional deliberation was coded as one-sided.

Pluralists and hyperpluralists, who predict open congressional deliberation, might object that analyzing congressional testimony will systematically

Table 6.6 Attempted Deliberative Partial Revision: A Closer Look

Type of Override Scenario	Name of Override Scenario	Common Congressional Attributes		Distinguishing Attributes			
		Open Congressional Deliberation	Partial Overrides	Expert Consensus Supporting Delegation	Expert Consensus Against Delegation	Post-Override Partisan Judicial Dissensus on Override Issue's Nondelegated Aspects	Post-Override Non-Partisan Judicial Dissensus on Override Issue's Nondelegated Aspects
Pluralist	Consensual delegation	X	X	X			
Hyperpluralist	Delegation by default	X	X		X		
	Partisan judicial resistance	X	X			X	
	Weak congressional signals	X	X				X

Key coding questions:
- Did the override effectively trigger judicial consensus on the nondelegated aspects of the override issue?
- If the override triggers judicial dissensus on the nondelegated aspects of the override issue, is post-override judicial dissensus partisan?
- If the override effectively triggers judicial consensus on the nondelegated aspects of the override issue, did an expert consensus support the overriding Congress's decision to delegate significant aspects of the issue to the courts?

undercount levels of participation. After all, there are back as well as front channels in Washington. As a result, groups may participate in congressional deliberations but fail to testify publicly. In addition, groups may have the opportunity to participate but believe their participation is fruitless, and hence voluntarily forego testifying on the override measure. If so, the process may offer ample opportunities for participation, even if not all groups choose to participate.

The response is two-fold. First, congressional testimony probably does reflect most participants on an issue. As Jeffrey Berry argues, groups have strong incentives to testify because testifying before Congress may legitimize participation in the policy-making process down the road; it may provide valuable public relations fodder for group newsletters and fund drives; and it may serve as a public platform for group leaders.[3] In addition, as an empirical matter, groups indicate that they routinely testify before Congress. Indeed, Kay Scholzman's and John Tierney's survey of Washington lobbyists found that 99 percent of their respondents testified on Capitol Hill.[4] Second, and more important, even if congressional testimony undercounts levels of participation, such bias is not problematic for the analysis. Indeed, it would only strengthen the finding that, contrary to capture theory, the passage of overrides is open.

Capture theorists might object that testifying in Congress is merely window dressing, providing a veneer of participation while the "real" decisions are made behind closed doors. If so, analyzing congressional testimony would systematically overcount levels of political participation in the override process and bias the findings toward open deliberations. Because the data show that the passage of overrides is open, such bias would be problematic.

It is tempting to dismiss this objection on methodological grounds, arguing that it cannot be falsified. On one hand, if congressional testimony is one-sided, the process is seen as captured. On the other hand, if a wide range of groups testifies, their testimony should be disregarded as cover for the real decision-making process. Thus, regardless of the observed pattern of interest group participation, one cannot disprove whether congressional testimony is symbolic. This response, however, is too facile.

A better response is to give capture theory the benefit of any doubt and take seriously the possibility that testifying before Congress is symbolic. Accordingly, the procedural analysis of congressional deliberations is buttressed with two substantive analyses. First, if testifying before Congress is window dressing and the real decisions were made behind closed doors, we would expect Congress to pass overrides that systematically benefit repeat players at the expense of one-shotters, who presumably lack the organizational wherewithal and long-standing political relationships to pursue their agendas effectively in multiple policy-making forums. Specifically, we would expect Congress to reverse court decisions that ruled against repeat players and in favor of one-shotters. Accordingly, I compared winners and losers under the overridden decisions versus winners and losers under the override statute, and evaluated whether repeat players used Congress as a kind of specialized court of appeals to overturn objectionable pre-override court cases.

Second, if Congress largely ignored testimony from competing interests, these interests would presumably denounce the override as unfair or arbitrary or defend the overridden decision. After all, having already testified before Congress, these groups would be well prepared to take their case to the media and relevant professional journals. Accordingly, I examined expert commentary on the override and overridden decisions, and assessed whether groups argued that the overriding Congress had acted unfairly or imprudently.

Determining the Comprehensiveness of the Override Bill.   The next issue in coding congressional override activity is whether Congress passes prescriptive overrides, which seek to resolve the override issue, or partial overrides that explicitly delegate significant aspects of the override issue to the courts. In addressing this issue, I performed a content analysis of the override bill and related legislative history. Specifically, as discussed in Chapter 4, an override was coded as a partial override if the overriding Congress (1) expressly directs courts to develop some significant aspect of the override issue; (2) explicitly remains neutral on an aspect of the policy area related to the override issue that divided the courts in the pre-override period; or (3) adopts an inherently vague standard of reasonableness or fairness (or their equivalent, such as an "all events" test). If none of these conditions were met, the bill was coded as a prescriptive override.

It is worth stressing that categorization turns on an independent assessment of Congress's stated intent as expressed in the statute and legislative history. As a result, coding partial overrides does *not* rest on an assessment of Congress's "actual" intent. Indeed, it is doubtful that any such thing exists.[5] At best, statutes and legislative history reflect a variety of intents, not all of which are consistent or readily apparent. In addition, no claims are made as to what judges may believe when construing the override or its legislative history. Finally, as discussed in Chapter 4, characterizing the scope of the override issue—as well as what portions of the override issue are delegated and nondelegated—turned on an assessment of the overriding Congress's stated understanding of the issue.[6]

Determining Whether the Override Triggers Judicial Consensus. Once the type of congressional override activity is determined, we must identify the underlying override scenario. A central issue at this stage is whether an override triggers judicial consensus on the nondelegated aspects of the override issue. Coding post-override judicial consensus was discussed at length in Chapter 4.[7] To reiterate briefly, the primary indicator of judicial consensus is consistent rule application under the override. The validity of this measure was checked by analyzing the following factors: (1) whether the judicial consensus emerged among judges appointed by Democratic and Republican presidents; (2) whether Congress sent subsequent signals indicating that courts had misconstrued the override; and (3) whether the winner in pre-override litigation lost in the post-override period. The primary indicators of judicial dissensus are circuit splits, reversals, and dissents on statutory grounds.

Determining Whether Post-Override Judicial Dissensus Is Partisan. If attempted deliberative revision or attempted partial deliberative revision failed to trigger judicial consensus on the nondelegated aspects of the override issue, the case involved hyperpluralism's partisan judicial resistance or weak congressional signals. As noted earlier, the partisan nature of post-override judicial dissensus was examined to distinguish these cases. If courts split along partisan lines following the passage of the override, the case was coded as partisan judicial resistance. If post-override judicial dissensus was non-partisan, the case was categorized as weak congressional signals.

The coding of partisan splits involved two steps, which have already been outlined. To reiterate: if the case involved a Supreme Court decision, the issue was whether Supreme Court justices split on the override issue along partisan lines, as indicated primarily in the sample by a split between Justices Rehnquist, who was appointed as a Supreme Court Justice by President Nixon and appointed as Chief Justice by President Reagan, and Justice Marshall, who was appointed by President Johnson.

If there was no Supreme Court decision, the issue was whether judges appointed by Democratic and Republican presidents interpreted the statute differently. I also examined whether judicial consensus spanned judges appointed by different Democratic and Republican presidents, recognizing that ideological differences exist among Democratic appointees, such as Johnson, Carter, and Clinton appointees, as well as Republican appointees, such as Ford, Reagan, and Bush appointees. Admittedly, such measures are not perfect, because not all judges toe their appointing president's party line. But they are reasonable measures. After all, numerous studies find a significant relationship between the party of the appointing president and judges' voting patterns in controversial policy areas.[8]

Determining Whether the Passage of Partial Overrides Is Consensual. In cases of attempted deliberative partial revision, where Congress passes a partial override following open congressional deliberations, we must assess whether Congress's decision to delegate was consensual or by default (in addition to assessing whether the override triggered judicial consensus). To identify consensual versus by default delegation, I examined whether experts supported the passage of a partial override, as indicated by a content analysis of the legislative history and contemporaneous expert commentary. If experts agreed that Congress should give courts some discretion on the override issue, the case was coded as consensual delegation. If experts urged Congress to pass a prescriptive override, but Congress failed to do so, the case was categorized as delegation by default.

This content analysis was corroborated in several ways. In cases of consensual delegation, the overriding Congress typically indicates that the overridden decision (or decisions) represents an anomalous interpretation of the original statute. I verified these claims with reference to the pre-override cases and secondary legal literature. In addition, in consensual delegation, policy-makers frequently assert that experts agree on the override issue involving a fact-intensive inquiry, which defies bright-line rules. Oftentimes this can be checked in the secondary literature, especially law review articles. For example, when the Trademark Clarification Act passed, legal commentators agreed that courts needed some discretion to adapt the definition of genericness on a case-by-case basis as well as to decide what constitutes relevant evidence of genericness. By contrast, when the Judicial Improvements Act passed, legal commentators agreed that Congress should have passed a prescriptive override aimed at ending wasteful litigation over where to litigate Tucker Act claims. Indeed, members of the overriding Congress conceded that the Judicial Improvements Act represented a stopgap procedural measure and that underlying jurisdictional issues would have to be revisited. Of course, law professors have their own political axes to grind, but in coding the cases, indications of broad expert consensus were sought.

Reliability.   In order to make credible inferences from the sample, coding procedures must be reliable. That is, the coding must measure actual variation in the cases, as opposed to idiosyncrasies of the analyst. To assess reliability, a third party independently coded a 30-percent random sample of the cases. I measured the degree of significance of inter-coder agreement using Kappa. As seen in Table 6.7, the analysis shows that had we coded the cases randomly (but with the probabilities equal to the overall proportion of cases), we would have expected agreement in about 26 percent of the cases. However, we agreed in all 30 cases (or 100 percent), which is significantly above that which would be expected by chance ($p < .001$).

Summary of Findings

As seen in Table 6.8, attempted deliberative revision is the predominant mode of congressional override activity, more than tripling the next most common mode, attempted deliberative partial revision. Specifically, there

Table 6.7   Inter-Coder Agreement

Scenario Type	Override Scenario	Coder 1	Coder 2
Pluralist	Effective deliberative revision	13	13
	Consensual delegation	3	3
	Judicially thwarted one-sided revision	1	1
Capture	Effective one-sided revision	3	3
Hyperpluralist	Delegation by default	1	1
	Partisan judicial resistance	4	4
	Weak congressional signals	5	5
	Totals	30	30

$N = 30$
Agreement: 100%
Expected agreement: 26%
Kappa = 1.0
$Z = 10.90$
$p < .001$

Table 6.8   Distribution of Congressional Override Activity

Comprehensiveness of the Override Bill	Openness of Congressional Deliberation on the Override Bill		Totals
	Open Deliberation ⟵⟶	One-Sided Deliberation	
Prescriptive Overrides ↕ Partial Overrides	Attempted deliberative revision: 74	Attempted one-sided revision: 5	79
	Attempted deliberative partial revision: 21	Attempted one-sided partial revision: 0	21
Totals	95	5	100

were 74 cases of attempted deliberative revision, 21 cases of attempted deliberative partial revision, 5 cases of attempted one-sided revision, and 0 cases of attempted one-sided partial revision.

Several trends bear emphasis. In 95 of 100 cases, congressional deliberations on the override bill were open. In addition, Congress typically tried to resolve the override issue. In 79 of 100 cases, Congress passed a prescriptive override. When Congress did engage in one-sided deliberations, it did not pass partial overrides in the sample; instead, it passed prescriptive overrides that sought to resolve the override issue in favor of groups that had testified without opposition.

Figures 6.1 and 6.2 depict the range of override scenarios in the sample. Figure 6.1 summarizes the overall distribution of pluralist, capture, and

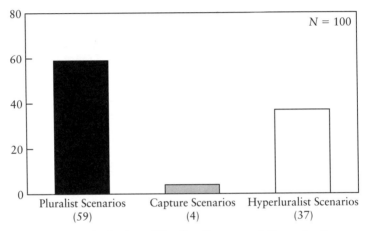

FIGURE 6.1   Distribution of Pluralist, Capture, and Hyperpluralist Override Scenarios

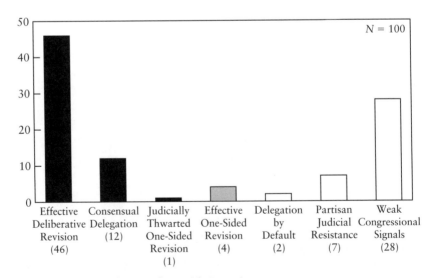

FIGURE 6.2   Distribution of Override Scenarios

hyperpluralist cases in the sample; Figure 6.2 breaks down the sample into specific override scenarios. (Note that Figures 6.1 and 6.2 are color coded: pluralist override processes are black; captured override processes are gray; and hyperpluralist override processes are white.) As seen in Figure 6.1, the sample encompassed pluralist, capture, and hyperpluralist override scenarios. Pluralist scenarios make up 59 of 100 cases; capture scenarios comprise 4 of 100 cases; and hyperpluralist scenarios account for the remaining 37 of 100 cases.

As seen in Figure 6.2, the sample also encompassed diverse types of override scenarios. It included examples of pluralism's effective deliberative revision, consensual delegation, and judicially thwarted one-sided revision; capture theory's effective one-sided revision; and hyperpluralism's delegation by default, partisan judicial resistance, and weak congressional signals.

Within this diversity, note several tendencies. The most common scenario is effective deliberative revision, accounting for nearly half—or 46 of 100—of all cases. The next most common scenario is weak congressional signals, which make up more than one-quarter of the cases—or 28 of 100—which more than doubles the next most common scenario, consensual delegation, which accounts for 12 of 100 of the cases.

Table 6.9 brings these perspectives together, organizing the distribution of override scenarios under each type of congressional override activity.

Table 6.9   Summary of Findings

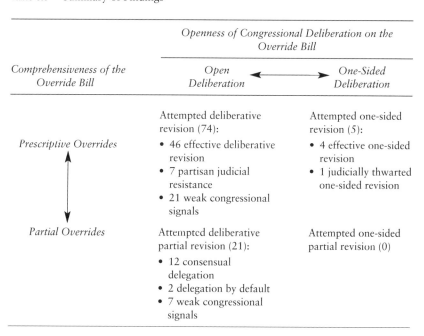

Comprehensiveness of the Override Bill	Openness of Congressional Deliberation on the Override Bill	
	Open Deliberation ←————→	*One-Sided Deliberation*
Prescriptive Overrides	Attempted deliberative revision (74): • 46 effective deliberative revision • 7 partisan judicial resistance • 21 weak congressional signals	Attempted one-sided revision (5): • 4 effective one-sided revision • 1 judicially thwarted one-sided revision
Partial Overrides	Attempted deliberative partial revision (21): • 12 consensual delegation • 2 delegation by default • 7 weak congressional signals	Attempted one-sided partial revision (0)

Using this table, we see that 46 of 74 cases (62 percent) of attempted deliberative revision involved effective deliberative revision, in which open congressional deliberations and the passage of a prescriptive override trigger judicial consensus on the override issue. In the 74 cases of attempted deliberative revision, 28 (38 percent) failed to trigger judicial consensus. Of these cases, 7 (25 percent) involved partisan judicial resistance and 21 (75 percent) involved weak congressional signals.

Under attempted deliberative partial revision, only 2 of 21 cases (9 percent) entailed delegation by default, in which experts unsuccessfully urged Congress to pass a prescriptive override. In the remaining 19 cases (91 percent), experts supported the passage of a partial override. Not all of these cases, however, involve pluralism's consensual delegation, because consensual delegation requires judicial consensus on the nondelegated aspects of the override issue. Instead, 12 of these 19 cases (63 percent) involved consensual delegation. In the remaining 7 cases (37 percent), the partial override did not trigger judicial consensus; it precipitated judicial dissensus on the nondelegated aspects of the override issue. In all 7 of these cases, post-override judicial dissensus was non-partisan, and the cases were coded as hyperpluralism's weak congressional signals.

Of the 5 cases of attempted one-sided revision in the sample, 4 involved capture's effective one-sided revision: cases in which the override triggers judicial consensus in favor of the winner in Congress. Only 1 case involved judicially thwarted one-sided revision, in which the override failed to trigger judicial consensus in favor of the winner in Congress.

Discussion

In discussing any sample, lessons from its variation and central tendencies should be considered. The sample's variation suggests that the current understanding of the override process needs considerable refinement. As noted in Chapter 2, the majority of override studies focus on whether—and under what conditions—Congress responds to the Supreme Court. This narrow focus on congressional override activity tends to ignore what happens after Congress acts and typically assumes that overrides will effectively resolve the override issue.

The data reveal a more subtle landscape. Most obvious, the data underscore that the passage of an override does not mark the end of the override process; instead, it typically marks the beginning of a new round of policy-making, which encompasses diverse patterns of court-Congress relations. Moreover, to the extent scholars are interested in congressional override activity, the data caution against treating all congressional responses to court decisions equivalently, because congressional override activity varies with respect to the diversity of interest group participation, the comprehensiveness of the override signal, and the degree of expert consensus on the appropriate congressional response to the courts. As a result, from a congressional perspective, we need to ask not only whether and under what conditions Congress acts but also what is the nature of congressional responses to the courts and what accounts for the significant variation in congressional override activity.

The data also cast serious doubt on simplistic normative characterizations of the passage of overrides. Overall, the literature typically overlooks whether the passage of overrides serves democratic values and important policy goals, such as broad political participation and legal certainty. Moreover, to the extent these issues are addressed at all, scholars tend to assert that either the passage of overrides embodies "healthy" pluralism or "unhealthy" capture. Again, the data depict a much more complex picture, indicating that the override process encompasses varied pluralist, capture, and hyperpluralist override scenarios.

As a result, we should not cavalierly assume that the passage of overrides is pluralistic or captured; rather, we should analyze the relative frequency of competing pluralist, capture, and hyperpluralist override scenarios and ask what accounts for the variation among them. On this score, the sample's central tendencies offer several important lessons, suggesting that the passage of overrides is typically pluralistic, rarely captured, and sometimes hyperpluralistic.

The Passage of Overrides Is Typically Pluralistic

Pluralism holds that fragmented power among diversely representative policy forums enriches American policy-making and democracy. It should provide interest groups multiple points of entry into the policy-making process, which should encourage broad political participation. It also should ensure tension among the branches of government, which are accountable to different political constituencies and approach policy-making differently. This combination of open policy-making and inter-branch tension should not only check the mischief of faction but also foster dynamic inter-branch dialogue over policy. This dialogue, in turn, should produce policy consensus and legal certainty, as Congress revisits and re-vises the law based on lessons learned from the other branches. From this perspective, the passage of overrides—as explicit cases of inter-branch policy-making—should feature open congressional deliberation, the passage of clear and comprehensive overrides, and post-override judicial consensus, regardless of the divisiveness of the underlying issues.

The data were generally consistent with these expectations. In 95 of 100 cases, the passage of overrides involved open congressional deliberation. In 79 of 100 cases, Congress passed prescriptive overrides that sought to resolve the override issue. As discussed in Chapter 4, the passage of overrides seems to increase significantly levels of judicial consensus on override issues, even though these issues had explicitly divided the courts in 89 of 100 cases.

That is not to say that the passage of overrides is always pluralistic; it is not. But a majority of the cases, 59 of 100, involve some form of pluralism. The most common scenario in the sample—representing 46 of 100, or almost half the cases—was effective deliberative revision, which embodies the pluralist ideal of open congressional deliberation, the passage of prescriptive overrides, and post-override judicial consensus.

The Passage of Overrides Is Rarely Captured

Capture theory, by contrast, fared poorly in the sample. To reiterate, modern capture theory posits that political participation in multiple and diversely representative policy forums is costly, and that these costs are not evenly distributed. As a result, policy-making should be one-sided, favoring well-organized and determined repeat players. This tendency should be particularly strong in the override process, because the override process, by definition, requires groups that possess sufficient political resources, allies, and determination to legislate and litigate. Put differently, from the perspective of modern capture theory, the passage of overrides should be an exclusive game, played by and for repeat players, such as regulated industries and governmental interests at the expense of one-shotters, such as convicted criminals and immigrants.

The data suggest otherwise. Contrary to capture theory, the passage of overrides in the sample was open. In 95 of 100 cases, competing groups first litigated in court and then lobbied in Congress on the override issues. In 84 of 100 cases, litigation continued after Congress acted, suggesting that groups typically litigated, then lobbied, and litigated again on override issues. Thus, despite the undoubted costs of lobbying and litigating an override issue, a wide range of groups vigorously participated in multiple stages of the override processes in the sample.

An analysis of winners and losers during the override process reinforced these findings. Specifically, if procedurally open congressional deliberations masked substantively one-sided lawmaking, most overrides should benefit repeat players at the expense of one-shotters, who presumably cannot muster the resources or allies to compete effectively in multiple policy-making forums. But repeat players did not systematically, or even usually, win in the sample. In 74 of 100 cases, the overriding Congress *reversed* judicial decisions that favored repeat players. In addition, one-shotters were not precluded from appealing to Congress and reversing unfavorable cases. In 17 cases, one-shotters successfully appealed to Congress to pass an override. Moreover, in 13 of these 17 cases, one-shotters successfully appealed to Congress, even though repeat players had won in the overridden decision. It should be added that public interest groups had not sponsored the initial litigation in these cases; instead, if these groups become involved at all, they did so long after the process was underway. Thus, contrary to capture theory, one-shotters seemed capable at initiating the process and finding political allies to help push their issues through multiple political forums.

The analysis of expert commentary at the time the overrides were passed lends further credence to the argument. If groups that testified before Congress believed their input was arbitrarily rejected, we would expect them to attack publicly the override as unfair or at least defend the overridden decisions. But they did not. Instead, to the extent there were any objections to the override at the time of its passage, these objections did not criticize Congress for ignoring competing viewpoints; rather, they criticized Congress for being too cautious and failing to pass prescriptive overrides that would attempt to resolve the underlying issues. Such criticisms are line with hyperpluralism, not capture theory.

Admittedly, there were 22 cases in which repeat players used the override process to reverse judicial decisions that favored one-shotters. But only 5 (23 percent) of these cases involved one-sided deliberation; thus, in most of these cases (77 percent), one-shotters did present their views to Congress. Moreover, none of the cases of one-sided deliberation involved the classic capture scenario in which a regulated industry benefited at the expense of the public or consumers. Instead, one-sided deliberation tended to involve relatively autonomous governmental entities, such as the Justice Department, which successfully overrode technical procedural rulings of the court without opposition. Thus, to find any cases of capture in the sample, the concept arguably had to be stretched.

The Passage of Overrides Is Sometimes Hyperpluralist

Consistent with pluralism, hyperpluralism predicts that fragmented political power will promote broad political participation. Contrary to pluralism, however, hyperpluralism predicts that open congressional deliberation will not result in the passage of prescriptive overrides that trigger judicial consensus. Instead, when faced with competing interest groups, members of Congress will enact vague or partial overrides that allow them to claim credit for passing legislation while avoiding policy stands that may anger well-organized groups. Moreover, even if members of Congress are willing to brave the storm of conflicting interest groups, hyperpluralists would expect independent federal judges to resist congressional oversight and apply the law based on their contested—and often partisan—understanding of what is fair in any given case. Finally, hyperpluralism predicts that congressional passing-the-buck and partisan judicial policy-making will be particularly prevalent when issues are divisive.

Contrary to these expectations, members of Congress did not shy away from competing groups or divisive issues in the sample. Instead, consistent with pluralism, Congress stepped up to the plate and passed prescriptive overrides following open deliberations in 74 of 100 cases, even though the override issues in the sample were highly contentious, as indicated by judicial dissensus in almost 90 percent of the cases. Moreover, when Congress passed partial overrides, its decision to delegate did not typically reflect a failure to reach accord. Indeed, in 19 of 21 (91 percent) of partial overrides in the sample, experts widely supported Congress's decision to give courts discretion on some aspect of the override issue, usually because the override issue was seen as involving a fact-intensive inquiry.

In addition, as seen in Chapter 4, the data suggest that the passage of overrides significantly increases judicial consensus. Indeed, overall levels of judicial consensus increased five-fold following the passage of overrides. Even when Congress passed partial overrides, it managed to resolve the nondelegated aspects of the override issue in 14 of 21 (67 percent) cases, despite the fact that strategic judges might view such overrides as weak signals, because Congress either invites judicial policy-making on significant aspects of the override issue or Congress admits it cannot reach accord on all aspects of the override issue. Thus, in the sample, Congress not only stepped up to the plate on tough issues, but it also managed reasonably effective swings.

The point is not that hyperpluralist accounts of the override process are wholly wrong. In 28 of 100 cases, the overriding Congress passed weak congressional signals, in which the override triggered non-partisan judicial dissensus. Indeed, in some cases, such as the National Defense Authorization Act of 1987, Congress admitted the override created confusion, not clarity. In 7 of 100 cases, the override process involved partisan judicial resistance, in which judges split on the override issue along partisan lines, despite the passage of prescriptive overrides. And, in 2 cases, Congress engaged in delegation by default, passing partial overrides despite an expert consensus for prescriptive overrides.

The point is that the sample seems to provide likely cases for hyperpluralism. In about 90 of 100 cases, the override issue was contentious enough to divide federal judges. In 95 of 100 cases, competing interest groups participated in congressional deliberations on the override bill. In 84 of 100 cases, disgruntled interests re-litigated the override issue after Congress acted. In all of the cases, diversely representative policy-making forums had a voice in defining and refining the meaning of the law, including the notoriously independent and ideologically diverse federal judiciary. Nevertheless, hyperpluralism did not predominate the sample. Instead, a majority of the cases—59 of 100—involved pluralism and the most common override in the sample was the pluralist ideal of effective deliberative revision.

The bottom line? The sample suggests that the passage of overrides is typically open, but that open deliberation tends to produce diverse pluralist and hyperpluralist override scenarios. The question remains: under what conditions does open congressional deliberation produce pluralist versus hyperpluralist override scenarios? The next chapter explores this question.

Notes

1. If partisan judicial consensus follows attempted deliberative revision (or partial revision), the issue is whether this consensus reflects judicial consensus under the law, or "ideological herding." If partisan consensus most likely reflected adherence to the override's language, then the case was coded as effective deliberative revision. If it most likely only reflects ideological herding (i.e., policymaking among like-minded judges), it was coded as partisan judicial resistance. As discussed in Chapter 4, the number of cases of post-override, partisan judicial consensus in the sample was very small. In the event, most of these cases were coded as involving effective deliberative revision because there was no evidence that the post-override judicial consensus violated the terms of the override. To the contrary, the winners and losers in court shifted after the passage of the override (consistent with the language of the override) and subsequent Congresses did not indicate that the courts had misconstrued the override. However, even if all cases of post-override, partisan judicial consensus following attempted deliberative revision were coded as partisan judicial resistance, the distribution of cases would remain substantially the same: the majority of cases would still be pluralistic, effective deliberative revision would still be the modal scenario, and weak congressional signals would still be the most common type of hyperpluralist override scenario.

2. Hyperpluralism is irrelevant to assessing either attempted one-sided revision or attempted one-sided partial revision, because it involves open congressional deliberation by definition.

3. Jeffrey M. Berry, *The New Liberalism: The Rising Power of Citizen Groups* (Washington, D.C.: Brookings Institution, 1999), 19.

4. Kay Scholzman and John Tierney, *Organized Interests and American Democracy* (New York: Harper and Row, 1986), 150.

5. Kenneth Shepsle, "Congress is a 'They' Not an 'It': Legislative Intent as Oxymoron," *International Review of Law and Economics* 12 (1992): 244–45; see also Frank Easterbrook, "Statutes' Domains," *The University of Chicago Law Review* 50 (1983): 547–48.

6. The coding of partial overrides in discussed in greater detail in Chapter 4 at pages 81–82.

7. See Chapter 4 at pages 83–89 and accompanying notes.

8. Chapter 2 cites a number of these studies, which include Thomas R. Marshall and Joseph Ignagni, "Supreme Court and Public Support for Rights Claims," *Judicature* 78 (1994): 146; Robert A. Carp, Donald Songer, C. K. Rowland, Ronald Stidham, and Lisa Richey-Tracy, "The Voting Behavior of Judges Appointed by President Bush," *Judicature* 76 (1993): 302; Neal C. Tate and Roger Handberg, "Time Binding and Theory Building in Personal Attribute Models of Supreme Court Voting Behavior, 1916–1988," *American Journal of Political Science* 35 (1991): 460; Neal C. Tate, "Personal Attribute Models of the Voting Behavior of U.S. Supreme Court Justices' Liberalism in Civil Liberties and Economic Decisions, 1946–1978," *American Political Science Review* 75: 355 (1981). See also Steve Alumbaugh and C. K. Rowland, "The Links Between Platform-Based Appointment Criteria and Trial Judges' Abortion Judgments," *Judicature* 74 (1990): 153; Ronald Stidham and Robert A. Carp, "Support for Labor and Economic Regulation among Reagan and Carter Appointees to the Federal Courts," *Social Science Journal* 26 (1989): 433; C. K. Rowland, Donald Songer, and Robert Carp, "Presidential Effects on Criminal Justice Policy in the Lower Federal Courts: The Reagan Judges," *Law & Society Review* 22 (1988): 191; Jon Gottshall, "Reagan's Appointments to the U.S. Court of Appeals: The Continuation of a Judicial Revolution," *Judicature* 70 (1986): 49–50; C. K. Rowland and Robert Carp, "Relative Effects of Maturation, Time Period, and Appointing President on District Judges' Policy Choices: A Cohort Analysis," *Political Behavior* 5, no. 1: 119–21.

7   Under What Conditions . . . ?
Patterns and Hypotheses

As seen in Chapter 6, almost all of the cases—95 of 100—involved open congressional deliberation, but open deliberation resulted in a range of congressional override activity. Specifically, 74 cases of open deliberation produced attempted deliberative revision: cases in which Congress passes prescriptive overrides that attempt to resolve override issues. The remaining 21 cases of open deliberation involved attempted deliberative partial revision, in which Congress passes partial overrides that explicitly delegate significant aspects of override issues to the courts.

Moreover, attempted deliberative revision did not always work. In 46 cases, attempted deliberative revision resulted in pluralism's effective deliberative revision, in which attempted deliberative revision triggers judicial consensus. In 28 cases, however, attempted deliberative revision resulted in hyperpluralism, in which attempted deliberative revision results in judicial dissensus. When attempted deliberative revision failed to trigger judicial consensus, 7 cases involved partisan, post-override judicial dissensus, or partisan judicial resistance; and 21 cases involved non-partisan, post-override judicial dissensus, or weak congressional signals.

This variation raises three main questions: When does Congress attempt to resolve override issues following open deliberation (i.e., when does Congress engage in attempted deliberative revision)? When does attempted deliberative revision trigger judicial consensus (i.e., when does attempted deliberative revision result in the pluralist ideal of effective deliberative revision)? What do these patterns suggest about the politics of court-Congress relations related to the passage of overrides?

This chapter probes these questions from the bottom up, using the data to explore the dynamics of open congressional deliberation and attempted deliberative revision. The analysis begins by setting forth the data's general lessons for open congressional deliberation and then turns to attempted deliberative revision. Based on these findings, I hypothesize that court-Congress relations in the sample mainly varied across two dimensions: (1) whether the override issue directly affects the federal budget, including the collection of tax revenue as well as the administration of federally funded programs, and (2) whether the override issue divides judges along partisan lines in the pre-override period, especially if the issue involves the statutory rights of "discrete, insular minorities," such as African Americans and immigrants.

The Dynamics of Open Congressional Deliberation

The Committee Connection

In his famous book, *Congressmen in Committees* (1973), Richard Fenno argues that members of Congress with different goals gravitate to specific types of committees. Members seeking influence and standing within Congress join "prestige" committees, such as the Appropriations and Ways and Means Committees, which deal with taxing and spending issues. Members most concerned with re-election enlist in "constituency" or "re-election" committees, such as the Agriculture Committees, which oversee large federal programs. Finally, members who want to "make good policy" sign up for "policy" committees, such as the Judicial Committees, which deal with an array of high-profile issues.[1] Other scholars, including Shep Melnick in his superb analysis of the interpretation of welfare rights, extend Fenno's analysis to court-Congress relations, arguing that each type of committee has a distinct political orientation to the courts.[2]

The cases build on these studies, suggesting that members of prestige committees and re-election committees are more likely than policy committees to pass prescriptive overrides following open deliberation.[3] The patterns are striking. As seen in Table 7.1, prestige and re-election committees reported out 30 override bills following open congressional deliberation in the sample. Of these, 29 (97 percent) were prescriptive overrides and 1 (3 percent) was a partial override. It should be added that a majority of these cases—19 of 30—involved tax issues and 18 of 19 (95 percent) tax overrides were prescriptive.[4]

By contrast, policy committees—which were typically Judiciary Committees in the sample—reported out 65 overrides following open deliberations. These overrides covered a wide range of issues, including civil rights, antitrust, intellectual property rights, civil and criminal procedure, and bankruptcy law. Of these overrides, 45 (69 percent) were prescriptive and 20 (31 percent) were partial. Thus, policy committees

Table 7.1   Cross-Tabulation of Committee Type Versus Attempted Deliberative Revision

Did Congress Engage in Attempted Deliberative Revision (i.e., Pass a Prescriptive Override Following Open Deliberation)?	Did a Prestige or Re-Election Committee Report Out the Override Bill?		Totals
	Yes	No	
Yes	29	45	74
(row %)	(39%)	(61%)	(100%)
(col. %)	(97%)	(69%)	(78%)
No	1	20	21
(row %)	(5%)	(95%)	(100%)
(col. %)	(3%)	(31%)	(22%)
Totals	30	65	95
(row %)	(32%)	(68%)	(100%)
(col. %)	(100%)	(100%)	(100%)

$N = 95$
Pearson chi-2(1) = 8.97
Pr. = .003

accounted for 20 of 21 (95 percent) partial overrides in the sample and, in percentage terms, were *ten times* more likely to pass partial overrides than prestige and re-election committees.[5]

It is not difficult to understand why prestige and re-election committees are more likely to pass prescriptive overrides than policy committees. The reasons boil down to money and pork. To elaborate, prestige committees have fiscal responsibility; indeed, a central reason these committees enjoy such high status is that they control Congress's bottom line. Given their fiscal responsibility, members of prestige committees have a strong interest in drafting detailed statutes that aim to prevent unpredictable court decisions that may undo delicate budget compromises, increase spending obligations, or reduce revenue collection. Similarly, members of re-election committees aim to garner support from key constituents by delivering programmatic benefits. As a result, they too have a strong interest in passing detailed laws that seek to prevent courts from disrupting (or delaying) the distribution of promised goods and services.

It should be emphasized that, contrary to capture theory, the key issue seems to be whether Congress's money is at stake and not the resources of the participating interest groups. Indeed, the data strongly imply that prestige committees' interest in controlling revenue trumps any interest in catering to powerful corporations. Accordingly, almost all tax overrides in the sample *reversed* judicial decisions over the objections of corporate interests, which sought to protect pre-override court decisions that established favorable tax loopholes and deductions.

By contrast, policy committees do not face such fiscal discipline. Accordingly, if negotiating specific prescriptive overrides is difficult, which is likely because members of policy committees tend to be more partisan, independent, and entrepreneurial than members of prestige and re-election committees, these committees seem more likely to settle for partial overrides. After all, passing partial overrides allows claiming credit for taking some action while sending tough issues back to the courts.

Passing partial overrides, moreover, may not be highly objectionable to the relevant interest groups. Why? As a political matter, once groups realize they cannot obtain prescriptive overrides from Congress, they may be satisfied with partial overrides that return issues to the courts, because these groups usually rely on litigation as part of their policy strategies.[6] Consistent with this argument, in 19 of 21 (91 percent) cases of attempted deliberative partial revision in the sample, diverse groups agreed that policy committees should pass partial overrides because the underlying issues dealt with highly complex matters, such as intellectual property rights, antitrust, and environmental law, where technology, markets, and science are in constant flux. Faced with such issues, although the relevant groups often disagreed on the specifics of the override, they recognized that any override should allow judges at least some discretion to adapt the law to changing circumstances.

One might counter that although in percentage terms policy committees passed fewer prescriptive overrides than prestige or re-election committees in the sample, in *absolute* terms they passed more prescriptive overrides than prestige or re-election committees (45 versus 29). However, closer scrutiny of these cases only seems to underscore the broader point: as a general matter, policy committees seem less likely to assert control over contested override issues than prestige committees. Specifically, unlike tax cases in which prestige committees passed prescriptive overrides over the objection of well-organized interests, policy committees seemed most likely to pass prescriptive overrides when there was a broad, preexisting consensus for the need of legal certainty and no clear winner existed under the override.

This pattern was most common in cases of administrative, civil, and criminal procedure, which made up about one-third of all prescriptive overrides passed by policy committees in the sample. The Comprehensive Crime Control Act of 1984 illustrates the point. In that case, courts had split on where drug-smuggling cases should be tried in the pre-override period.

Some cases, such as *United States v. Lember,* held that drug import cases must be brought in the port of entry.[7] Other courts specifically rejected *Lember,* holding that drug smuggling is a "continuing" crime for which cases can be brought in any district where the drugs were transported.[8]

A range of interest groups descended on Congress to clarify the rules, including various representatives of the Justice Department, the ACLU, law professors, and Democratic and Republican members of Congress. In response, Congress passed a prescriptive override, which states that drug smuggling constitutes a "continuing offense for which venue is appropriate in any district in which the imported object or person moves. This is designed to overcome the decision in *United States v. Lember.*"[9] As with most procedural overrides, it is difficult to identify a clear "winner" under the override a priori. Although federal prosecutors may initially choose the venue of cases, criminal defendants have a right to challenge venue. Consequently, in this case and others like it, passing a prescriptive override involved not necessarily taking sides among the interests, but attempting to clarify the law for the benefit—and with the support—of contending interests.

The Federal Government Connection

Although the patterns were not as pronounced, the data also suggest that Congress is more likely to pass prescriptive overrides following open deliberations when the federal government has a direct stake in reversing court decisions. As seen in Table 7.2, governmental interests sought an override after losing in court in 57 cases of open deliberation in the sample. In 48 (84 percent) of these cases, Congress passed prescriptive overrides that sought to resolve the override issue. In 9 (16 percent) of these cases, Congress passed partial overrides, which sent significant aspects of the override issue back to the courts (where the governmental interests had already lost). By contrast, private interests sought an override after losing in court in 38 cases of open congressional deliberation. In 26 (68 percent) of these, Congress passed prescriptive overrides, and in about one-third—12 of 38 (32 percent)—Congress passed partial overrides. Consequently, in percentage terms, Congress was half as likely to pass partial overrides when the federal government had a direct stake in reversing court decisions.

The converse was also true. Congress was more likely to pass partial overrides when the issue involved private interests exclusively. As seen in Table 7.3, in 19 cases of open congressional deliberation, the override issue pitted private interests against one another, meaning the government did not participate in the pre-override litigation (either as a party or amicus curiae). In 8 (42 percent) of these cases, Congress passed partial overrides. In 76 cases of open congressional deliberation, the government directly

Table 7.2   Cross-Tabulation of Governmental Pre-Override Litigation Loser Versus Attempted Deliberative Revision

Did Congress Engage in Attempted Deliberative Revision (i.e., Pass a Prescriptive Override Following Open Deliberation)?	Did a Governmental Entity Lose in the Pre-Override Litigation and Seek an Override?		Totals
	Yes	No	
Yes	48	26	74
(row %)	(65%)	(35%)	(100%)
(col. %)	(84%)	(68%)	(78%)
No	9	12	21
(row %)	(43%)	(57%)	(100%)
(col. %)	(16%)	(32%)	(22%)
Totals	57	38	95
(row %)	(60%)	(40%)	(100%)
(col. %)	(100%)	(100%)	(100%)

$N = 95$

Pearson chi-2(1) = 3.30

Pr. = .07

participated in the pre-override litigation. In 13 (17 percent) of these cases, Congress passed a partial override. Therefore, in percentage terms, Congress was more than twice as likely to pass partial overrides when the federal government did not participate in the pre-override litigation.

These findings augment existing override studies, which find that governmental agencies outperform other groups, including business interests, at placing decisions on Congress's agenda and securing the passage of overrides.[10] Specifically, the data add that governmental entities are not only adept at passing overrides but also skilled at working with committees to craft more comprehensive overrides. Of course, from the perspective of capture theory, the question remains as to whether governmental interests parlay their legislative victories into courtroom victories. This issue will be addressed when the analysis turns to the dynamics of attempted deliberative revision.

Other Factors Considered

A number of factors seemed relevant to individual cases, but surprisingly did not seem to play a role in the passage of prescriptive overrides in the sample. For example, based on the famous snail-darter case and the Civil Rights Act of 1991, one might expect the public salience of override issues

Table 7.3   Cross-Tabulation of Private Interests Versus Attempted
Deliberative Revision

Did Congress Engage in Attempted Deliberative Revision (i.e., Pass a Prescriptive Override Following Open Deliberation)?	Did Private Interests Exclusively Participate in the Pre-Override Litigation?		Totals
	Yes	No	
Yes	11	63	74
(row %)	(15%)	(85%)	(100%)
(col. %)	(58%)	(83%)	(78%)
No	8	13	21
(row %)	(38%)	(62%)	(100%)
(col. %)	(42%)	(17%)	(22%)
Totals	19	76	95
(row %)	(20%)	(80%)	(100%)
(col. %)	(100%)	(100%)	(100%)

$N = 95$
Pearson chi-2(1) = 5.52
Pr. = .02

to affect congressional activity following open deliberations in one of two ways. On one hand, as in the snail-darter case, it may increase the likelihood of prescriptive overrides, because members of Congress might be motivated to assert control over issues when the public and the media are watching. Alternatively, as in the Civil Rights Act case, it may be more difficult for members of Congress to broker detailed compromises on publicly salient issues, because interest groups may be less likely to compromise when the media spotlight is on and their members are scrutinizing their actions.

To assess this factor, I analyzed national media coverage of the passage of the override. Specifically, I coded the cases using a dummy variable denoting whether *The New York Times Index* specifically mentioned the override bill (1 for a specific reference, 0 otherwise).[11] Using this proxy, 23 cases of open congressional deliberation involved publicly salient override issues. As seen in Table 7.4, of these cases, Congress passed 5 (22 percent) partial overrides and 18 (78 percent) prescriptive overrides. 72 cases of open congressional deliberation involved nonpublicly salient issues. Of these cases, 16 (22 percent) resulted in partial overrides and 56 (78 percent) resulted in prescriptive overrides. These identical percentages suggest that the public salience of issues did not greatly affect congressional override activity following open deliberation.

Table 7.4   Cross-Tabulation of the Override Issue's Public Salience Versus Attempted Deliberative Revision

Did Congress Engage in Attempted Deliberative Revision (i.e., Pass a Prescriptive Override Following Open Deliberation)?	*Was the Override Issue Publicly Salient?*		
	Yes	*No*	*Totals*
Yes	18	56	74
(row %)	(24%)	(76%)	(100%)
(col. %)	(78%)	(78%)	(78%)
No	5	16	21
(row %)	(24%)	(76%)	(100%)
(col. %)	(22%)	(22%)	(22%)
Totals	23	72	95
(row %)	(24%)	(76%)	(100%)
(col. %)	(100%)	(100%)	(100%)

$N = 95$
Pearson chi-2(1) = .002
Pr. = .96

Similarly, one might expect divided government to emerge as a significant factor in the sample. Specifically, although some have argued that divided government does not affect the *overall* output of Congress,[12] others maintain that divided government does affect the content of laws enacted.[13] Extending the logic of these studies to the override process suggests alternative views. One view holds that divided government may encourage the passage of partial overrides. The theory is that divided government increases the already high bargaining costs of negotiating bills through Congress. Faced with increased bargaining costs, members of Congress will find it difficult to force consensus among contending factions and hammer out prescriptive overrides, as in the case of the Civil Rights Act of 1991.

The competing view traces its roots to spatial models of separation of powers, which indicate that divided government should result in greater deadlock among the elected branches of government, and hence a much wider range of irreversible court decisions.[14] The implication is that court decisions that do trigger overrides during divided government are objectionable enough to galvanize opposition on both sides of the aisle. Under these circumstances, the elected branches should be highly motivated to craft prescriptive overrides.

Table 7.5   Cross-Tabulation of Divided Government Versus Attempted
Deliberative Revision

Did Congress Engage in Attempted Deliberative Revision (i.e., Pass a Prescriptive Override Following Open Deliberation)?	Was There Divided Government When the Override was Passed?		Totals
	Yes	No	
Yes	54	20	74
(row %)	(73%)	(27%)	(100%)
(col. %)	(79%)	(74%)	(78%)
No	14	7	21
(row %)	(67%)	(33%)	(100%)
(col. %)	(21%)	(26%)	(22%)
Totals	68	27	95
(row %)	(72%)	(28%)	(100%)
(col. %)	(100%)	(100%)	(100%)

$N = 95$
Pearson chi-2(1) = .32
Pr. = .57

Neither argument finds much support in the sample. As seen in Table 7.5, 68 cases of open congressional deliberation involved overrides passed during divided government, as indicated by more than one party controlling the House, Senate, and presidency; 14 (21 percent) of these cases resulted in partial overrides and 54 (79 percent) resulted in prescriptive overrides. Congressional activity during unified government in the sample was similar. There were 27 cases of open congressional deliberation that involved overrides passed during unified government, meaning that one political party controlled the House, Senate, and presidency. Of these cases, 7 (26 percent) resulted in the passage of partial overrides and 20 (74 percent) resulted in the passage of prescriptive overrides.

The Dynamics of Attempted Deliberative Revision

The Committee Connection (Again)

In the sample, prestige and re-election committees were not only more likely to pass prescriptive overrides than policy committees but also more likely to produce judicial consensus when they engaged in attempted deliberative revision. As seen in Table 7.6, 29 cases of attempted deliberative revision

Table 7.6   Cross-Tabulation of Committee Type Versus Effective Deliberative
Revision

Did Attempted Deliberative Revision Result in Judicial Consensus (i.e., Effective Deliberative Revision)?	Did a Prestige or Policy Committee Report Out the Override Bill?		Totals
	Yes	No	
Yes	22	24	46
(row %)	(48%)	(52%)	(100%)
(col. %)	(76%)	(53%)	(62%)
No	7	21	28
(row %)	(25%)	(75%)	(100%)
(col. %)	(24%)	(47%)	(38%)
Totals	29	45	74
(row %)	(39%)	(61%)	(100%)
(col. %)	(100%)	(100%)	(100%)

$N = 74$
Pearson chi-2(1) = 3.81
Pr. = .05

involved prestige or re-election committees reporting out the override bill. Of these cases, 22 (76 percent) resulted in effective deliberative revision, in which attempted deliberative revision triggers judicial consensus, and only 7 (24 percent) failed to trigger judicial consensus. By contrast, 45 cases of attempted deliberative revision involved policy committees reporting out the bill. Of these cases, 24 (53 percent) resulted in effective deliberative revision and 21 (47 percent) failed to trigger judicial dissensus. Thus, in percentage terms, prestige and re-election committees were about 50 percent more likely than policy committees to engage in effective deliberative revision and about half as likely to pass prescriptive overrides that failed to result in judicial consensus.

The explanation is relatively straightforward. Because prestige and re-election committees deal with Congress's fiscal bottom line and the delivery of pork, it makes sense that these committees not only pass prescriptive overrides but also develop effective institutional mechanisms for monitoring courts and reversing objectionable decisions. Faced with comprehensive follow-up signals and extensive control mechanisms, politically savvy federal judges should be more likely to apply the letter of the law, knowing that errant decisions are more likely to trigger congressional reversals. It is worth stressing that this pattern was particularly prominent in tax cases. Specifically, 18 of 19 (95 percent) tax overrides were prescriptive overrides, and 16 of 18 (89 percent) prescriptive tax overrides triggered judicial consensus or effective deliberative revision. In sum, the data suggest that policy and re-election committees control courts better than policy committees, passing more comprehensive and effective overrides, especially when the issue involved the collection of tax revenues.

Equally important, the mode of judicial statutory interpretation in these cases was highly deferential to Congress. Recall the *Textron* case discussed in Chapter 5, which typified the courts' approach to tax law in the sample. In that case, the majority of judges applied the tax code strictly, even though a literal reading of the law produced unintended double deductions. Recognizing that their strict adherence to the letter of the law produced absurd results, judges urged Congress (or the IRS) to override their decision. In justifying this approach, judges stressed the norm of congressional supremacy in matters of statutory interpretation and the importance of legal certainty in the area of tax law. Thus, in tax cases, members of Congress seemed to care greatly about the issues and invested the needed time and energy to control policy, whereas judges seemed to have little interest in making policy and applied the law as they found it.

Judicial Partisanship

Of course, judges were not always deferential to Congress in the sample, which raises the issue of which conditions tend to produce judicial resistance to congressional oversight. Although the patterns are less pronounced, the data suggest that attempted deliberative revision was less effective in the sample when the override issue divided courts along partisan lines in the pre-override period. As seen in Table 7.7, 18 cases of attempted deliberative revision involved pre-override partisan judicial dissensus. A minority of those cases—8 of 18 (44 percent)—resulted in effective deliberative revision. By contrast, 56 cases of attempted deliberative revision did not involve pre-override partisan judicial dissensus. A substantial majority of these cases—38 of 56 (68 percent)—resulted in effective deliberative revision.

It is not difficult to understand why partisan judicial dissensus is more intractable than non-partisan judicial dissensus. If an issue divides judges along partisan lines under the original statute, passing a prescriptive override—regardless of how specific or credible—will not change judges' underlying partisan preferences. By contrast, if the override issue involves non-partisan issues, such as good-faith confusion over ambiguity or technical flaws in the pre-override statute, passing a prescriptive override can eliminate the ultimate source of disagreement among judges.

Table 7.7   Cross-Tabulation of Pre-Override Partisan Judicial Dissensus Versus Effective Deliberative Revision

Did Attempted Deliberative Revision Result in Judicial Consensus (i.e., Effective Deliberative Revision)?	Did the Override Issue Divide Judges Along Partisan Lines in the Pre-Override Period?		Totals
	Yes	No	
Yes	8	38	46
(row %)	(17%)	(83%)	(100%)
(col. %)	(44%)	(68%)	(62%)
No	10	18	28
(row %)	(36%)	(64%)	(100%)
(col. %)	(56%)	(32%)	(38%)
Totals	18	56	74
(row %)	(24%)	(76%)	(100%)
(col. %)	(100%)	(100%)	(100%)

$N = 74$
Pearson chi-2(1) = 3.17
Pr. = .075

The point resonates with the comments of judges, who argue that not all legal issues are equally divisive or ideologically charged from the perspective of the bench. For example, Justice Patricia Wald once explained as follows: "A large portion of our cases (particularly administrative law cases) have no apparent ideology to support or reject at all. . . . For my part, I cannot even imagine having personal feelings about the appropriate regulatory standards for 'retrofitted cell-burners' as opposed to 'wall-fired electric utility boilers.'"[15] In the absence of an important ideological stake in the issue, it makes sense that judges are more likely to acquiesce to congressional oversight.

In my judgment, it also accords with the broader judicial politics literature. Specifically, as noted in Chapter 3, judicial behavioralists have strenuously argued that ideological preferences offer a parsimonious explanation of Supreme Court voting patterns on contentious legal issues, such as the scope of civil liberties.[16] At the same time, scholars have found that the law matters more in less politically charged areas, including cases where the Court invites an override.[17] These views need not be seen as mutually exclusive; instead, to the extent the law is conceived as an external constraint, it makes sense that it will work better in some areas than others. Perhaps this is what Frank Cross has in mind when he analogized the law to "ropes binding a judicial Houdini" and noted: "If we try to constrain judges with law, it is imperative to understand which brand of rope and which type of knot are most effective and inescapable."[18] The data add that it is also crucial to understand when judges are most determined to wriggle free from the law and congressional oversight.

It should be added that attempted deliberative revision seemed particularly ineffective when the override involved the statutory rights of what Justice Stone once called "discrete and insular minorities"[19] or, as Lawrence Tribe describes them, groups that are "perennial losers in the political process" due to "widespread, insistent prejudice," such as African Americans or immigrants.[20] In fact, only 1 of 10 cases involving the rights of these groups produce judicial consensus, and not a single civil rights override in the sample brought about judicial consensus.

Equally important, the mode of judicial statutory interpretation differed sharply from the deferential mode in my tax cases. Specifically, whereas judges in tax cases sought to apply the law as written and often invited Congress to override their decisions, judges seem more inclined to make policy based in their (contested) understanding of the law's purpose when minority rights were at stake and, in the sample, never asked Congress to set the record straight.

There are at least two reasons why judicial resistance may be likely in these cases. First, these issues are highly divisive among judges; indeed, in contrast to technical administrative issues, it would be hard to imagine federal judges not having personal feelings about the scope of minority rights. Under these circumstances, it seems less likely that passing overrides will reduce conflict among judges because changing the law will not change judges' individual partisan preferences. Second, under the Equal Protection Clause, judges have long asserted a special role in scrutinizing statutes that affect "suspect" classes, such as race or national origin, or "semi-suspect" classes, such as gender and illegitimacy.[21] As a result, it is not surprising that this mind-set tends to spill over to interpreting the statutory rights of these groups, and that federal judges act particularly independent from—and distrustful of—Congress in these cases.

Other Factors Considered

Several factors arguably played an important role in specific cases, but surprisingly did not seem to play a significant role in affecting post-override judicial consensus in the sample. For example, one might expect that the public salience of the override issue may affect judicial behavior following attempted deliberative revision. Why? Strategic judges may be more likely to defer to Congress when the media spotlight is on because they believe members of Congress are more likely to monitor and reverse errant decisions on these issues. As seen in Table 7.8, however, public

Table 7.8   Cross-Tabulation of the Override Issue's Public Salience Versus Effective Deliberative Revision

Did Attempted Deliberative Revision Result in Judicial Consensus (i.e., Effective Deliberative Revision)?	Was the Override Issue Publicly Salient?		
	Yes	No	Totals
Yes	10	36	46
(row %)	(22%)	(78%)	(100%)
(col. %)	(56%)	(64%)	(62%)
No	8	20	28
(row %)	(29%)	(71%)	(100%)
(col. %)	(44%)	(36%)	(38%)
Totals	18	56	74
(row %)	(24%)	(76%)	(100%)
(col. %)	(100%)	(100%)	(100%)

N = 74
Pearson chi-2(1) = .44
Pr. = .51

salience—as indicated by reference in *The New York Times Index*—did not seem to matter. Specifically, 18 cases of attempted deliberative revision involved publicly salient issues; 10 (56 percent) resulted in effective deliberative revision. Of attempted deliberative revision cases, 56 involved non-publicly salient issues and 36 (64 percent) resulted in effective deliberative revision. Thus, it appears the glare of the media spotlight, or at least coverage in *The New York Times,* did not significantly affect the level of judicial deference to Congress in the sample.

More surprising, various attributes of the contending interest groups did not seem to affect the likelihood of effective deliberative revision in the sample. For example, based on cases like the Fine Improvements Act, one might expect that governmental entities would be more likely to win in court after securing the passage of a prescriptive override. After all, these groups have extensive litigation experience and a proven track record in seeking legislative relief from unfavorable decisions on the override issue. Under these circumstances, politically savvy judges may be more likely to apply prescriptive overrides faithfully because they know governmental entities care about these issues and have the wherewithal to appeal to Congress for reversals of errant decisions.

Although plausible, the data did not support this argument. As seen in Table 7.9, governmental entities successfully lobbied for prescriptive

Table 7.9   Cross-Tabulation of Governmental Pre-Override Litigant Loser Versus Effective Deliberative Revision

Did Attempted Deliberative Revision Result in Judicial Consensus (i.e., Effective Deliberative Revision)?	Did a Governmental Entity Lose in the Pre-Override Litigation and Seek an Override?		Totals
	Yes	No	
Yes	31	15	46
(row %)	(67%)	(33%)	(100%)
(col. %)	(65%)	(58%)	(62%)
No	17	11	28
(row %)	(61%)	(39%)	(100%)
(col. %)	(35%)	(42%)	(38%)
Totals	48	26	74
(row %)	(65%)	(35%)	(100%)
(col. %)	(100%)	(100%)	(100%)

$N = 74$

Pearson chi-2(1) = .44

Pr. = .56

overrides after losing in court in 48 cases of attempted deliberation revision. In 31 (65 percent) of these cases, the override produced effective deliberative revision. However, private litigants were similarly effective: in 15 of 26 (58 percent) cases in which private interests had successfully secured the passage of a prescriptive override after losing in court, the override triggered judicial consensus. In short, although governmental entities may enjoy an advantage in Congress, the data do not suggest that they enjoy similar advantages in court.

Based on cases involving effective court challenges to overrides, as in the ADEA case, one might expect that the willingness and capacity of contending interest groups to litigate would affect the likelihood of effective deliberative revision. To elaborate, interest group and public law scholars maintain that certain groups have greater capacity—both resources *and* willingness—for long-term, strategic litigation that looks beyond outcomes in particular cases and seeks to shape the meaning of the rules.[22] Applying this logic to the override process, some groups should be more likely to bring test cases designed to exploit any ambiguity in the override. Such cases, in turn, are likely to divide the courts as judges struggle to apply the override to hard cases. This line of reasoning implies a "strategic litigant" hypothesis: if a strategic litigant wins during the pre-override litigation (and thereafter loses in Congress), the probability of effective deliberative revision will decrease.

Assessing this argument requires identifying strategic litigants: groups that have the resources and willingness to sustain systematic legal challenges to override. I used two proxies for strategic litigants. Primarily, groups that initiated successful lawsuits in the pre-override period, or "voluntary litigants," and thereafter lost in Congress, would be most likely to bring effective challenges to the override.[23] Secondarily, I assumed that repeat players who won in the pre-override litigation, and thereafter lost in Congress, would be likely to bring effective lawsuits challenging the override. To reiterate, repeat players are entities that litigate frequently, such as the following: large corporate interests (such as tobacco companies); public interest groups (such as the NAACP or National Resource Defense Council); or governmental entities (such as the EPA or SEC). Using these proxies, I probed the strategic litigant hypothesis with dummy variables denoting whether a voluntary litigant won in the pre-override litigation (1 if yes, 0 if not) and, alternatively, whether a repeat player won the initial round of litigation (1 if repeat player, 0 if otherwise).

Using these proxies suggests that strategic litigants did not play a significant role in the sample. As seen in Table 7.10, 35 cases of attempted

Table 7.10   Cross-Tabulation of Voluntary Pre-Override Litigant Winner Versus Effective Deliberative Revision

Did Attempted Deliberative Revision Result in Judicial Consensus (i.e., Effective Deliberative Revision)?	Did a Voluntary Litigant Win in the Overridden Decision?		
	Yes	No	Totals
Yes	23	23	46
(row %)	(50%)	(50%)	(100%)
(col. %)	(66%)	(59%)	(62%)
No	12	16	28
(row %)	(43%)	(57%)	(100%)
(col. %)	(34%)	(41%)	(38%)
Totals	35	39	74
(row %)	(47%)	(53%)	(100%)
(col. %)	(100%)	(100%)	(100%)

N = 74
Pearson chi-2(1) = .36
Pr. = .55

deliberative revision involved voluntary litigants, who had won in the pre-override period but lost in Congress. In 12 (34 percent) of these cases, the override failed to trigger judicial consensus. However, involuntary litigants fared about as well. Specifically, there were 39 cases in which an involuntary litigant had won in the pre-override period but lost in Congress. In 16 (41 percent) of these cases, the override failed to trigger judicial consensus. Similarly, as seen in Table 7.11, there was no statistically significant correlation between the secondary proxy for strategic litigants—repeat players that won in the overridden decision—and post-override judicial consensus.

Finally, and perhaps most surprising, the data suggest that judges did not significantly adapt their decisions to changes in the partisan composition of Congress. More specifically, positive political theory assumes that in order to prevent Congress from reversing their decisions, strategic judges interpret the law dynamically, adjusting their reading of statutes so that the marginal cost of overriding their decisions will outweigh any benefit from a policy shift.[24] Under this logic, all things being equal, judicial dissensus should be more likely under older statutes because it is more likely that judges have shifted their interpretations of the law to reflect ideological changes in Congress.

Table 7.11   Cross-Tabulation of Repeat Player Pre-Override Litigant Winner Versus Effective Deliberative Revision

Did Attempted Deliberative Revision Result in Judicial Consensus (i.e., Effective Deliberative Revision)?	Did a Repeat Player Win in the Overridden Decision?		
	Yes	No	Totals
Yes	36	10	46
(row %)	(78%)	(22%)	(100%)
(col. %)	(65%)	(53%)	(62%)
No	19	9	28
(row %)	(68%)	(32%)	(100%)
(col. %)	(35%)	(47%)	(38%)
Totals	55	19	74
(row %)	(74%)	(26%)	(100%)
(col. %)	(100%)	(100%)	(100%)

N = 74
Pearson chi-2(1) = .99
Pr. = .32

The data offered little support for this argument. Overall, the effectiveness of overrides in the sample was stable over time. Compare the most recent overrides in the sample, those passed during the 101st Congress (1990–1991), versus the oldest overrides in the sample, those passed during the 94th Congress (1974–1975). In both sets of cases, the percentage of overrides that triggered post-override judicial consensus is about 60 percent.

More telling is that if judges adapt their decisions to partisan shifts in Congress, courts should have shifted their interpretations of statutes after the historic 1994 congressional elections in order to calibrate their decisions to the new, more conservative House of Representatives and committee chairs. Contrary to this expectation, only one case in the sample involved an observable shift in statutory interpretations following the 1994 election. Thus, inconsistent with strategic models that posit dynamic statutory interpretations over time, the overall patterns of judicial consensus were generally stable over time and the patterns of judicial dissensus were generally contemporaneous in the sample.

Of course, these findings do not mean that strategic models of judicial voting behavior are necessarily wrong, or that judges never adapt their decisions to reflect the preferences of key members of Congress. It merely underscores that, in a policy-making system of multiple veto points, and in an era of divided government, judges may—quite rationally—believe that enough members of a lawmaking coalition will prefer their interpretations to the status quo and, thus, block any attempts at overrides.[25]

Building a Theory of the Politics of Court-Congress Relations and the Passage of Overrides

The findings in Chapters 6 and 7 suggest a framework for understanding court-Congress relations in connection with the passage of overrides. Specifically, the data in Chapter 6 show that the passage of overrides is remarkably open, featuring contending interest groups that are adept at moving from courts to Congress and back again. In this environment, capture is rare and the crucial issue is which conditions tend to produce pluralistic versus hyperpluralistic patterns of court-Congress relations. This chapter probed the data on these issues, which point to two hypotheses I call the "congressional salience hypothesis" and the "judicial salience hypothesis."

The congressional salience hypothesis holds that if override issues directly affect the federal budget, including both the collection of tax revenues as well as the administration of federal programs, Congress is more likely to pass prescriptive overrides following open deliberations. The theory is that when policy-making is open, passing prescriptive overrides is usually costly and risky for members of Congress. Hammering out specific agreements among rival factions is often time-consuming and complex, because members of Congress must try to find common ground among contending viewpoints. It is risky because passing prescriptive overrides often requires members of Congress to assert control over contested policy issues, which may anger well-organized interests. Passing partial overrides, by contrast, allows members of Congress to send the thorniest aspects of override issues back to the courts while claiming some credit for reversing objectionable court decisions.

Given the costs and risks of passing prescriptive overrides following open deliberation, it seems to follow that members of Congress need some reason to take the policy-making lead and pass prescriptive overrides, which take sides on contested issues. The congressional salience hypothesis holds that the simplest motivation is the most powerful: controlling its budget in the forms of preserving tax revenue and guarding the administration of federal programs.

The corollary is that when diverse groups converge on Congress and seek clarification of the law, and there is no clear winner under the new rules, the risks and costs of passing prescriptive overrides are low. Under these circumstances, members of Congress—even members of fractious policy committees—are more likely to step up to the plate and pass prescriptive overrides.

The judicial salience hypothesis holds that if the override issue engenders pre-override partisan splits among judges—especially if it affects the rights of discrete, insular minorities—the probability of judicial consensus following attempted deliberative revision will decrease. The theory is that the United States features politically selected judges, who are notoriously independent. Under these circumstances, it is not enough for Congress to pass prescriptive overrides; judges must be willing to defer to congressional oversight. The judicial salience hypothesis suggests that judges are least deferential when they have an ideological stake in the override issue, especially when the issue involves the rights of discrete, insular minorities, an area in which the courts have long asserted a special role. By contrast, if judges are not likely to see the issue in ideological terms, they will be more willing to defer to Congress.

Put differently, whereas the data suggest that leading members of Congress believe taxing and spending represents their core institutional mission, judges believe that shaping minority rights represents their core institutional mission. Accordingly, just as leading members of Congress are willing to take political risks and expend resources when controlling its bottom line, judges seem willing to risk congressional overrides and

Table 7.12   Summary of Hypotheses

Does the Override Issue Directly Affect the Federal Budget?	Did the Issue Divide Judges Along Partisan Lines Prior to the Passage of the Override?	
	Yes	*No*
Yes	Hyperpluralism, especially partisan judicial resistance (e.g., immigration law)	Pluralism, especially effective deliberative revision (e.g., tax law)
No	Hyperpluralism, especially weak congressional signals (e.g., civil rights)	Pluralism, especially consensual delegation (e.g., intellectual property rights)

challenge existing precedent when defining minority rights, even if inconsistent or partisan rule application threatens the appearance of neutrality that arguably bolsters the courts' legitimacy.

These hypotheses can be integrated into a single framework, which is summarized in Table 7.12. The vertical dimension is the congressional salience hypothesis, which concerns whether the override issue directly affects the federal budget. The horizontal dimension is the judicial salience hypothesis, which concerns whether the override issue divided judges along partisan lines in the pre-override period. The result is four ideal types of policy areas, which should feature different patterns of court-Congress relations when policy-making is open:

- *Federal money/partisan judicial splits.* If the override issue directly affects the federal budget and has split the courts along partisan lines in the pre-override period, both Congress and the courts have a stake in the issue. As a result, the passage of overrides is likely to result in hyperpluralism, especially partisan judicial resistance, in which Congress passes prescriptive overrides but partisan conflicts among judges in the pre-override period spill into the post-override period. Although the numbers were small, these patterns were most pronounced in immigration and social welfare cases in the sample, where Congress and the courts engaged in a hyperpluralistic struggle over issues that resulted in persistent legal uncertainty.

- *Federal money/no partisan judicial splits.* If the override issue directly affects the federal budget but has not divided judges along partisan lines in the pre-override period, Congress has a strong stake in the issue, but courts do not. Accordingly, the passage of overrides is likely to result in the pluralist ideal of effective deliberative revision, in which Congress takes the policy-making lead and courts try to apply the law as written. In the sample, this pattern characterized the area of tax law, where Congress passed prescriptive overrides following open deliberation and these overrides triggered judicial consensus, as courts strived to apply the statutory language literally, even if adhering to the statute's plain language produced absurd policy results.

- *Private cost/partisan judicial splits.* If an override issue does not directly affect the federal budget but has split the courts along partisan lines under the original statute, the passage of overrides is likely to result in persistent judicial dissensus, which is the hallmark of hyperpluralism. Specifically, absent a clear stake in the override issue, Congress is likely to pass vague overrides that allow credit-claiming but pass the buck to the courts. By contrast, courts do have a stake in the issue. As a result, even if Congress manages to pass reasonably clear prescriptive overrides, or agencies manage to promulgate relatively clear rules, courts are likely to exploit any ambiguity in the law to avoid congressional oversight. This pattern was typical in the cases involving employment discrimination law, in which the cost of compliance mainly fell on private employers and typically benefited minority groups.

- *Private cost/no partisan judicial splits.* If the override issue neither directly affects the federal budget nor divides judges along partisan lines under the original statute, neither Congress nor the courts have a strong stake in the outcome. Accordingly, Congress and the courts are more likely to share power, and pluralism's consensual delegation seems most likely to emerge. Thus, Congress tends to pass partial overrides, which reverse specific cases under the original statute and direct courts to develop significant aspects of the issues on a case-by-case basis. Following the override, courts tend to acquiesce to Congress's reversal of specific decisions and, at Congress's request, continue to adapt the law to individual cases. Although the numbers are small, this pattern seemed to emerge in intellectual property rights cases in the sample, in which the override distributed uncertain costs and benefits among contending business interests.

The next chapter concludes the analysis, considering the broader implications of the data for the pluralist, capture, and hyperpluralist debate as well as suggesting several avenues of future inquiry.

Notes

1. Richard F. Fenno Jr., *Congressmen in Committees* (1973; reprint, Berkeley, Calif.: IGS Press, 1995), 1–14.

2. R. Shep Melnick, *Between the Lines: Interpreting Welfare Rights* (Washington, D.C.: Brookings Institution, 1994), 264–69; see also Robert A. Katzmann, *Institutional Disability: The Saga of Transportation Policy for the Disabled* (Washington, D.C.: Brookings Institution, 1986), 18, 44–78; Mark Miller, "Congressional Committees and the Federal Court: A Neo-Institutional Perspective," *Western Political Quarterly* 45 (1992): 956–57, 959 (examining attitudes of members of different types of committees toward the courts).

3. In the vast majority of the cases, the policy committees were the Judiciary Committees, and the non-policy committees involve prestige committees, especially the House Ways and Means and Appropriation Committees and Senate Finance Committees.

4. These findings generally comport with David Epstein and Sharyn O'Halloran's transaction cost analysis of delegation to executive agencies, which finds that Congress delegates to agencies least in the area of tax law (*Delegating Powers: A Transaction Cost Politics Approach to Policy Making Under Separation of Powers* [Cambridge: Cambridge University Press, 1999], 197–201).

5. A few methodological notes bear emphasis. First, the goals are hypothesis generation, not hypothesis testing. Thus, I am using cross-tabulations to explore patterns in the sample, not to rigorously test competing hypotheses. I believe that examining bivariate relationships is an instructive first step for generating hypotheses based on the sample because, as seen in the Chapter Appendix, the correlations among the independent variables are low, with the exception of the variables for "governmental pre-override litigation loser" and "private litigants only during the pre-override period," which seek to measure the flip sides of the same argument. Second, and obviously, it would be inappropriate to use the data for both hypothesis generation and hypothesis testing. To the extent one wanted to test the hypotheses, one would need fresh data. Finally, it is worth noting, even if one were inclined to deduct various hypotheses and use the data to test them, 95 cases of open congressional deliberation may be insufficient to use techniques of logit regression given the number of variables that would be tested. See Scott Long, *Regression Models for Categorical and Limited Dependent Variables* (Thousand Oaks, Calif.: Sage Publications, 1997), 53–54; S. B. Green, "How Many Subjects Does It Take to Do a Regression Analysis," *Multivariate Behavioral Research* 26 (1991): 499 (arguing that logit regression requires $n = 50 + 8*P$, where P is number of predictor variables).

6. See generally Melnick, *Between the Lines,* 264–69 (explaining why policy committees may be more likely to delegate to courts).

7. See, *United States v. Lember,* 319 F.Supp. 249, 252 (E.D.Va. 1970).

8. See, for example, *United States v. Jackson,* 484 F.2d 1167, 1178 (10th Cir. 1973) (affirming district court and rejecting *Lember*), rehearing denied Nos. 72-1792, 72-1793, 72-1653, certiorari denied 414 U.S. 1159 (1974); *U.S. v. Godwin,* 546 F.2d 145, 146 (5th Cir. 1977) (rejecting *Lember* and reversing the district court's ruling on venue).

9. United States Code Congressional and Administrative News (U.S.C.C.A.N.) (1984): 3538.

10. William Eskridge Jr., "Overriding Supreme Court Statutory Interpretation Decisions," *The Yale Law Journal* 101 (1991): 348–53.

11. Alternatively, one could search for newspaper coverage of the overridden decision, but newspapers, such as *The New York Times,* tend to cover Supreme Court decisions as a matter of course. Thus, coverage of the overridden decision may not measure issue salience, but reflect the allocation of resources by the newspaper itself.

12. David Mayhew, *Divided We Govern* (New Haven, Conn.: Yale University Press, 1991); see also Sara Binder, "The Dynamics of Legislative Gridlock, 1947–96," *American Political Science Review* 93, no. 3 (1999): 519 (refining Mayhew's analysis).

13. See Epstein and Halloran, *Delegating Powers,* 11 (analyzing delegation to federal agencies).

14. See Matthew McCubbins, Roger Noll, and Barry Weingast, "Structure and Process, Politics and Policy: Administrative Arrangements and the Political Control of Agencies," *Virginia Law Review* 75 (1989): 431; Eskridge, "Overriding Supreme Court Statutory Interpretation Decisions," 372; Rafael Gely and Pablo T. Spiller, "A Rational Choice Model of Supreme Court Statutory Interpretation Decisions with Applications to the *State Farm* and *Grove City* Cases," *Journal of Law, Economics, and Organization* 6 (1990): 263; Pablo T. Spiller and Rafael Gely, "Congressional Control or Judicial Independence: The Determinants of U.S. Supreme Court Labor-Relations Decisions, 1949–1988," *RAND Journal of Economics* 23, no. 4 (1992): 463; see also John Ferejohn and Charles Shipan, "Congressional Influence on Bureaucracy," *Journal of Law, Economics, and Organization* 6 (1990): 1.

15. Patricia Wald, "A Response to Tiller and Cross," *Columbia Law Review* 99 (1999): 237.

16. See Jeffrey A. Segal and Harold J. Spaeth, *The Supreme Court and the Attitudinal Model* (Cambridge: Cambridge University Press, 1993) (providing the classic statement of this view).

17. See generally Howard Gillman, "What's Law Got to Do with It? Judicial Behavioralist Test the 'Legal Model' of Judicial Decision Making," *Law & Social Inquiry* 26, no. 2 (Spring 2001): 465 (collecting authority); Lori Hausegger and Lawrence Baum, "Inviting Congressional Action: A Study of Supreme Court Motivations in Statutory Interpretation," *American Journal of Political Science* 43, no. 1 (1999): 162.

18. Frank B. Cross, "Political Science and the New Legal Realism: A Case of Unfortunate Interdisciplinary Ignorance," *Northwestern University Law Review* 92 (1997): 326.

19. *U.S. v. Carolene Products Co.*, 304 U.S. 144, 152, n. 4 (1938) (coining the term).

20. Lawrence H. Tribe, *American Constitutional Law*, 2nd ed. (New York: Foundation Press, 1988), 1454.

21. Judge Stone articulated this theory in a famous footnote in *Carolene Products* as follows: "[P]rejudice against discrete and insular minorities may be a special condition, which tends seriously to curtail the operation of those political processes ordinarily to be relied upon to protect minorities, and which may call for a correspondingly more searching judicial inquiry" (304 U.S. at 152 fn 4).

22. Kim Sheppele and Jack Walker Jr., "The Litigation Strategies of Interest Groups," in *Mobilizing Interest Groups in America: Patrons, Professions and Social Movements*, ed. Jack Walker Jr. (Ann Arbor: University of Michigan Press, 1991); Marc Galanter, "Why the 'Haves' Come Out Ahead: Speculations on the Limits of Legal Change," *Law & Society Review* 9 (1974): 95.

23. I thank Judy Gruber from my dissertation committee for this argument.

24. The seminal work for this approach is Brian Marks, "A Model of Judicial Influence on Congressional Policy-Making: *Grove City College v. Bell (1984)* (Ph.D. diss., Washington University, St. Louis, Mo., 1984); see also Eskridge, "Overriding Supreme Court Statutory Interpretation Decisions," 372; Edward P. Schwartz, Pablo T. Spiller, and Santiago Urbiztondo, "A Positive Theory of Legislative Intent," *Law and Contemporary Problems* 57 (1994): 72.

25. Jeffrey A. Segal, "Separation-of-Powers Games in the Positive Political Theory of Congress and the Courts," *American Political Science Review* 91, no. 1 (March 1997): 28.

Correlations of Factors Examined

	Non-Policy Committee	Governmental Loser	Private Interests	New York Times	Divided Government	Judicial Partisan Split	Voluntary Litigant Winner	Repeat Player Winner
Prestige or Re-Election Committee Reporting ("Non-Policy Committee")	1.0000	—	—	—	—	—	—	—
Governmental Pre-Override Litigation Loser ("Governmental Loser")	.1079	1.0000	—	—	—	—	—	—
Private Litigants Only During the Pre-Override Period ("Private Interests")	-.2058	-.6186	1.0000	—	—	—	—	—
The New York Times Index Mentions Override Bill ("New York Times")	-.2022	.0362	-.0224	1.0000	—	—	—	—
Divided Government at the Time Override Passes ("Divided Government")	.2015	.2200	-.2796	.0648	1.0000	—	—	—
Pre-Override Judicial Partisan Split ("Judicial Partisan Split")	-.1890	-.1465	.0035	.2178	-.1017	1.0000	—	—
Voluntary Litigant Pre-Override Litigation Winner ("Voluntary Litigant Winner")	.0262	.2161	-.0061	-.0019	-.0920	-.0675	1.0000	—
Repeat Player Pre-Override Litigation Winner ("Repeat Player Winner")	-.1094	-.2292	-.0035	.2156	-.1037	.0395	.1588	1.0000

$N = 95$

Conclusion

8 Broader Implications and Avenues for Future Inquiry

This chapter wraps up the analysis, considering the broader implications of the data for the pluralist, capture, and hyperpluralist debate and charting future avenues of inquiry. As discussed in Chapter 1, pluralism, capture theory, and hyperpluralism make competing assumptions about court-Congress relations and the implications of fragmented lawmaking power. Specifically, pluralism assumes that fragmented lawmaking power creates multiple access points for political participation, and that diverse groups will take advantage of these opportunities when their interests are at stake. Moreover, the U.S. system of separate institutions sharing power promises ongoing dialogue and feedback among the branches, which eventually should promote broad policy consensus. From this perspective, when multiple branches of government contribute to the process, policy-making should be open and effective.

Modern capture theory, or public choice theory, disagrees. It emphasizes the costs of participating in a complex, fragmented policy-making process and argues that these costs fall disproportionately on diffuse interests and one-shotters in two ways. First, diffuse interests and one-shotters are less likely to overcome the free rider, or collective action, problem that creates a threshold barrier to political action. Second, even if these groups are mobilized for action in one branch of government, one-shotters are unlikely to have either the resources or the political allies needed to pursue policy goals in multiple forums, which are designed to approach lawmaking differently and respond to distinct constituencies. Thus, when groups must make their voices heard in more than one branch of government, policy-making should be one-sided in favor of well-organized interests.

Hyperpluralists take a different tack. They agree with pluralists that fragmented lawmaking power creates ample opportunities for political participation and that a wide array of groups will assert their interests in the process. However, fragmented political power also limits the ability of any one branch to resolve conflict and force consensus. As a result, when diversely representative lawmakers join in the process, policy-making should be open but ineffective, because either Congress will pass the buck or independent, politically selected federal judges will resist congressional oversight.

As striking examples of inter-branch relations in the fragmented American policy-making system, the passage of overrides stands on crucial fault lines among these views. Accordingly, although the passage of overrides is not typical of all inter-branch relations, and hence cannot "prove" pluralism, capture theory, or hyperpluralism, it can serve as an engineer's stress test to reveal the relative strength of these views' assumptions under extreme conditions and offer some insights about the system's underlying dynamics. Specifically, data on the passage of overrides offers an interesting optic to view three core points of tension in the pluralist, capture, and hyperpluralist debate: (1) whether inter-branch relations in the fragmented American policy-making process promote open or one-sided lawmaking; (2) whether, and under what conditions, Congress tends to pass the buck to the courts on divisive and contested issues; and (3) whether, and under what conditions, Congress is able to rein in independent, politically selected federal judges. These insights, in turn, suggest several general hypotheses about the workings of contemporary court-Congress relations.

Broader Implications

Overall, the data are consistent with pluralism, suggesting that inter-branch policy-making in a system of fragmented power promotes open policy-making and judicial consensus. The majority of cases in the sample—59 of 100—involved some form of pluralism, and the most common pattern of inter-branch policy-making by far, representing 46 of 100 cases, was the pluralist ideal of effective deliberative revision: cases in which congressional deliberation is open, Congress passes prescriptive overrides that aim to resolve contested issues, and judicial consensus emerges after Congress acts. More specifically, the data support pluralism on at least three counts, which are detailed in the following sections.

Inter-Branch Policy-Making Promotes Broad Political Participation

Contrary to modern capture theory, the data show that the passage of overrides is almost always open, despite the undoubted costs of litigating and lobbying on the underlying issues. In fact, competing interest groups were remarkably adept at moving from the courts to Congress and back again. Thus, in every case, contending interest groups litigated under the original statute; in 95 of 100 cases, these interests or their representatives then testified before Congress, and in 84 of 100 cases, these groups returned to the courts.

In addition, the procedural openness of the override process did not mask substantive outcomes that systematically favored repeat players. Indeed, the overriding Congress *reversed* judicial decisions that favored repeat players in 74 of 100 cases. Similarly, the data offered almost no support for capture's prediction that inter-branch policy-making will give privilege to powerful corporate interests or regulated industries. Even in the 5 cases of one-sided congressional deliberation, none involved a regulated industry unilaterally reversing unfavorable court decisions. Instead, these cases involved relatively autonomous governmental entities, such as the Justice Department, which successfully overrode technical procedural rulings of the court without opposition. Moreover, to the extent that capture theory should be stretched to include governmental agencies—a point that is contestable—governmental agencies did not seem to enjoy similar advantages in court.

The pattern of court-Congress relations in tax cases further buttresses the point. Tax overrides are theoretically interesting cases from the perspective of capture theory because they represent likely cases for corporate favoritism. Why? Members of Congress can use tax policy to transfer wealth from the general public to narrow corporate interests without risking media or public scrutiny. Moreover, tax provisions are passed as part of large omnibus provisions. As a result, in the unlikely event that the media or public gets wind of objectionable tax breaks, members of Congress can always claim that they voted for the bill as a whole, despite individually flawed provisions. Nevertheless, in almost all the tax overrides in the sample, the overriding Congress reversed court decisions over the objections of corporations, which sought to protect court-approved tax loopholes under the original statute.

These data accord with other studies. The findings of diverse interest group participation in a wide range of policy areas is consistent with the well-documented surge in interest group activity in Washington since the 1960s, especially among public interest groups that seek to represent diffuse interests.[1] The findings of intense interest group activity across the branches of government resonate with careful case studies of American policy-making, which show interest groups often combine lobbying and litigation in their political strategies.[2] As a result, it seems reasonable to ask: If the costs of participating in multiple forums did not prevent a broad range of groups from lobbying and litigating in connection with the passage of overrides, or systematically advantage repeat players, why should we expect these costs to do so in other settings, especially when Washington is teeming with diverse interest groups, many of which are adroit in Congress and the courts?

Capture theorists might rejoin that even if the passage of overrides is open and the costs of advocating in multiple policy-making forums does not bar broad participation, the data fail to address processes that prevent certain types of groups from mobilizing in the first place as well as keep some issues off congressional agendas.[3] Admittedly, the data are not designed to test these arguments directly and, clearly, the group formation and agenda-setting processes warrant further study. At the same time, there was little evidence that historically disadvantaged groups were precluded from initiating the passage of overrides. Specifically, in about 20 percent of the sample (17 of 100 cases), these groups successfully appealed to Congress for overrides in areas such as civil rights, social welfare policy, immigration, criminal law, and Native American affairs. In 13 (76 percent) of these cases, they successfully appealed to Congress, even though repeat players had won in the overridden decision. It is worth stressing that these issues were not publicly salient and that public interest groups, such as the NAACP, ACLU, or others, did not sponsor the initial litigation in these cases. Thus, if a wide range of historically disadvantaged groups were able to initiate the override process without the help of political sponsors or media coverage, one might ask why they could not initiate other political processes and find allies among the growing ranks of public interest groups in Washington.

Congress Is Willing to Assert Control Over Contested Issues

Hyperpluralists agree with pluralists that the fragmented American policy-making process should be open and responsive to diverse interests. However, whereas pluralists assume that open policy-making will eventually result in consensus among diversely representative lawmakers, hyperpluralists argue that the combination of fragmented power, weak parties, and active interests groups in the United States is a recipe for congressional passing-the-buck because passing vague or partial laws allows members of Congress to claim some credit for passing laws, avoid controversial policy stands, and send tough issues to the courts. From this perspective, when the underlying issues are contentious and contending interests descend on Capitol Hill, Congress should pass vague or partial statutes.

The data suggest that this view may be overstated. To elaborate, 89 of 100 original statutes in the sample triggered explicit judicial dissensus, as indicated by circuit splits, dissents, and reversals on statutory grounds. In 95 of 100 cases, contending interest groups testified before Congress on the override issue. Nevertheless, in 74 of 100 cases, Congress engaged in attempted deliberative revision: cases in which Congress passes prescriptive overrides that attempt to resolve the override issue following open deliberation. Moreover, when Congress did pass partial overrides following open deliberation, delegation did not appear to involve passing-the-buck. Instead, in 19 of these 21 cases (91 percent), the legislative record and contemporaneous expert commentary indicated that Congress's decision to give courts discretion on significant aspects of the override issue was widely supported.

The point is not that hyperpluralism is wrong, even from the perspective of the passage of overrides. After all, hyperpluralists may fairly counter that the data indicate Congress did not always assert control over the issues following open deliberation; rather, it passed partial overrides in 21 of 100 cases. Moreover, the data do not include cases where override bills die on the floor or in committee, which may (but do not necessarily) reflect hyperpluralist dynamics.[4] Thus, the crucial issue is not whether members of Congress *always* pass the buck or *always* assert control over issues, but *under what conditions* open deliberation produces detailed statutes, such as prescriptive overrides, that seek to resolve contested issues.

The data point to two factors. First, prestige and re-election committees, which deal with tax and spending issues and the oversight of large federal programs, were substantially more likely to pass prescriptive overrides than policy committees, which tend to deal with high-profile issues that do not directly affect the federal budget. Second, and related, Congress was more likely to enact prescriptive overrides following open deliberation when federal agencies had lost in court and sought an override.

The pattern was most pronounced in tax law, in which Congress passed prescriptive overrides to preserve tax revenue over the objection of well-organized interests, which had benefited from court-sanctioned tax breaks. These tax cases suggest a gloss on standard accounts of why members of Congress may pass legislation that provide general benefits over the objection of well-organized interests. For example, James Q. Wilson's famous account of the politics of regulation argues that when the perceived benefits of a policy are diffuse and costs are concentrated, congressional action turns on the efforts of political entrepreneurs, such as Ralph Nader, who mobilize latent public support (often through the media and high-profile court actions) and link reform to widely accepted values (like consumer safety).[5] In the sample, however, tax cases did not involve entrepreneurial politics. They involved budgetary politics, which features Washington insiders on the powerful prestige committees who typically work outside the glare of the media spotlight.

Martha Derthick and Paul Quirk counter that a political entrepreneur is not always needed to pass diffuse benefits over entrenched industry opposition. Specifically, in *The Politics of Deregulation*, they analyze airline, trucking, and telephone service deregulation in the United States.[6] In each case, diffuse consumer interests triumphed over well-organized, active industry groups without the help of a political entrepreneur. In fact, they argue that the public was generally satisfied with the services provided by regulated industries, there was no scandal or crisis to mobilize latent public support, and high-profile activists offered only tepid support.[7] To explain these anomalous but highly significant cases, Derthick and Quirk stress the role of ideas and policy elites in the process. Perhaps most controversially, Derthick and Quirk argue that the concept of deregulation grew into a kind of political "symbol turned fashion" that gained independent causal significance in Washington.[8] Again, this explanation seems inapplicable to the tax overrides in the sample, which rode the subtle tides of the budgetary process as opposed to waves of public policy fashion.

The data suggest another, more prosaic reason why members of Congress may stand up to powerful interest groups: preserving its bottom line. Specifically, the data suggest that Congress is more likely to assert detailed control over issues that directly affect the federal budget, especially the collection of tax revenue, even if the issues are divisive and involve well-organized opposition. This may be particularly true in an age of federal budget deficits, in which vague or poorly crafted statutes could invite expansive court decisions that create unfunded judicial mandates, which could undo delicate budgetary compromises and force scarce federal resources to be siphoned away from other priorities.[9]

Congress Can Significantly Increase Levels of Judicial Consensus

Hyperpluralism also stresses that the American system of fragmented law-making power features politically selected and independent judges, who are likely to resist congressional oversight. The data qualify this argument. On one hand, using a variety of comparisons, the data suggest that the passage of overrides significantly increases levels of judicial consensus. For example, about 10 percent of the original statutes involve high levels of judicial consensus. Following the passage of overrides, this percentage increased *five-fold*, to about 50 percent. On the other hand, in about half the cases, judicial dissensus persisted after Congress acted. The key question, then, is what conditions tend to produce judicial consensus following open deliberation?

The data suggest that two factors affect the probability of judicial consensus following open deliberations. First, and not surprising, the passage of overrides is less likely to produce judicial consensus when the underlying issue divides judges along partisan lines in the pre-override period, especially where the issue involves the statutory rights of discrete, insular minorities. Thus, some override issues tend to defy congressional control, even when Congress sends multiple signals to the courts. Second, the type of committee reporting on the override bill significantly affected the chances of judicial consensus following open deliberations. Specifically, not only were prestige committees and re-election committees more likely to pass prescriptive overrides than policy committees, but these committees were also more likely than policy committees to pass prescriptive overrides that triggered judicial consensus. Hence, the data suggest that prestige and re-election committees control courts better than policy committees by sending more detailed and effective legislative signals.

Pulling the Pieces Together

When viewed from the passage of overrides, current court-Congress relations appear remarkably open, reflecting a broader trend of increased interest group activity in federal lawmaking. When policy-making is open, the central issue is whether and under what conditions openness produces pluralist or hyperpluralist patterns of court-Congress relations. The data suggest that court-Congress relations vary across two dimensions: (1) whether the issue affects the federal budget directly, especially if the issue affects the collection of tax revenue, and (2) whether the issue has traditionally divided judges along partisan lines, especially if the issue affects the rights of discrete insular minorities.

Combining these dimensions suggests four hypotheses about contemporary court-Congress relations. First, if an issue directly affects the federal budget and the rights of discrete, insular minorities, we would expect either a hyperpluralist tug-of-war where Congress and the courts fight to control the issue, or congressional jurisdiction stripping in which Congress prevents judges from hearing issues and thus bars judicial interference with its prerogatives over spending issues. Second, if an issue directly affects the federal budget but does not affect the rights of discrete, insular minorities, we would expect the pluralist ideal of open and effective congressional signals, in which Congress seeks to resolve contested issues and courts seek to apply the law as written. Third, if an issue does not directly affect the federal budget but does affect the rights of discrete, insular minorities, we would expect either hyperpluralistic passing-the-buck in which Congress enacts vague or partial laws that allow credit-claiming but sends tough issues back to the courts, or hyperpluralistic judicial partisanship in which judges read the law along partisan lines, despite reasonably clear laws or interpretive guidelines. Finally, if the issue neither affects the federal budget nor the rights of discrete, insular minorities, we would expect Congress and the courts to share power consistent with the wishes of the underlying interest groups. Thus, if the groups want clear rules, Congress will pass comprehensive statutes; if the groups want to give courts the discretion to adapt the law to changing policy environments, Congress will delegate to the courts. Either way, courts will tend to work within the broad interpretative framework established by Congress.

Avenues for Further Inquiry

As noted in Chapter 1, this book is intended as a beginning, not a culmination, of inquiry. After all, assessing court-Congress relations in an age of statutes is a vast and complex task, and it is unrealistic to expect any single set of cases to provide leverage on every dimension of the debate over the nature of inter-branch relations. Accordingly, I have sought to advance understanding of contemporary court-Congress relations several steps by integrating legal and social science approaches to studying inter-branch relations and rethinking the outcomes to be explained.

To elaborate, legal scholars tend to concentrate on the quality of individual court cases and the proper role of courts in the policy-making process. These valuable normative analyses, however, often ignore basic explanatory questions, especially what issue, institutional, and interest group factors tend to produce specific patterns of judicial behavior. Political scientists, by contrast, rarely study the quality of legislative output in the same way legal scholars study the quality of judicial output. As a result, their valuable explanations of political behavior are often divorced, at least on the surface, from normative assessment.

In this study, I have sought to illustrate one way to bridge this gap: creating a typology of observable patterns of court-Congress relations that are normatively distinct and analyzing the conditions that tend to produce the most common patterns. Put differently, by conceptualizing the outcome to be explained in terms of pluralist, capture, and hyperpluralist categories of interaction, I have attempted to further normative and empirical research agendas. Normatively, I have evaluated the quality of policy outcomes by assessing whether the passage of overrides serves the democratic value of openness and the policy goal of legal certainty. Empirically, I have generated hypotheses based on recurring patterns of court-Congress relations in a relatively large sample of cases that cover a diverse range of issue, institutional, and interest group contexts.

In conclusion, I will briefly identify three avenues of further inquiry.

Exploring Variation in Court-Congress Relations Across Issue Areas. The most obvious next step involves collecting data outside the passage of overrides to test the hypotheses of court-Congress relations presented earlier. In analyzing these data, key questions would include the following: Are court-Congress relations open? Does Congress send more detailed signals when the issue directly affects the federal budget? Do courts act differently when the issue tends to be ideologically divisive, especially if the rights of discrete, insular minorities are at stake? Do Congress and the courts share policy-making power when an issue affects neither Congress's bottom line nor the definition of minority rights?

Rules of Law and Separations of Power?   Another possibility is a more open-ended inquiry into the meaning of the rule of law and separation of powers doctrine in the current age of statutes and an era of heightened adversarial legalism. To elaborate briefly, traditional conceptions of the rule of law and separation of powers doctrine hold that each branch should have a specialized niche in the policy-making process: Congress should make the law, agencies should implement the law, and courts should apply the law as written (as long as it is constitutional). This division of labor ultimately rests on the ideal of legislative supremacy in statutory matters, in which Congress serves as the principal lawmaker and courts serve as faithful agents.

The data suggests that contemporary court-Congress relations imperfectly adhere to the traditional principal-agent model. On one hand, the passage of overrides seems to increase overall levels of judicial consensus on the override issues, which suggests that Congress—as principal—is able to use its legislative powers to rein in courts as its agent. In addition, in the important area of tax law, court-Congress relations in the sample were consistent with the standard ideal: Congress generally made the law, courts applied it literally, and if a strict application of the statute produced absurd policy results, courts invited Congress to pass new laws.

On the other hand, in half of the cases, the passage of overrides failed to produce judicial consensus consistent with the language of the statute, which suggests that either Congress does not always serve as a strong and effective principal or courts are not always faithful agents. Indeed, in some cases, Congress did not even try to take the policy-making lead. In intellectual property rights, for instance, Congress seemed content to monitor the courts' decisions and allow judges to create the governing standards. In addition, in the cases of civil rights overrides, courts were far from faithful agents. Instead, they seemed to resist congressional oversight, applying the law along partisan lines, even if Congress managed to pass reasonably clear overrides.

This variation in court-Congress interaction suggests that the United States features not a uniform rule of law and separation of powers doctrine, but norms about *modes of statutory interpretation* and *divisions of labor* among the branches of government, which may vary across policy areas.[10] This finding is consistent with studies that show American government no longer features branches of government, but instead a bramble of policy makers, each of which serves legislative, executive, and judicial functions.[11]

It also suggests that each branch of government has core issues that it guards jealously from other branches, and non-core issues that it seems willing to share with, or pass off to, other branches. Further identifying and explaining this variation—how it has developed, how it affects policy outcomes, its normative implications, and the conditions that produce different patterns of court-Congress relations—offers a potentially fruitful endeavor for both legal scholars and political scientists.

Modeling Consistent Versus Discordant Rule Application.   Finally, I hoped to have illustrated a fresh approach to studying judicial decisions, which can be elaborated in future studies. Specifically, scholars have long realized the importance of uncertainty in shaping political and legal behavior. Judicial behavior scholars have spent less time, however, considering conditions that tend to produce legal uncertainty. Instead, studies of judicial decisions tend to focus on the determinants of judges' votes on individual cases, especially Supreme Court cases.[12] This study shifts the unit of analysis from judicial decisions in individual cases to patterns of rule application over time and across policy areas. This shift suggests a new line of studies that would model how issue, institutional, and interest group settings affect the probability of consistent, non-partisan rule application.

The common thread among these research agendas is a conviction that we must move beyond standard studies of American policy-making, which tend to look at either (1) individual institutions and actors in the process, such as Congress, the Supreme Court, the president, and agencies; or (2) specific outcomes, such as votes in individual Supreme Court decisions or the passage of individual statutes. Put simply, we must recognize that policy in the United States emanates from interaction among branches of government, not from the edicts of any single institution standing in splendid isolation.[13] In grappling with this complexity, we have tended to either simplify, using formal models to capture the higher mathematics of strategic interaction, or focus narrowly, using case studies as a window into the process. This book suggests a middle road: examining a relatively large number of cases in some detail to discover recurring patterns within the ongoing, inter-branch dialogue that defines—and refines—American law and policy-making. I hope that this road becomes more traveled.

Notes

1. See, for example, Allen L. Cigler and Burdett A. Loomis, *Interest Group Politics* (Washington, D.C.: CQ Press, 1995), 1–6, 10–20, 25–28; see also Jeffrey M. Berry, *The New Liberalism: The Rising Power of Citizen Groups* (Washington, D.C.: Brookings Institution, 1999), 16–33.

2. See, for example, R. Shep Melnick, *Between the Lines: Interpreting Welfare Rights* (Washington, D.C.: Brookings Institution, 1994), 135–82 (detailing a strategy of rights that allowed advocates of special education programs to translate relatively narrow court victories into the passage of major federal legislation).

3. For a classic version of this argument, see Peter Bachrach and Morton Baratz, "Two Faces of Power," *American Political Science Review* 56 (1962): 947.

4. It is equally plausible that the failure to pass any override—similar to the decision to pass a partial override—may reflect a broad policy consensus, which is consistent with pluralism. The key point is that the data on the passage of overrides do not imply hyperpluralism is wrong, but underscore the issue of what conditions tend to produce pluralist versus hyperpluralist patterns of court-Congress relations.

5. James Q. Wilson, "The Politics of Regulation," in *The Politics of Regulation,* ed. James Q. Wilson (New York: Basic Books, 1980), 370.

6. Martha Derthick and Paul Quirk, *The Politics of Deregulation* (Washington, D.C.: Brookings Institution, 1985).

7. Ibid., 11.

8. Ibid., 53–55.

9. See Melnick, *Between the Lines,* 267.

10. See generally Keith E. Whittington, *Constitutional Construction: Divided Powers and Constitutional Meaning* (Cambridge, Mass.: Harvard University Press, 1999); Howard Gillman, *The Constitution Besieged: The Rise and Demise of Lochner Era Police Powers Jurisprudence* (Durham, N.C.: Duke University Press, 1993) (both works discussing the political construction of constitutional meaning).

11. See, for example, Malcolm M. Feeley and Edward L. Rubin, *Judicial Policy-Making in the Modern State: How the Courts Reformed America's Prisons* (Cambridge: Cambridge University Press, 1999), 314–16.

12. See Jeffrey A. Segal and Harold J. Spaeth, *The Supreme Court and the Attitudinal Model* (Cambridge: Cambridge University Press, 1993), 32–33, 62–65.

13. See generally Mark Miller and Jeb Barnes, ed. *Making Policy, Making Law: An Inter-Branch Perspective* (Washington, D.C.: Georgetown University Press, forthcoming 2004); Michael McCann, "How the Supreme Court Matters in American Politics: New Institutionalist Perspectives," in *The Supreme Court in American Politics: New Institutionalist Interpretations,* ed. Howard Gillman and Cornell Clayton (Lawrence: University of Kansas Press, 1999), 63–97; Edward L. Rubin, "The New Legal Process, the Synthesis of Discourse, and the Microanalysis of Institutions," *Harvard Law Review* 109 (1996): 1424–33 (advocating the detailed analysis of how legal and political processes unfold in a variety of institutional contexts).

Appendix

Summary of Overrides Analyzed

Case Number	Name of Override	Overridden Case(s)	Override Issue
1	Immigration Act of 1990, Pub. L. No. 101-649, Sec. 601, 104 Stat. 4978, 5067 (1990)	*Matter of Longstaff,* 716 F.2d 1439 (5th Cir. 1983); *Boutilier v. INS,* 387 U.S. 118 (1967)	Exclusion of gay aliens
2	Crime Control Act of 1990, Pub. L. No. 101-647, Sec. 3103, 104 Stat. 4789, 4916 (1990)	*Pennsylvania Dept. of Public Welfare v. Davenport,* 495 U.S. 552 (1990)	Dischargeability of criminal restitution obligations in consumer bankruptcy
3	Inventions in Outer Space, Pub. L. No. 101-580, 104 Stat. 2863 (1990)	*Decca Ltd. v. U.S.,* 191 U.S.P.Q. 439 (Ct. Cl. 1976); see also *Deepsouth Packing Co. v. Laitram,* 406 U.S. 518 (1972), superseded on other grounds by Patent Amendments Act of 1984, Pub. L. No. 98-622, 98 Stat. 3383	Extraterritorial effect of U.S. patents for inventions in outer space
4	Copyright Remedy Clarification Act, Pub. L. No. 101-553, 104 Stat. 2749 (1990)	*BV Engineering v. UCLA,* 858 F.2d 1394 (9th Cir. 1988) et al.	States' sovereign immunity for copyright violations

5	Clean Air Act Amendments, Pub. L. No. 101-549, Sec. 228(b), 104 Stat. 2399, 2507-08 (1990)	*Ced's Inc. v. EPA, 745* F.2d 1092 (7th Cir. 1984)	Scope of Clean Air Act provisions concerning "tampering" with auto emission devices
6	Clean Air Act Amendments, Pub. L. No. 101-549, Sec. 228(d), 104 Stat. 2399, 2510-11 (1990)	*U.S. v. Hill Petroleum,* No. 85-0814C (W.D. La. July 29, 1986)	Calculating remedies for violations of fuel standards based on multiday averaging period
7	Clean Air Act Amendments, Pub. L. No. 101-549, Sec. 706, 104 Stat. 2399, 2682 (1990)	*West Penn. Power v. EPA,* 860 F.2d 581 (3d Cir. 1988)	Finality of EPA decisions for appellate purposes
8	Clean Air Act Amendments, Pub. L. No. 101-549, Sec. 707(h), 104 Stat. 2399, 2683-4 (1990)	*New York v. Thomas,* 613 F. Supp. 1472 (D.D.C. 1985), reversed on other grounds, 802 F.2d 1443 (D.C. Cir. 1986)	Jurisdiction of D.C. Circuit of U.S. Court of Appeals over certain EPA decisions
10	Civil Service Due Process Amendments, Pub. L. No. 101-376, 104 Stat. 461 (1990)	*U.S. v. Fausto,* 484 U.S. 439 (1988)	Federal employees' right of appeal under the Tucker Act
11	Financial Institutions Reform, Recovery and Enforcement Act of 1989, Pub. L. No. 101-73, Sec. 212(a), 103 Stat. 183, 240 (1989)	*Continental Casualty v. Allen,* 710 F.Supp. 1088 (N.D. Tex. 1989)	Enforceability of insurance contract provisions which provide that coverage ends upon the appointment of a receiver
12	Insider Trading & Securities Fraud Enforcement Act of 1988, Pub. L. No. 100-704, Sec. 3(b)(2), 102 Stat. 4677, 4680 (1988)	*U.S. v. Carpenter,* 791 F.2d 1024 (2d Cir. 1986), affirmed by an equally divided court in 484 U.S. 19 (1987) (on securities law issues)	Scope of insider trader liability under "misappropriation" of information theory
13	Insider Trading & Securities Fraud Enforcement Act of 1988, Pub. L. No. 100-704, Sec. 5, 102 Stat. 4677, 4680-81 (1988)	*Moss v. Morgan Stanley,* 719 F.2d 5 (2d Cir. 1983)	Scope of insider trader liability to "contemporaneous" traders
14	Patent & Trademark Office Authorization, Pub. L. No. 100-703, Sec. 201, 102 Stat. 4674, 4676 (1988)	*Morton Salt v. Suppiger Co.,* 314 U.S. 632 (1941)	Whether patent misuse is a valid defense to an infringement suit

15	Judicial Improvements & Access to Justice Act, Pub. L. No. 100-702, Sec. 501, 102 Stat. 4642, 4652 (1988)	*Hohri v. U.S.*, 482 U.S. 64 (1987)	Scope of Federal Circuit Court jurisdiction over mixed "little" Tucker Act claims
16	Trademark Law Revision Act of 1988, Pub. L. No. 100-667, Sec. 132, 102 Stat. 3935, 3946 (1988)	*Bernard Food Indust. v. Dietene Co.*, 415 F.2d 1279 (7th Cir. 1969)	Scope of false advertising claims under the Langham Act
17	Review of Tribal Constitutions & Bylaws, Pub. L. No. 100-581, 102 Stat. 2938 (1988)	*Coyote Valley Band of Pomo Indians v. U.S.*, 639 F.Supp. 165 (E.D. Cal. 1986)	Rules governing ratification of tribal constitutions
18	Intellectual Property Licenses in Bankruptcy, Pub. L. No. 100-506, 102 Stat. 2538 (1988)	*Lubrizol Enterprises, Inc. v. Richmond Metal Finishers, Inc.*, 756 F.2d 1043 (4th Cir. 1985), certiorari denied 106 S.Ct. 1285 (1986)	Treatment of intellectual property licenses under bankruptcy law
19	Foreign Relations Authorization Act, FY 1988–89, Pub. L. No. 100-204, 101 Stat. 1331, 1399 (1987)	*Reagan v. Abourezk*, 785 F.2d 1043 (D.C. Cir. 1986)	Exclusion of aliens on national security grounds
20	Omnibus Reconciliation Act of 1987, Pub. L. No. 100-203, Sec. 9307(d), 101 Stat. 1330, 1330-357 (1987)	*AMP, Inc. v. U.S.*, 820 F.2d 612 (3d Cir. 1987)	Allowable deductions for contributions to qualified benefit pension plans
21	Omnibus Reconciliation Act of 1987, Pub. L. No. 100-203, Sec. 9343(c), 101 Stat. 1330, 1330-372 (1987)	*Calfee, Halter & Griswold v. Comm'r*, 88 T.Ct. 641 (1987)	Conditions under which employer contributions to pension funds may be returned
22	Omnibus Reconciliation Act of 1987, Pub. L. No. 100-203, Sec. 10222, 101 Stat. 1330, 1330-410 to 1330-411 (1987)	*Woods Inv. Co. v. Comm'r*, 85 T.Ct. 274 (1985)	Rules for computing basis in subsidiary's stock when filing a consolidated tax return

23	Omnibus Reconciliation Act of 1987, Pub. L. No. 100-203, Sec. 10225, 101 Stat. 1330, 1330-413 (1987)	*Textron, Inc. v. U.S.,* 561 F.2d 1023 (1st Cir. 1977)	Treatment of loss carryforward in connection with corporations for which shareholders have claimed worthless stock exemptions
24	Criminal Fine Improvements Act, Pub. L. No. 100-185, Sec. 3, 101 Stat. 1279 (1987)	*U.S. v. King,* 824 F.2d 313 (4th Cir. 1987); *U.S. v. Mayberry,* 774 F.2d 1018 (10th Cir. 1985)	Interplay between the Assimilative Crimes Act and Crime Control Act as applied to special assessments into the federal victims' fund
25	Water Quality Act, Pub. L. No. 100-4, Sec. 406(e), 101 Stat. 7, 73 (1987)	*NRDC v. EPA,* 790 F.2d 289 (3d Cir. 1986)	Scope of EPA's authority to approve issuance of removal credits
26	National Defense Authorization Act for Fiscal Year 1987, Pub. L. No. 99-661, Sec. 952, 100 Stat. 3816, 3945-49 (1986)	*U.S. v. Rogerson,* 785 F.2d 296 (Fed. Cir. 1986)	Scope of offsets against defective pricing in government contracts
27	Criminal Law & Procedure Technical Amendments Act of 1986, Pub. L. No. 99-646, Sec. 63, 100 Stat. 3592, 3614-15 (1986)	*U.S. v. Lopez-Flores,* 592 F.Supp. 1302 (W.D. Tex. 1984)	Scope of federal criminal laws governing ransom demands
28	Criminal Law & Procedure Technical Amendments Act of 1986, Pub. L. No. 99-646, Sec. 68, 100 Stat. 3592, 3616 (1986)	*U.S. v. Culbert,* 548 F.2d 1355 (9th Cir. 1977)	Scope of federal extortion laws
29	Futures Trading Act of 1986, Pub. L. No. 99-641, Sec. 103, 100 Stat. 3556, 3557 (1986)	*CFTC v. Nahas,* 738 F.2d 487 (D.C. Cir. 1984)	Scope of Future Trading Commission's subpoena power
30	Immigration Reform & Control Act of 1986, Pub. L. No. 99-603, Sec. 112, 100 Stat. 3359, 3381-83 (1986)	*U.S. v. Anaya,* 509 F.Supp. 289 (S.D. Fla.), affirmed by 685 F.2d 1272 (11th Cir. 1982)	Scope of boat owner's liability for knowingly transporting undocumented immigrants

31	Quiet Title Actions, Pub. L. No. 99-598, 100 Stat. 3351 (1986)	*Block v. North Dakota,* 461 U.S. 273 (1983)	Application of statute of limitations on state quiet title suits against the federal government
32	Age Discrimination in Employment Amendments of 1986, Pub. L. No. 99-592, 100 Stat. 3342 (1986)	*Johnson v. Mayor & City Council of Baltimore,* 472 U.S. 353 (1985)	Application of Age Discrimination in Employment Act (ADEA) to local firefighters and law enforcement officials
33	False Claims Amendments Act of 1986, Pub. L. No. 99-562, Sec. 5, 100 Stat. 3153, 3158 (1986)	*U.S. v. Ueber,* 299 F.2d 310 (6th Cir. 1962)	Burden of proof for federal government under the False Claim Act
34	Tax Reform Act of 1986, Pub. L. No. 99-514, Sec. 1501, 100 Stat. 2085, 2388 (1986)	*Miller v. Comm'r,* 733 F.2d 399 (6th Cir. 1984) et al.	Deduction of casualty loss covered by insurance but which was not claimed by insured taxpayer
35	Tax Reform Act of 1986, Pub. L. No. 99-514, Sec. 1501, 100 Stat. 2085, 2742-43 (1986)	*Asphalt Products Co. v. Comm'r,* 796 F.2d 843 (6th Cir. 1986)	Method for calculating the negligence penalty in which taxpayer negligently paid only a portion of taxes
36	Electronics Privacy Act, Pub. L. No. 99-508, Sec. 301(a), 100 Stat. 1848, 1868-72 (1986)	*U.S. v. New York Tel. Co.,* 434 U.S. 159 (1977)	Rules governing electronic surveillance, especially pen registers
37	Superfund Amendments & Reauthorization Act of 1986, Pub. L. No. 99-499, Sec. 127(d), 100 Stat. 1613, 1693 (1986)	*Middlesex County Sewerage Auth. v. National Sea Clammers Ass'n,* 453 U.S. 1 (1981)	Availability of citizen suits under the Marine Protection, Research and Sanctuaries Act
38	Judicial Improvements Act of 1985, Pub. L. No. 99-336, Sec. 3, 100 Stat. 633, 637 (1986)	*Lambert Run Coal Co. v. B&O R. Co.,* 258 U.S. 377 (1922), affirmed by *Franchise Tax Bd. v. Construction Trust,* 463 U.S. 1, 24 (1983)	Clarification of removal jurisdiction of U.S. district courts

39	Trademark Clarification Act., Pub. L. No. 98-620, Sec. 102, 98 Stat. 3335 (1984)	*Anti-Monopoly, Inc. v. General Mills Fun Group, Inc.,* 684 F.2d 1316 (9th Cir. 1982)	Meaning of "generic terms" under trademark law
40	Local Government Antitrust Act of 1984, Pub. L. No. 98-544, 98 Stat. 2750 (1984)	*Community Communications Co. v. City of Boulder,* 455 U.S. 40 (1982); *City of Lafayette v. Louisiana Power & Light,* 435 U.C. 389 (1978)	Scope of local government immunity against antitrust suits
41	Central Intelligence Information Act, Pub. L. No. 98-477, Sec. 2(c), 98 Stat. 2209, 2211-2212 (1984)	*Terkel v. Kelley,* 599 F.2d 214 (7th Cir. 1979); *Painter v. FBI,* 615 F.2d 689 (5th Cir. 1980)	Interplay between Freedom of Information Act and Privacy Act as applied to first-person requests for governmental files
42	Comprehensive Crime Control Act of 1984, Pub. L. No. 98-473, Sec. 1005, 98 Stat. 1837, 2138-39 (1984)	*Busic v. U.S.,* 446 U.S. 398 (1980); *Simpson v. U.S.,* 435 U.S. 6, 10 (1978)	Sentencing for crimes involving dangerous weapons
43	Comprehensive Crime Control Act of 1984, Pub. L. No. 98-473, Sec. 1104, 98 Stat. 1837, 2143-44 (1984)	*U.S. v. Loschiavo,* 531 F.2d 659 (2d Cir. 1976) et al.	Scope of federal bribery laws
44	Comprehensive Crime Control Act of 1984, Pub. L. No. 98-473, Sec. 1106, 98 Stat. 1837, 2145 (1984)	*U.S. v. Kaplan,* 586 F.2d 980 (2d Cir. 1978)	Intent requirement under federal bank robbery statute
45	Comprehensive Crime Control Act of 1984, Pub. L. No. 98-473, Sec. 1107, 98 Stat. 1837, 2145-46 (1984)	*Williams v. U.S.,* 458 U.S. 279 (1982)	Scope of federal criminal law that makes it a crime to knowingly make a false statement or report to influence the actions of a federally insured bank
46	Comprehensive Crime Control Act of 1984, Pub. L. No. 98-473, Sec. 1109(a), 98 Stat. 1837, 2147-48 (1984)	*U.S. v. Bedwell,* 456 F.2d 448 (10th Cir. 1972)	Scope of federal criminal law that makes it a crime to convey a weapon from place to place in a federal prison

47	Comprehensive Crime Control Act of 1984, Pub. L. No. 98-473, Sec. 1204(a), 98 Stat. 1837, 2152 (1984)	*U.S. v. Lember,* 319 F.Supp. 249 (E.D. Va. 1970)	Venue for drug-smuggling cases
48	Drug Price Competition & Patent Term Restoration Act, Pub. L. No. 98-417, Sec. 202, 98 Stat. 1585, 1603 (1984)	*Roche Prods. v. Bolar Pharmaceutical Co.,* 733 F.2d 858 (Fed. Cir. 1984)	Scope of patent protection for "experimental use"
49	Deficit Reduction Act of 1984, Pub. L. No. 98-376, Sec. 82, 98 Stat. 494, 598 (1984)	*Edward L. Stephenson Trust v. Comm'r,* 81 T.C. 283 (1983)	Treatment of multiple trusts for tax purposes
50	Deficit Reduction Act of 1984, Pub. L. No. 98-369, Sec. 91, 98 Stat. 494, 598-601 (1984)	*Harold v. Comm'r,* 192 F.2d 1002 (4th Cir. 1951); *Crescent Wharf v. Comm'r,* 518 F.2d 772 (9th Cir. 1975)	Timing of business deductions of costs that can be estimated but have not been accrued
51	Deficit Reduction Act of 1984, Pub. L. No. 98-369, Sec. 131, 98 Stat. 494, 662-64 (1984)	*Dittler Bros. v. Comm'r,* 72 T.C. 896 (1979)	Scope of provisions governing asset transfers to foreign companies
52	Shipping Act of 1984, Pub. L. No. 98-237, Sec. 7, 98 Stat. 67, 73-74 (1984)	*FMC v. Aktiebolaget Svenska Amerika Linien,* 390 U.S. 238 (1968); *Carnation Co. v. Pacific Westbound Conf.,* 383 U.S. 213 (1966)	Application of antitrust laws to shipping "conferences"
53	Supplemental Appropriations Act of 1983, Pub. L. No. 98-63, Ch. VII, 97 Stat. 301, 323-24 (1983)	*Meade Township v. Andrus,* 695 F.2d 1006 (6th Cir. 1983) (as amended on denial of rehearing)	Definition of units of government under Payments in Lieu of Taxes Act
54	Futures Trading Act of 1982, Pub. L. No. 97-444, Sec. 225, 96 Stat. 2294, 2315-16 (1982)	*Board of Trade of the City of Chicago v. SEC,* 677 F.2d 1137 (7th Cir. 1982)	Competing jurisdiction of SEC and Commodities Futures Trading Commission over certain government mortgage-backed securities
55	Futures Trading Act of 1982, Pub. L. No. 97-444, Sec. 225, 96 Stat. 2294, 2315-16 (1982)	*Board of Trade of the City of Chicago v. CFTC,* 605 F.2d 1016 (7th Cir. 1979)	District court jurisdiction over CFTC's emergency orders

56	Tax Equity & Fiscal Responsibility Act of 1982, Pub. L. No. 97-248, Sec. 228, 96 Stat. 324, 493 (1982)	*Rickey v. U.S.,* 592 F.2d 1251 (5th Cir. 1979)	Application of entity attribution rules to the sale of stock by an estate
57	Federal Tort Claims—National Guard, Pub. L. No. 97-124, 95 Stat. 1666 (1981)	*Maryland v. U.S.,* 381 U.S. 41 (1965)	Application of Federal Tort Claims Act to the National Guard
58	Immigration & Nationality Act Amendments of 1981, Pub. L. No. 97-116, Sec. 8, 95 Stat. 1611, 1616 (1981)	*Reid v. INS,* 420 U.S. 619 (1975); *INS v. Errico,* 385 U.S. 214 (1966)	Scope of immigration laws that bars deportation of aliens who gain entry in to the U.S. who are married to a U.S. citizen and not otherwise excludable
59	Military Justice Amendments of 1981, Pub. L. No. 97-81, Sec. 5, 95 Stat. 1085, 1088–89 (1981)	*U.S. v. Larneard,* 3 M.J. 76 (CMA 1977)	Notice requirements to court-martialed soldiers
60	Lacey Act Amendments of 1981, Pub. L. No. 97-79, Sec. 2(d), 95 Stat. 1073, 1073 (1981)	*U.S. v. Molt,* 599 F.2d 1217 (3d Cir. 1979)	Application of Lacey Act to violations of non-wildlife protection laws
61	Marine Mammal Protection Act, Pub. L. No. 97-58, Sec. 2(2), 95 Stat. 979, 981 (1981)	*People of Togiak v. U.S.,* 470 F.Supp. 423 (D.D.C. 1979)	Application of the Marine Mammal Protection Act to Alaskan tribes
62	Omnibus Budget Reconciliation Act or 1981, Pub. L. No. 97-35, Sec. 1118(e)(3) & 1119(d), 95 Stat. 357, 631-32, 633 (1981)	*Gebbie v. U.S. R.R. Retirement Bd.,* 631 F.2d 512 (7th Circ. 1980)	Eligibility of retirees for dual benefits under the Railroad Retirement Act
63	Economic Recovery Tax Act of 1981, Pub. L. No. 97-34, Sec. 266, 95 Stat. 172, 265-66 (1981)	*Consolidated Freight Lines, Inc. v. Comm'r,* 37 BTA 576 (1939), affirmed by 101 F.2d 813 (9th Cir. 1939)	Scope of business deductions
64	Miscellaneous Revenue Act of 1980, Pub. L. No. 96-596, Sec. 2, 94 Stat. 3469, 3469-74 (1980)	*Adams v. Comm'r,* 72 T.C. 81 (1979)	Jurisdiction of tax court to enforce "second tier" excise tax on foundations

65	Bankruptcy Tax Act of 1980, Pub. L. No. 96-589, Sec. 5(f), 94 Stat. 3389, 3406 (1980)	*Meyer v. Comm'r*, 383 F.2d 883 (8th Cir. 1967)	Whether discharge of debts in bankruptcy creates taxable income
66	Equal Access to Justice Act, Title II of the Small Business Export Expansion Act of 1980, Pub. L. No. 96-481, 94 Stat. 2321, 2325-30 (1980)	*Pealo v. Farmers Homes Admin.*, 562 F.2d 744 (D.C. Cir. 1977); *Alyeska Pipeline v. Wilderness Soc'y*, 421 U.S. 240 (1975)	Scope of 28 U.S.C. Sec. 2412, which establishes the so-called American Rule for payment of attorneys' fees
67	Installment Sales Revision Act of 1980, Pub. L. No. 96-471, Sec. 2(a), 94 Stat. 2247, 2250 (1980)	*J.K. Griffith v. Comm'r*, 73 T.C. No. 76 (1980)	Tax treatment of third-party guarantees of sales of property
68	Antitrust Procedural Improvements Act of 1980, Pub. L. No. 96-349, Sec. 2, 94 Stat. 1154, 1154-56 (1980)	*U.S. v. GAF Corp.*, 449 F.Supp. 351 (S.D.N.Y. 1978)	Department of Justice's powers to issue civil investigative demands for materials discovered during private antitrust litigation
69	Antitrust Procedural Improvements Act of 1980, Pub. L. No. 96-349, Sec. 5, 94 Stat. 1154, 1157 (1980)	*Illinois v. General Paving Co.*, 590 F.2d 680 (7th Cir. 1979)	Use of government antitrust judgments in Clayton Act cases
70	Soft Drink Interbrand Competition Act, Pub. L. No. 96-308, 94 Stat. 939 (1980)	*In the Matter of the Coca-Cola Company*, et al., 91 FTC 517 (1978); see also *U.S. v. Arnold, Schwinn & Co.*, 388 U.S. 365 (1967)	Application of Sherman Antitrust laws to exclusive territorial arrangements used in the soft drink industry
71	Civil Rights of Institutionalized Persons Act, Pub. L. No. 96-247, 94 Stat. 349 (1980)	*U.S. v. Mattson*, 600 F.2d 1295 (9th Cir. 1979); *U.S. v. Solomon*, 563 F.2d 1121 (4th Cir. 1977)	Federal government's standing under the Developmentally Disabled Assistance and Bill of Rights Act
72	Endangered Species Act Amendments of 1978, Pub. L. No. 95-632, Sec. 7, 92 Stat. 3751, 3752-60 (1978)	*TVA v. Hill*, 437 U.S. 153 (1978) (the famous "Snail Darter" case)	Whether courts may balance benefits of governmental projects versus the threat to endangered species under the Endangered Species Act

73	Revenue Act of 1978, Pub. L. No. 95-600, Sec. 365, 92 Stat. 2763, 2854-55 (1978)	*Bongiovanni v. Comm'r*, 470 F.2d 921 (2d Cir. 1972); *Thatcher v. Comm'r*, 533 F.2d 114 (9th Cir. 1976)	Taxability of asset and liability transfer among related corporate entities
74	Bankruptcy Reform Act of 1978, Pub. L. No. 95-598, Sec. 101, 92 Stat. 2549, 2555 (1978)	*Toucy v. N.Y. Life Ins. Co.*, 314 U.S. 1 (1941)	Bankruptcy court jurisdiction to stay state court actions
75	Bankruptcy Reform Act of 1978, Pub. L. No. 95-598, Sec. 101, 92 Stat. 2549, 2557 (1978)	*In re Bank of Crowell*, 53 F.2d 682 (N.D. Tex. 1931) (district court case reported in F.2d)	Application of federal bankruptcy laws to banks
76	Bankruptcy Reform Act of 1978, Pub. L. No. 95-598, Sec. 101, 92 Stat. 2549, 2564 (1978)	*Massachusetts Mutual Life Ins. Co. v. Brock*, 405 F.2d 429 (5th Cir. 1968)	Standards governing the granting of bankruptcy debtors' attorney and trustee fees
77	Bankruptcy Reform Act of 1978, Pub. L. No. 95-598, Sec. 101, 92 Stat. 2549, 2584 (1978)	*U.S. v. Embassy Restaurant*, 359 U.S. 29 (1958)	Priority status of wage claims under bankruptcy laws
78	Bankruptcy Reform Act of 1978, Pub. L. No. 95-598, Sec. 101, 92 Stat. 2549, 2594 (1978)	*Lines v. Frederick*, 400 U.S. 18 (1970); *Lockwood v. Exchange Bank*, 190 U.S. 294 (1903)	Whether unpaid vacation pay and other employee benefits constitute property of the "bankruptcy estate"
79	Bankruptcy Reform Act of 1978, Pub. L. No. 95-598, Sec. 101, 92 Stat. 2549, 2598-99 (1978)	*In re King Porter Co.*, 446 F.2d 722 (5th Cir. 1971)	Treating of floating liens as bankruptcy "preferences"
80	Bankruptcy Reform Act of 1978, Pub. L. No. 95-598, Sec. 101, 92 Stat. 2549, 2619 (1978)	*In re Rosenbaum Grain Corp.*, 112 F.2d 315 (7th Cir. 1940)	Need for tracing proceeds in administering commodity contracts in bankruptcy
81	Bankruptcy Reform Act of 1978, Pub. L. No. 95-598, Sec. 101, 92 Stat. 2549, 2624 (1978)	*American United Mutual Life Ins. Co. v. City of Avon Park*, 311 U.S. 138 (1940)	Application of the fair and equitable test in the confirmation of bankruptcy plans

82	Contract Disputes Act of 1978, Pub. L. No. 95-563, Sec. 10(a), 92 Stat. 2383, 2388 (1978)	*U.S. v. Bianchi & Co.,* 373 U.S. 709 (1963)	Standard of appellate court review under the Wunderlich Act, which governs government contract disputes
83	Contract Disputes Act of 1978, Pub. L. No. 95-563, Sec. 8(g), 14(h), 92 Stat. 2383, 2387, 2390 (1978)	*S & E Contractors, Inc. v. U.S.,* 406 U.S. 1 (1972)	Procedures for appeals under the Wunderlich Act
84	Age Discrimination in Employment Act Amendments of 1978, Pub. L. No. 95-256, Sec. 2, 92 Stat. 189, 189 (1978)	*McMann v. United Airlines,* 434 U.S. 192 (1977)	Application of ADEA to mandatory retire-ment plans adopted prior to the act's passage
85	Age Discrimination in Employment Act Amendments of 1978, Pub. L. No. 95-256, Sec. 4(b), 92 Stat. 189, 190-1 (1978)	*Ott v. Midland-Ross Corp.,* 523 F.2d 1367 (6th Cir. 1975)	Statute of limitations under ADEA
86	Clean Water Act of 1977, Pub. L. No. 95-217, Sec. 61, 67(b), 91 Stat. 1566, 1598, 1606 (1977)	*Minnesota v. Hoffman,* 543 F.2d 1198 (8th Cir. 1976)	Application of state water regulations to federal facilities
87	Food & Agriculture Act of 1977, Pub. L. No. 95-113, Sec. 1301, Stat. 913, 962-3 (new Sec. 5[d]) (1977)	*Hein v. Burns,* 402 F.Supp. 398 (S.D. Ia. 1975), reversed by 429 U.S. 288 (1977) et al.	Calculation of govern-mental benefits as income for purposes of determining food stamp eligibility
88	Clean Air Act Amendments of 1997, Pub. L. No. 95-95, Sec. 120, 91 Stat. 685, 720 (1977)	*Northern States Power Co. v. State of Minn.,* 447 F.2d 1143 (8th Cir. 1971), affirmed by 405 U.S. 1035 (1972) (Douglas and Stewart dissenting from affirmance)	Power of states to regulate radioactive effluents
89	Clean Air Act Amendments of 1997, Pub. L. No. 95-95, Sec. 127, 91 Stat. 685, 731 ff. (1977)	*FRI v. Sierra Club,* 412 U.S. 541 (1973), affirmed by equally divided Court, 344 F.Supp. 253 (D.D.C. 1972)	Application of Clean Air Act to substantial deterioration of pris-tine areas

90	Clean Air Act Amendments of 1997, Pub. L. No. 95-95, Sec. 305, 91 Stat. 685, 772-77 ff. (1977)	*Kennecott Copper Corp. v. EPA*, 462 F.2d 846 (D.C. Cir. 1972)	Standards of agency disclosure of rationales for decision-making
91	Federal Land Policy and Management Act of 1976, Pub. L. No. 94-568, 90 Stat. 2697 (1976)	*McGlotten v. Connally*, 338 F.Supp. 448 (D.D.C. 1972)	Non-profit tax status of discriminatory social clubs
92	Copyrights Act, Pub. L. No. 94-553, Sec. 101, 90 Stat. 2541, 2541-44 (1976)	*White-Smith Publishing Co. v. Apollo Co.*, 209 U.S. 1 (1908)	Application of copy-right protection to new copying technology
93	Copyrights Act, Pub. L. No. 94-553, Sec. 108, 90 Stat. 2541, 2546-48 (1976)	*Williams & Wilkins Co. v. U.S.*, 487 F.2d 1345 (Ct. Cl. 1973), affirmed by an equally divided Court, 420 U.S. 376 (1975)	Scope of the "fair use" exception to copyright law
94	Copyrights Act, Pub. L. No. 94-553, Sec. 411, 90 Stat. 2541, 2583 (1976)	*Vacheron & Constantin-Le Coultre Watches, Inc. v. Benrus Watch Co.*, 260 F.2d 637 (2d Cir. 1958)	Procedural require-ments for bringing infringement suits
95	Tax Reform Act of 1976, Pub. L. No. 94-455, Sec. 208, 90 Stat. 1520, 1541-42 (1976)	*Burck v. Comm'r*, 63 T.Ct. 556 affirmed by 533 F.2d 768 (2d Cir. 1976)	Deduction of prepaid interest by taxpayers using cash method accounting
96	Tax Reform Act of 1976, Pub. L. No. 94-455, Sec. 601(a), 90 Stat. 1520, 1569-72 (1976)	*George H. Newi*, T.C. Memo. 1969-131, affirmed by 432 F.2d 998 (2d Cir. 1970)	Rules governing home office deductions
97	Tax Reform Act of 1976, Pub. L. No. 94-455, Sec. 1051, 90 Stat. 1520, 1643-47 (1976)	*Burke Concrete Accessories, Inc.*, 56 T.C. 588 (1971)	Rules for filing consolidated returns for U.S. and foreign corporations
98	Tax Reform Act of 1976, Pub. L. No. 94-455, Sec. 1201(a), 90 Stat. 1520, 1660-67 (1976)	*Tax Analysts & Advocates v. IRS*, 505 F.2d 350 (D.C. Cir. 1974)	Interplay between the Freedom of Information Act and the tax code

99	Tax Reform Act of 1976, Pub. L. No. 94-455, Sec. 1204(b), 90 Stat. 1520, 1696-97 (1976)	*Laing v. U.S.*, 496 F.2d 853 (2d Cir. 1974)	Procedural rules governing challenges to termination assessments by IRS
100	Hart-Scott-Rodino Antitrust Improvements Act of 1976, Pub. L. No. 94-435, Sec. 102, 90 Stat. 1383, 1384-87 (1976)	*U.S. v. Union Oil Co. of Calif.*, 343 F.2d 29 (9th Cir. 1965)	Department of Justice's power to issue civil investigative demands related to incipient as well as past violations

Index